CLAUDIA LEWIS is a Distinguished Specialist in Children's Literature at Bank Street College in New York City, where she teaches literature, language, reading readiness, and creative writing. She is the author of five books for children, one of which, *When I Go to the Moon*, enjoys international popularity.

How did the day taste?

Like ice cream, like French fries,
like cherry soda, like clouds, like if you
took a big bite of the world, you'd have
too much air in your stomach and fly away
like a balloon.

Primary Class
Annunciation School
(see page 125)

A big bite of the world:

children's creative writing

Claudia Lewis

A SPECTRUM BOOK

PRENTICE-HALL, INC., Englewood Cliffs, New Jersey 07632

Library of Congress Cataloging in Publication Data

LEWIS, CLAUDIA LOUISE (date)
   A big bite of the world.

   (A Spectrum Book)
   Includes bibliographies.
   1. Creative thinking (Education)   2. Creative writing
(Elementary education)   3. English language—Composition
and exercises.   I. Title.
LB1062.L48   372.6   79-13925
ISBN 0-13-076273-3
ISBN 0-13-076265-2 pbk.

To the memory of Lucy Sprague Mitchell
and to Barbara Biber and
Charlotte B. Winsor with gratitude and love

Editorial production and
   interior design by Carol Smith
Cover design by Judith Kazdym Leeds
Manufacturing buyer: Cathie Lenard

© 1979 by Prentice-Hall, Inc.
Englewood Cliffs, New Jersey 07632

A SPECTRUM BOOK

Printed in the United States of America

10 9 8 7 6 5 4 3 2 1

PRENTICE-HALL INTERNATIONAL, INC., London
PRENTICE-HALL OF AUSTRALIA PTY., LIMITED, Sydney
PRENTICE-HALL OF CANADA, LTD., Toronto
PRENTICE-HALL OF INDIA PRIVATE, LIMITED, New Delhi
PRENTICE-HALL OF JAPAN, INC., Tokyo
PRENTICE-HALL OF SOUTHEAST ASIA PTE., LTD., Singapore
WHITEHALL BOOKS, LIMITED, Wellington, New Zealand

Contents

Preface   vii

Introduction

What do we mean by creative writing?   1
References, 8

Chapter one

The inventive threes, fours, fives   9
Inventive, searching, 11; Curiosity, questions, solutions, 13; The attempt to organize concepts, 15; Self-expression, 19; Pattern, repetition, rhythm, 23; Playfulness, 25; Poetry: symbol and magic, 27; Individuality and nurturing, 28; Involvement, 31; Sound, color, movement, 32; Exposure to books, 34; Prologue to the elementary years, 35; References, 38

Chapter two

Prerequisite to creativity: the school setting   39
Engagement in a rich curriculum, 41; Experiences outside the classroom, 57; References, 62

Chapter three
The sixes and sevens: beginning to write 65
Dictation, 67; Writing begins, 81; A new perspective emerges, 97; Writing ability evolves, 105; The beginnings of poetry, 110; References, 126

Chapter four
The eights and nines:
growing into the middle years 129
Reflections of the new independence, 133; Moving toward reality, 144; The new perspective writings, 149; Drawing the threads together, 152; When is it poetry?, 162; References, 171

Chapter five
The nines and tens:
self-discovery and self-understanding 173
Self-discovery through poetry, 176; Self-declaration through stories, 201; New awareness, new maturity, 212; Growth and discovery through drama, 219; From Majikton to outer space: half-magic worlds and science fiction, 238; Moving beyond the horror story, 246; Exploring characters, situations, experiences, 252; References, 265

Chapter six
Eleven, going on twelve:
new awareness and abilities 269
Reality, 272; Creativity through poetry, 285; Inventive, searching, 298: References, 306

A final word 309
Looking ahead, 310

vi

Contents

Preface

During my long association with Bank Street College of Education and my eight years of summer teaching at Portland State University, my work has taken me into public and private schools, inner-city and middle-class areas. I have become acquainted with teachers, student teachers, and parents, and it is to them that this book owes its very existence. They are the ones who have established the atmospheres, conceived of approaches, stimulated and helped the children with their stories, poems, and plays, and delightedly shared all of this with me.

A few of these people are named in connection with specific projects because I am quoting them or because the writing becomes awkward without the use of names. To list all of the people who have contributed their ideas and provided the children's writings I am using so liberally would take another volume. However, I would like to extend my special acknowledgment to:

New York City private schools
  Annunciation School: Marion Bunche
  Bank Street School for Children: Nancy Brumm, Betty Crowell,
    Judith Gutman Freed, Ellen Galinsky, Patsy Gesell, Diane
    Ginsberg, Sari Grossman, Robie Heilbrun Harris, Barbara

McAllister, Hanna McElheney, Sue Monell, Muriel Morgan, Deborah Salzer, Marilyn Chandler Schwartz, David Wickens, Elaine Wickens, Pearl Zeitz, Robert Cohen, Hugh McElheney, Scott Spear, Eleanor Crosby, Ursula Krainock, Dolly Levin, Peggy Nelson Wegman

City and Country School: Jane Ling and student teacher

Dalton School: Miss Brownell, Mrs. Horowitz, Peggy Parish, Margaret Santry, Marjorie Trimble, Cathie Weisel, Julie Cantor, Joan Hotchkis, Claire Henshaw McNeill

Hartley House: Margery Baumgartner

Little Red School House: Clara Antin, Margaret Wertham, Lois Wolf

New Lincoln School: Shizu Proctor

Brooklyn private schools

St. Ann's Episcopal School: Pamela Graham, Mary Grishaver, Carolyn Voigt

Oregon Private Schools

Gatlin-Gabel School, Portland: Sandra Stone Peters

St. Mary's Academy, The Dalles: Sister Stella Maris

The Cathedral School, Portland: Sister Stella Maris

New York City public schools

P.S. 1: Sophia Neaman

P.S. 70: Michael Mager

P.S. 84: Shelly Alpert, Julie Cantor, Sandra Coler, Caroline Zinsser

P.S. 108: Ruth Dermer, Aurora Jorgenson, Rose Marien, Elizabeth Stone

P.S. 121: Virginia Kwarta

P.S. 122: Judith Scholder

P.S. 134: Jane Drucker

P.S. 157: Maude Robinson

P.S. 165: Rebecca Elfant

Long Island and New Jersey public schools

Jamaica Avenue School, Plainview, Long Island: Ruth Kaufman

Westmoreland School, Fairlawn, New Jersey: Lee Bennett Hopkins

Oregon public schools
  Ardenwald School: Deborah Howe
  Seth Lewelling School: Patricia Herienger, Peter Hinds, Gerald
    Scovil, Janet Witter

Parents
  Sue Barasch, Joan Blos, Hannah Smith, Lorraine Smithberg

I am deeply indebted to all of these people, and this book is theirs as well as mine.

The scores of children whose writings appear in this book are unnamed because I feel they are entitled to their privacy. However, they emerge unforgettably on the pages. They have taught me; they have told me indirectly many things about themselves; they have pointed to new directions; they have stirred and astonished me; and here I am holding onto the comets they are shooting across space. Indeed, I have written this book because of them—who they are and what they have to say to all of us.

My final acknowledgment is to the continuing influence of Lucy Sprague Mitchell—founder of Bank Street College of Education, my own teacher there in the early days, and later my colleague. A great deal of what I have learned about language has come from her, both from her teaching and from her being. She sharpened my awareness, gave me "intake," and encouraged my "outgo," to use her own expressions. And by being entirely herself she demonstrated gloriously what it can mean to be a spirited human being who follows her own truth.

What do we mean by creative writing?

Introduction

War

But why to kill a human body.
   To exchange thoughts,
and help each other.
   But just because the thoughts don't
latch, combine or go together
   Destroyed was blood, bone
brain that so carefully
put together make a human being.
But not just that have you destroyed
for God and love still
stand in sorrow.

9-year-old girl[1]

In this poem we see a child struggling to express thoughts that are almost too heavy and dimly grasped to put into words. Obviously she has glimpsed that poetry is the right vehicle for such a burden of feeling. The result is crude but authentic; the power comes through.

A few months later the same child wrote a story which she enclosed in a thank-you letter to an adult friend who had sent her a list of poetry books. "I have written a story for you called Punpkin Pie and I," she wrote. "Pumkin Pie is a cat. I will give it to you with this letter. Thankyou again for the list of books."

Pumpkin Pie and I

> It was a usual day. But no one but I was home. It was a nice day but the sun was so hot you would think the sun would turn itself crisp like bacon. I was going to stay inside and read. But a stray cat which I named pumpkin Pie was sitting lazy like in the hot sun. As he lay in our back yard his eyes seemed to say "lets go on an adventurful journy across the sea." So under the tricky spell from Pumpkin Pie's eyes I packed a lunch containing crackers, cheese, milk, ¼ of an apple, and two candy Bars. Pumpkin Pie and I are people who like to Pretend. We make big things out of small and small out of big.
>
> I got my bathing suit on and turned the water on the green green grass.
>
> Finley It was deep enough to cover the tips of your toes. And the sun and the clouds were reflected in the shimmering water. I called Pumpkin pie over and we went threw the water like it wasn't a sea at all. After the water my pink new tenishoes went squish squish in the grass.
>
> Oh pumpkin pie there is an air plane we know. Rember Robin Red vest. Oh and there goes glamours bluebird. Such a lovely blue. Finley it got dark and mother is finishing dinner dishes. Soon I went to bed after giving Pump. Pie some brown cat food. Soon I was asleep after my adventrful day

In this story we see the child's delight in her own imagination and in her sensory responses to the sun, the wet grass, the picnic food. We see the writer at work, finding—apparently with great ease—the words that can give experience new life.

These two effective but very different pieces of writing from the same child clearly indicate that creative writing can and should fulfill more than one purpose and that the discovery of a style that is appropriate for the content is in itself a part of the creative process.

Let us turn to some second-graders. They are making a careful study in their classroom of all the steps in the development of frogs. This science project includes daily observation and note-taking. Two boys, examining a mass of frog's eggs, comment: "It looks like they weave webs out of water." "Looks like a jellyfish that swallowed beads." Science, yes; but also poetry. What we call it is immaterial. The important thing is that the boys are observing closely and are finding imaginative and startlingly accurate ways of describing what they see—"startling" because of the unexpected likenesses they are perceiving. The ability to make such links lies at the heart of the creative process.

The same could be said of the experience chart below, dictated by a group of third-graders. The intention was not to dictate poetry for poetry's sake. The children were helping a primary class across the hall with their reading. This chart—printed by the teacher on large experience-chart sheets—was intended to provide some interesting reading matter to be read aloud to the beginners. But the accurate observation and the clear images created effective surprise and made this a powerful piece of writing.

Horned Toad

Prickly, soft-bottomed,
    eyes like black diamonds,

The horned toad scrambles
    along on his black-spotted
    stomach,

Stops, lifts his needle-horned
    Triceratops head,

Flattens out his snake skin-
    scaley, stripey self,

Shuffles along on pine-cone
    feet

Looking at the ground
with his eyes like
    Concord grapes.

Slips, slides, shoots along,

Dives into the gravel,
    and digs in

With his Stegosaurus
   tail.[2]

Whatever the form, whatever the product, it is the underlying process that is important for the child and determines whether he is thinking and writing creatively or not.

The following story, by a seven-year-old boy who wrote easily and well, probably represents one of his most creative efforts. The story reveals an attempt—no doubt on a preconscious level—to look at a problem, to ask "Who am I? What am I doing? What can I become?" In short, the child is involved in a significant process of discovery of self and organization of feeling, as children so often are when they write what they simply call a "story." The boy, of course, is himself the "sneaky baby." At the time of writing he was having trouble at home with "sneaky" behavior that erupted because of his feelings about a younger brother.

The Sneaky Baby

Once there was a little baby. He was real sneaky. Like one night he turned on all the lights and woke everybody up in the house.

One day he was going to his grandmother's and he made the car go without anybody in it. And then they went next door to the gas station and bought a car and then they went to grandmother's.

On the way they passed a boat station. The baby jumped out of the car and onto a boat and he made the boat go. The boat was going 100 m.p.h.

In 20 years the baby came back from the navy. And he was a tall man. And he did not turn on all the lights in the night.

He did not make the car go without anybody in it.

And they went to grandmother's and the man did not jump out of the car.

He said "Hi grandmother."

"Hi Grandson."

And then they ate dinner.

---

[2]From *Somebody Turned on a Tap in These Kids*, edited by Nancy Larrick (Delacorte Press, 1971). Copyright © 1971 by Nancy Larrick Crosby. Reprinted by permission of the publisher.

If we focus on creative writing as a process that can lead children toward various forms of discovery, then we will escape the pitfall of too much reliance on labels and topics. In fact, we would do well to forget our old categories and "topics for creative writing." If we approach children without an array of preconceived ideas of what is appropriate for them, they themselves will teach us much about their capacities to imagine, to feel, to discover, and to find effective ways of putting their discoveries into words. Our century is exposing children to new forms in all the arts and hurtling them forward into experiences we did not have in childhood. As we know, many of our boys and girls are rocketing their thoughts into space, where we are slow to follow. Fifteen or twenty years ago, what eight-year-old boy would have remarked while looking at a picture of a church: "The steeple is a nosecone to shoot people up to heaven." What eleven-year-old girl would have written a poem like this one:

Alone in a spot in the Universe
Far off among stars that shine bright,
Our little world lives 'til this
    Little world dies.
'Til then, spins with all its might.
Far off in an unknown galaxy,
Far off by the stars secured,
Another world spins and twirls,
Intelligence far above our own,
Superior to our race.
Yes, off in the stars another small world
Stays snugly in its place.

Of course, children do not usually write like this in an atmosphere that does not encourage them to do so. Though it is common to think of children—the younger ones especially—as natural artists, the process takes nurturing. More exactly, the individuality of the children takes nurturing. What we have been implying every time we have used the word process is that a child is there at the center, able to make his own observations, honest and trusting enough to react in his own way to what he sees, and equipped with the knowledge and skills that must underlie any significant effort. After all, as teachers we are primarily concerned with the growth of children. Writing is one of the tools. When the result is creative, it is a measure of the quality of growth.

No one has expressed this better than Robert Henri in his book *The Art Spirit*. He is referring to artists; we are referring to children, but this makes little difference. The common core is the vitality of the individual. "When the artist is alive in any person, whatever his kind of work may be, he becomes an inventive, searching, daring, self-expressing creature. He becomes interesting to other people. He disturbs, upsets, enlightens, and he opens ways for a better understanding. Where those who are not artists are trying to close the book, he opens it, shows there are still more pages possible."[3]

Any teacher can translate these words; can see in them a description of boys and girls she has known. Perhaps preschool teachers especially can recognize here their inventive, searching, daring, self-expressing threes, fours, and fives. The task for elementary school teachers is partly one of trying to help their growing children retain these vital qualities, while at the same time they are learning new skills and acquiring the knowledge and understanding that carry them toward adulthood.

In fact, a look at preschool children in action may give us our best overall introduction to this question of creativity—What is it? How do we know? What are the signs?

As I think of this large subject, I visualize an enormous room of many walls and corners, uncertain in shape, its ceilings undefined, some of its areas ready for occupancy, others still of unclear dimensions, the doors everywhere standing open. I do not propose to be able to bring this room into entirely clear focus. I believe, though, that the youngest children—the threes, fours, and fives—can teach us a good deal of what we need to know about it.

References

HENRI, ROBERT. *The Art Spirit*. Philadelphia: J. B. Lippincott Company, 1960.

The inventive threes, fours, fives

Chapter one

Three-year-olds can clearly show us what is meant by the onrush toward learning through searching. Everything new must be touched, manipulated, tried on, tried out. Unexpected uses are discovered; new juxtapositions are explored.

Inventive, searching

A little boy sits at a table looking around at the yellow world through a piece of yellow cellophane the teacher has just brought in for collage work. He suddenly realizes there is something else new in the room—the small turtle he was watching earlier, over in the aquarium in the corner. New cellophane plus new turtle—what will be the result? The little boy rushes over to the turtle and peers intently through his new yellow eyepiece, and fortunately no adult stops him with a preconceived notion that collage materials belong only on the collage worktable. We do not know what the boy thought about his yellow turtle. What was important was his effort to bring two new unknowns together.

In another three-year-old room the four or five children who are early arrivals discover laid out on the table some playthings they have not seen before. These are flat, rubbery, wheel-like objects about the size of pancakes, with small cutout pieces to be taken out and fitted in. Puzzles, yes; but since they bear little resemblance to the large jigsaw puzzle boards familiar to the children, they are not recognized as puzzles. What are they? In ten minutes' time numerous uses are discovered. First, one child begins to make a pile of the small cutout pieces. As the other children hand the pieces to her she sings out, "I have a penny!"

But in a moment another child begins to prop up some of the little pieces in the holes. She sees instantly that she has made a birthday cake. "Happy birthday to David," she sings. But by this time two others have discovered that they can make "sandwiches" by fitting two of the wheels together. They pretend to eat, and talk of mustard sandwiches and peanut butter sandwiches.

Now there is discovery that these round objects roll beautifully on the floor. One or two children roll them, while three others jump to their feet, grasping the wheels in their fists. They face each other and begin rhythmical mock striking movements. Do they feel they have boxing gloves on? Once again, here are children who are profiting from the freedom to experiment in their own ways with the materials they have been given.

Shift the scene to a city park, where a group of three-year-olds have been taken for a picnic on a warm day in May. This is new territory for all of them, and their way of enjoying it is to explore it thoroughly in the three-year-old manipulatory manner—touching, feeling, doing. One child asks to be held up so that he can touch the leaves on the trees; another finds some crumbled dirt on the ground and busies himself throwing great handfuls just to see the "smoke" fly; another walks around collecting all the little sticks he can find; others throw sticks into the brook to see the splash, watch the flow. And as they scramble around on the rocks, all of them discover something about the properties of rubber soles. With all their lively senses, the three-year-olds touch, try, and learn.

Just as young children manipulate sticks and stones, so also they manipulate words to learn them, master them, enjoy them. Two four-year-olds sitting on the edge of a story circle, listening to a farm story, whisper to each other over and over, "hayloft," "apple orchard," "hayloft," "apple orchard."

In another room a five-year-old is heard repeating an enigmatic phrase, "The galaxy of the army, the galaxy of the army." When asked what he means, he explains, "The galaxy of the army is that man with all the stars on his helmet." A misconception, to be sure, but one can only be impressed by the boy's interest in the word and effort to understand it and apply its meaning in his own way.

Curiosity, questions, solutions

Children in the preschool years constantly show us that they do not take our ordinary world for granted. They wonder about anything and everything, trying to figure out reasons, answers, and inner workings. A four-year-old is walking to school with his teacher one day in the autumn. "What is on the top of those trees that makes the leaves fall down?" he asks. A three-year-old produces a definition for herself: "Tomorrow is the day we sleep for." A four-year-old suddenly announces out of nowhere, while he sits quietly eating at the lunch table: "There are nineteen people in this room, and the nineteenth is the turtle."

A group of four-year-olds who always use the elevator in their school to go down to the music room are having some trouble with the situation. As might be expected—since all of us seem to be corner-loving creatures—there is usually a grand rush for the corners, with ensuing struggle and unhappiness. One day the teacher discusses the problem with the children before they leave their room for the walk down the hall to the elevator. What can they do? What can they think of to make it easier for everyone? Is there a solution? Yes. One little girl makes a proposal that seems to satisfy the whole group. She holds up a small piece of paper, folded over once. This fold makes a corner, she points out. If each child had a piece of folded paper like this and held it up beside him, then each child would have a corner to stand in. Incredible solution! But incredible only to the adult, who never would have thought of it. The children walk calmly and happily down the hall to the elevator, each holding his piece of folded paper up beside him. The problem is solved, at least for the time being. How fortunate that no adult tells them it is nonsense; fortunate because the children are all having the opportunity to imagine and to take first steps in the learning of symbolic satisfaction.

Because young children are so ready to give their attention to problems, an alert teacher can find opportunities to carry on thought-provoking discussions with them at almost any time of day. At a four-year-old lunch table, where all are munching potato chips, the teacher asks: "Do you know where potato chips come from?"

First child:	"They have a yellow mix and they put on salt."
Second child:	"A hardening machine—that makes them hard."
Third child:	"Hey, I know—potato—potato chip!"
Fourth child:	"That's funny. I don't taste the potato in the chip."

Here are the beginnings of that group discussion process which teachers can use to stimulate children to think critically, examine premises, and arrive at new learnings as they toss the ball of thought back and forth.

These beginnings are evident also in the following excerpt from a long discussion—or thinking game—with a small group of five-year-olds on "The Fastest Things in the World." The children influence each other as they express their thoughts, stimulate each other to extend their concepts, and correct each other in the interests of clarification. They begin, as might be expected, by mentioning all the kinds of motor-driven objects and machines they can think of (omitted here). Then they move on to the less obvious:

- As fast as when you paint, the drip goes.

- Fast as rain and snow come down.

- Fast as sleighs go down the hill.

- Fast as you throw snowballs.

- Fast as sticks and pebbles and bricks when you throw them.

- Fast as sometimes weather vanes go.

- Fast as a ball.

- Fast as you plaster.

- Fast as shades come down.

- Fast as rock swings when you crane it up.

- Fast as a swing.

- Fast as blood comes out.

- Fast as firecrackers.

- Fast as birds fly away.

- Fast as eagles.

- Fast as guns.
  He means fast as bullets.

- Fast as cannonballs.

- Fast as a waterfall.

- Fast as dogs go down steps.

- Fast as dogs run.

- Fast as you look in the mirror.

- Fast as kittens run.

- Fast as when the milk comes up when you blow the straw.

- Fast as machines when you milk cows.

- Fast as paper machines go.
  Fast as printing machines—that's what he means.

The attempt to organize concepts

Similes

Even without the teacher's stimulus, preschool children are busy putting two and two together, sorting out their impressions, relating new discoveries to old. It is their ability to make analogies, to think in terms of vivid similes, that has led adults to call them natural poets.

The process is related to the making of poetry, to be sure, but it is also basic to scientific creation. As J. Bronowski has put it: "All the discoveries of science, all works of art are explorations—more, are explosions—of a hidden likeness."[1]

The preschooler, of course, is unaware that he is a poet or a scientist. All that he is doing is learning, in the way that is natural to him. He is organizing his concepts, the first step in a gradual process of learning how to generalize and think abstractly. If he delights us with the freshness of his images, it is because he is still anchored to the concrete; his senses are receptive, alive; and he will say what he thinks.

A three-year-old has found an insect on its back, struggling to right itself. She bends over and lightly touches it. "It feels like rubber pants." A five-year-old trying to describe the look of water glinting with sun and shadow under a bridge says, "It rattles around. The shadows crawl around like a worm, with the water." Another, listening to a story of a lighthouse, comments that the stairs go "like a drill." A four-year-old describes a rather complicated process: "Thinking is like little movies in your eyes." And finally, a little girl of four-and-a-half, talking to her mother about the moon and the sun, sees a likeness uniquely related to her own experience. She links the disappearing moon with the melting of marshmallows in her cup of hot chocolate:

Morning rises
And the moon is not there.
The sun is in the moon's place.

The moon is magic
Like the cups I use
To melt my marshmallows.[2]

Likenesses and differences

Preschool teachers, recognizing that sorting out likenesses and differences presents a challenge that is met with enthusiasm, help their

[1]J. Bronowski, *Science and Human Values* (Harper & Row, 1965), p. 19.

[2]Claudia Lewis, "Language and Literature in Childhood" from *Elementary English*, May 1967, Vol. 44, p. 518. © 1967 by the National Council of Teachers of English. Reprinted by permission.

children extend their thinking in this way. "How Is Skippy Like Us?" and "How Is Skippy Not Like Us?" demonstrate the ability of five-year-olds to observe closely, express their thoughts absolutely candidly, and learn as they think and discuss together. Skippy was their pet guinea pig, an important member of their classroom over a long period.

How Is Skippy Like Us?

- He has a face.

- He has ears.

- He has hair.

- He has feet.

- He cries like us.

- He climbs like us. He's a good climber.

- He has a house like us. He has a cage. He has a box.

- He sleeps like us.

- He has nipples like us.

- He has a penis like boys?

- He has a nose.

- He has teeth—little tiny teeth.

- He has a tongue like us. Sometimes he sticks his tongue out like we do. I have seen him do that at rest time, when he is on my mat.

- He bites like us.

- He drinks like we do.

- He likes us and we like him.

- He likes to be with me on my rest mat. He makes little sounds.

- He likes to hide.

- He runs.

- He cries when he is hungry. That's how we know he needs some food.

- He eats like us.

    No, he doesn't. He can't use a fork.
I mean, he has to eat like us or he will die.

- He has to have water. He likes a lot of water.

- He climbs in his water.

- He makes plop-plop in his water.

    We don't do that.

How Is Skippy Not Like Us?

- He does not eat with silver, like a knife and fork and a spoon, like us.

- He does not have hands like us. He has four feet—two in front and two in back.

- He doesn't have as big ears as we have.

- He doesn't have clothes and shoes.

- He doesn't have a coat.

    Yes, he does have a coat—his hair is a coat.
    He is all covered with hair and that is his coat.

- He doesn't stand up like we do. He doesn't stand up real real tall.

    He can't. He's really very little. He will never be as big as we are.
    He's tiny.

- He does not walk like us.

- He crawls.

- He doesn't know how to tie, or how to draw, or how to write a five.

- He can't sit down and watch TV how we do that—Indian style.

- He can't hold things.

- He doesn't talk.

    Oh yes, he squeaks.
    And he purrs.
    But he doesn't know words—he doesn't talk words.

The inventive threes, fours, fives

- He can't write.

- He isn't as big as us.

- He can't pick things up like we do.

- He can't run as fast as we can.

- He can't ice skate, or ski, or roller skate, or wear shoes.

- He can't wear PF Flyers and Keds to run faster.

- He can't sew or weave.

- He can't build buildings.

- He can't brush his teeth.

- He is softer than we are. But he can't talk to us.

- Yeah, he just goes squeeek, squeeek, squeeek.

- No, sometimes he goes peeeep peeeep peeeeeep.

Self-expression

The young child who chants a song to himself or dictates a story is often finding emotional release and comfort. The process, of course, is one well known to artists of any age. What may be overlooked, in the case of children, is the amount of organization of thought and feeling that is taking place. It is doubtful that self-expression without this ordering component leads to any lasting satisfaction. The "Bird Song" below, chanted by a little girl, is a beautiful demonstration of the use of words in a time of trouble to sum up, relieve, and transform the burden of feeling. Spontaneously the child finds a symbol for herself, sings rhythmically, and even gives structure to her refrain. Note the gradually diminishing repetition as she calls out to the bird: at first, when the emotion is high, she chants the word four times, then later three times feels right to her, then two, and finally at the end she is simply singing "Birdie." This little four-year-old girl was a child from a city slum, away from her family, in the country on a vacation. A letter had come from her grandmother, whom she called mother. At the counselor's suggestion, she dictated this reply:

I hope you ain't cryin'.
I am fine in the country.
I sleep in that house all alone.
My mother sent this, huh?
Did my mother really send this?
O.K. I hope you'll be all right. Goodbye.

Immediately afterward she sang her "Bird Song":

Bird, bird, bird, bird—
pidge, pidge, pigeon, pidge—
he's in the cage,
he's in the cage,
and maybe he's going to climb out.
Oh, I don't care, he's shut.

Birds, birds, birds, birds—
all the birds got real eyes:
teeny teeny teeny beady ones.
They got teeny teeny teeny beady ones.
They got teeny teeny teeny little nose,
and teeny teeny teeny little tail.

Bird, bird, bird—
he's in—the—cage.
I think he's chopped up,
I don't know is he chopped up or not.

You haven't got no mommy,
has no father or mommy
'cause he's lost.
'Cause I think the cage was open.
I think he have to go sleep in the street.
He's cryin' for his mama.

Bird, bird—
your mommy will come back.
I don't know will your mommy come or not.
Goodbye, goodbye.

I hope you take care of yourself.
Your mommy be right back.

Birdie—
I hope you ain't cryin'.
You ain't cryin'. I know you ain't cryin'.
But I hope you ain't cryin'.
Goodbye.[3]

Another four-year-old girl draws a series of pictures and dictates stories to go with them, again illustrating the ability of a young child to use the story as a vehicle for organizing ideas and feelings. Ideas are perhaps uppermost here. The self-expressing process is, of course, as important for the self that is learning concepts and integrating new knowledge as it is for the self that is surrounded by a sea of troubles. The following stories reveal not only the child's unique idea of what to say about a picture, but suggest that she is attempting to order her ideas about the passage of time and the metamorphoses of the seasons and of human growth.[4] I call her "Ann Wilson Rogers"—a name of her own inspiration. She combines in it the name of one of her friends in the group—Ann Wilson—and her own last name, Rogers. Ellen is the assistant teacher who wrote down the stories for the child on her seven pages of pictures:

This is a rainbow. It is night time and the sun is half going away. The sky is black and there is one little flower, because it is going to snow and that's the last flower that has to go.

This is winter. What do you think happened then? It became windy. Look at the left blue side that is colored. Printing all the letters by Ellen.

Now it is summer. It is hot. It doesn't have as much smoke and fire as the other picture. What do you think happened then?

[3]Margery Baumgartner, *Developing Children's Personalities Through Use of Language* (unpublished Master's thesis, Bank Street College of Education, 1958), pp. 49–50. Reprinted by permission of the author.
[4]Claudia Lewis, "Creating Stories: Learning, Discovery, Delight" in *Offspring*, May 1965, Vol. VI, No. 2.

This is a little girl. Her whole name is Ann Wilson Rogers. She is walking in the grass and it is very, very high and very, very cool. She cries for her sister to get her out. Her whole sister's name is Margery Ellen Rogers. Printed all of the letters by Ellen.

Look at her man that she is going to marry and his name is Henry and she is on the beach where the sun is out and there are high mountains to climb on.

This is a tree. Look at its branches and there is a red flower. If you look on the left of the tree you'll see the red flower. The sun is out and the sky is blue. It is not night and it is not raining.

Now Ann Wilson is married. She is holding a red balloon and some pink roses and she is bouncing her baby on the other arm.

Finally, here is a five-year-old at the threshold of true story creation. She has a character and a plot. That is to say, her character is in trouble with an adversary. Stories of this kind—though with more expertly developed plot and resolution—pour from children of six, seven, and eight when they are given the opportunity to write or dictate them. This is self-expression in symbolic form, representing an effort to organize and clarify. Though it does not solve a child's problem, it gives him the sense of mastery that always comes from the effort to give shape and coherence to ideas and feelings. And when a sympathetic listener is beside him, taking down what he dictates, this in itself may encourage both self-knowledge and capacity for empathy.

The Cuckoo Clock Bird

Once upon a time there was a silly little bird and its name was the Cuckoo Clock Bird. And its mother hated it and that's why its name was so silly. And his mother took very good care of him even though she did not like him because she wanted him to grow up quicker so that he could go find a new home and she wouldn't have to see him. And she treated him the best in the family even though.

And his mother just couldn't stand the way he chirped. He was very sad and he was very nice. And his father hated him and gave him spankings all day and all night. And his bedtime was nine o'clock in the morning. He got up, and then he stayed up until nine o'clock and then he had to go to bed for the whole night.

When he got up he had lots of fun. He went to parties, but he was never allowed to eat any candy or junk. His mother just couldn't stand giving him junk. And he was a very healthy little bird, but he was very sad. And he jumped all day when he was up. And he got up at eight and then had to go to bed at nine.[5]

Pattern, repetition, rhythm

We have seen above how easily a little girl expressed her feelings in poetic form as she sang her "Bird Song." The delight young children take in rhythm and repetition leads them into constant use of and play with chants, songs, and patterned stories and games. Indeed, pre-school children often appear to be more at home with these basically aesthetic elements of language than they are with purely utilitarian words and sentences. To be at home with them—in one form or another—is crucial for any artist, child or adult.

A three-and-a-half-year-old little girl had been swinging one morning at the nursery school. As she rode home with her mother on the bus later on, she began to chant a swing song—as good a way as any of telling her mother what she had been doing and enjoying during the morning:

Oh—I go swinging in my swing, in my swing, in my swing
All day long.

[5]Marilyn Chandler Schwartz, *Children's Original Stories Seen as an Expressive Medium and Their Implications for Teaching* (unpublished Master's thesis, Bank Street College of Education, 1960), p. 126. Reprinted by permission of the author.

And I swing up in the sky
I go high
All day long.

Then—my swing breaks.
So—I hang it in the sky.
I get long strings on
And I hang it in the sky.
So I get on—
And I swing so high
And I swing so high.

And I fly so high
I come to the moon
And I say to the moon,
"Hi!"
I say, "Hi, can I come on?"
And the moon says, "Yes."
So I get on.[6]

And we go around the world
And we go around the world
And we go around the world
And I never get tired.

Then—I go down sometimes and up
And down till I am home.

And then I am tired
And get in my bed
And the moon goes by
And that is the end!

In another spirit entirely, five three-year-olds seated around a snack table spontaneously create a patterned game. It begins with one of them, a girl, laughingly reporting something that must have been a joke at home: "My daddy had to take my head off!" The children respond to this by laughing and touching their heads, as though trying to take them off. "Let's take our head off!" they say.

Soon another child touches her nose—"Let's take our nose off!" All

[6]Claudia Lewis, "Creating Stories: Learning, Discovery, Delight" in *Offspring*, May 1965, Vol. VI, No. 2.

the others follow with gestures. Then, various other children take the lead:

"Let's take our eyes off!"

"Let's take our ears off!"

"Let's take our neck off!"

"Let's take our teeth out!"

Before they had finished, they were taking their bottoms off in true three-year-old fashion. All of this was accompanied with gesture and much laughter and chiming together. In this effortless and highly pleasurable way the children were learning to communicate with each other, as well as to participate in a delightful process of rudimentary story-making. They were using enumerations and repetitions characteristic of classic nursery tales which have been favorites for many generations.

Playfulness

I want to emphasize playfulness, not only because it is so characteristic of the preschool child's use of language, but because playfulness is basic in any consideration of the roots of creativity. It implies the relaxation and lack of inhibition that can help an individual find his own style; it implies inventiveness, or perhaps the restlessness and responsiveness that can lead to invention. If a child in the elementary years, or later—indeed, if any writer working with words—succeeds in becoming an innovator, it is partly because he is challenged by language as a plaything and he approaches words in the spirit of trying, testing, juggling; he has broken free from clichés and old forms and free from nets that may confine him as a person.

Preschool children often seem to have easy access to a private, playful language they all understand, a language that can help them bridge the gulfs in the early days of nursery school and bring them into contact with one another, just as their patterned games do.

In a four-year-old room, early in the year, six children are sitting quietly around a table, working with play-dough. Soon one little boy breaks the silence. As he rolls a small ball of dough in his hands he says, "I'm a ball maker. I'm a booga-ball maker." The little girl opposite him picks up a word and repeats it: "Booga-ball." This brings both children together in laughter. Before long the little boy is chanting:

"Break the moon to pieces
Break the baboon to pieces."

Pure silliness? Perhaps, but silliness that serves a purpose. It is not stopped by the teacher. She sees that it is productive, not destructive.

More often than not the preschool child plays with words and their sounds and rhythms just for his own enjoyment. He needs no collaborators. He invents, combines, and ranges all around the alphabet. Five-year-old Roger, down on the floor, working away at his block building, accompanies himself:

"Crister and a craster,
Plister and a plaster,
Mister and a master."

During the outdoor playtime a four-year-old girl sees a student teacher taking notes. She approaches her and asks to dictate something. The playful words of nonsense, rhyme, and strange reason that come pouring out may have been released by the fact that she was in a playful mood; was receptive to whatever ideas made their appearance; was trustful that she "had something to say"; and felt that since she was dictating, she was taking that step over the threshold that separates fact from fancy. She was free—or perhaps even obliged—to move about among concepts that were symbols and words that were tinged with incantatory magic. In short, it was up to her to make a poem. She experimented first with phrases that combined numbers and the names of letters and colors. Then came this delicate, playful construction:

EE for lunch,
BB DD for brunch,
A B Ho, Ho, hop, hop;
GG three three
A B C C

I E G G
A brunch,
Six five three,
HH EE GB.[7]

Poetry: symbol and magic

We have seen a number of poems in the making as we have listened to the preschool children. Not all of them have sprung from an urge so manifestly playful as the one that produced "EE for lunch." The "Bird Song" was sung for solace; the little girl who went swinging on the moon was caught up in the enjoyment of rhythm. But all three were using language more highly charged than prose; and no one had to tell them, teach them, talk with them about the ways and means. They had exposure, to be sure, in the read-aloud story sessions in their school programs; exposure, perhaps to Margaret Wise Brown's poetic concepts and words, to Wanda Gag's refrains, or to the rhythmic patterns in the beloved *Caps for Sale* by Esphyr Slobodkina. Undoubtedly this exposure offered teaching of a kind, or persuasion and invitation.

At the same time it is evident that the ease with which preschool children sing and chant and dictate what we call poetry is related to their full-bodied responsiveness, their emotional vitality. They have not closed themselves up against the appeal of rhythm and incantation; the sudden griefs and joys that rock them lead them to expressiveness that takes its color and movement from the mood. And because language is one of their playthings, they easily discover the magical edges of words.

There is much more to say, of course, about the writing of poetry, and some of it will be said as we move into the elementary years. For the time being, here is one more preschool child, a girl aged five, dictating at home a poem that seems to come straight from the frosty, midnight spot she has stepped into in her imagination. Her words are

[7]From *Somebody Turned on a Tap in These Kids*, edited by Nancy Larrick (Delacorte Press, 1971). Copyright © 1971 by Nancy Larrick Crosby. Reprinted by permission of the publisher.

charged with her excitement in her own playful, daring inventiveness:

Now would you like to go out
In the cold of the night
And tell a secret to the moon?

In the dark dark frosty snow
There will be your snowman
Waiting for you.

What was your secret you told to the moon?
That your snowman would have babies
In the frosty cold night?
Oh! Wouldn't it be too bad if your snowman melted?

Individuality and nurturing

Our consideration of the inventiveness of preschool children has led
us straight to poetry. It would be a mistake, however, to stop there or
to imply that creative writing is creative only when something "poetic" is the outcome. As we have stressed earlier, the outcome is not as
important as the process. We are interested in the individual who is
using himself in whatever ways he can to become an "inventive,
searching, daring, self-expressing creature." What we call the poetic
creations of young children often are impressive just because they
carry the stamp of individuality—that is, they reveal a child's fresh,
unique, honest way of seeing. This honesty can be encouraged by the
teacher, whatever the medium involved. Indeed, such encouragement is implicit in any preschool or elementary school program that
promotes creative thinking and expression—implicit in the total atmosphere, the total array of expectations, the everyday approach.

A group of five-year-olds who live in New York City have been
taken to visit the heliport on the top of the Pan Am Building. Later on
at school they draw pictures of any aspect of the trip they choose and
dictate comments to go with them. These dictated stories are not
poems. All are straightforward prose. Yet the varieties of approach
indicate that here indeed are individuals writing. They have not been

told what they should say about their pictures or what pictures they should draw. They are not prodded to rehearse in any set fashion what they have learned, though they have already had a chance to discuss the trip together. Instead they have been given a very rich experience and offered an opportunity to relive it in their own ways. Bob can give his vivid, brief description, his eye completely on the helicopter, while Sara ranges into a long account that reveals her paramount interest in human relationships. In this way the children are encouraged to rely upon themselves, to know and to believe in their own abilities. They are encouraged to feel that there are no sanctions against being different.

Bob

This is a propeller and it goes around fast. It goes around so fast that it makes air. It goes to the Pan Am Building and to the Kennedy Airport. It stands up like a dog.

The End

Sara

We went to the Pan Am Building and when we got there, he said, "The helicopter hasn't came yet so you can go out on the runway if the wind isn't blowing so hard. I'll look at the wind socks and see if it isn't so windy." He looked at the wind socks and said, "Too bad, you can't go out on the runway. But still it's a good view from the window and the door." (They had an automatic door.) We were very unhappy but suddenly we saw the helicopter come down and we asked Barbara for our "Happy Helicopter" books.

And the boys got up on little shelves and then all of the teachers got the boys down, but some got down theirselves. And then the teacher said, "Don't ever get up there again!" And the girls stood on chairs and some of the boys stood on chairs and when the helicopter took off we saw the helicopter take off. When we went to the subway station we saw my mother, Mary. (Our last name is Henson). When we went on the subway we had Charms. We each got seconds of Charms. We rode on the subway to school. And the teacher bumped my head on Natalie's head.

And I cried and I was very angry at Debbie after I got over crying. Then we went on the roof and after we came down from the roof we set our places. Then we went to discussion. And then we had lunch. Then we had rest time and went home.

The End

But shouldn't Sara be helped to focus her expression a little more? Shouldn't Bob be encouraged to broaden his observations? These questions might well be asked, and the teacher herself might answer them affirmatively, but the ways of working on these needs must extend over time and be absorbed into her whole approach to the children; she cannot expect growth through inexpert pruning, and she actually does see growth. Bob's story, for instance, represents a giant step for him, compared with his earlier efforts.

We stated at the very outset that the individuality of children takes nurturing. It is in the preschool, where teachers are usually trained to work with the needs of individuals uppermost in their minds, that this nurturing process is especially evident. If it often disappears from sight in the elementary years, what is to blame? Large classrooms? Academic pressures? Misconceptions about learning or the goals of learning?

In the preschool the teacher is usually aware of what the Saras and Bobs need to help them develop mastery—as aware as she can be in light of current knowledge. These children do not come to school merely to play Batman all day long; and the teacher has no fears that by cutting off this play she is cutting off creativity. She knows that some children need to be pulled back to reality from too much withdrawal into fantasy. She senses that for each child she must establish a suitable balance between structuring and permissiveness. She knows that all have a tremendous urge to learn and that it is up to her to provide the materials and many of the problems they can profitably attack, as well as the atmosphere and the broad range of experiences that encourage learning. She must meet the needs to explore, to question, to make and do; the need to feel growing mastery—all while she is constantly learning from the children and respecting their autonomy.

Some of her children may be trying to express themselves in impoverished language that cannot take them very far. For the present, she accepts the impoverishment as she accepts the children, avoiding any injurious focusing on inadequacies. However, she watches her own speech, helps the children find the words they need, searches for stories and songs full of suitable repetition, and encourages the talking and thinking that lead to language development. In addition she may want to make some use of the games and techniques suggested in such language programs as the Peabody, Bank Street, Lavatelli (a Piaget program), and others.[8]

Involvement

Because the materials for work and play that are generally offered to threes, fours, and fives seem so uniquely well suited to them, it is in the preschool that one can find almost a model of the deep interest and involvement that are crucial for creative accomplishment. Where such involvement is lacking, what is to motivate expression that has the mark of an individual personality grappling with new awareness and new interactions? It is always engagement with life that develops the individual, from the earliest years to the last.

The engagement of preschool children is often especially evident in their dramatic play. As they try on and test out the roles of mother, father, space pilot, fireman, bride—even as they curl up and "become" the kittens they have just seen—they are caught up in learning. They are exploring their concerns and discovering what they know, as well as what they feel and fear and long for. They are also mastering, in their imaginings, the problems they confront. Play is their proving ground.

Their involvement shows itself, too, as they work with blocks, paints, wood, cellophane, and clay; or while they gather about the teacher to listen to stories or enter into discussions that open up new concepts for them. Wherever they are—out on the street with the teacher, questioning the workmen there; on the playground swinging to the moon; or in the science corner, observing their guinea pigs—

[8]For an excellent description and evaluation of available programs, see Elsa Bartlett Jaffe, "Selecting Preschool Language Programs," in *Language in Early Childhood Education*, Courtney B. Cazden, ed. (National Association for the Education of Young Children, 1972).

they are at work learning about the world and about themselves.

There are preschool children, of course, who do not find it easy to become involved, to throw themselves headlong into play and exploration and learning. They may be timorous, inhibited, inarticulate, or chaotically scattered. Some of them may not know what it is to feel that sudden punishments will not descend upon them; to some the simple learning of communication through the unfamiliar use of blocks, crayons, and paints presents a large hurdle, a frightening risk of defeat; to many—no matter whether from ghetto or middle class homes—the learning of trust in an adult, in her unfailing presence, her understanding, her ability to meet needs, becomes the major, all-consuming task.

When such children are in their care, teachers always try to supply some of what has been lacking, to take any steps they can that will turn the tide. Fortunately, it is hard for anyone to believe that a young child cannot eventually learn to become receptive and involved, cannot learn to take joy in a world to be explored.

Sound, color, movement

Teachers in the elementary grades often discover that when their children are given opportunities to paint, work with clay, pantomime, improvise dramatic scenes, or move to music, their writing takes on new quality; it reflects a more expressive individual, a child who has discovered, through the other arts, new dimensions to work with in language.

In the preschool rooms, children experience the arts in richly interrelated ways. They sing and chant as they jump on the jouncing boards; they sing as they paint; they discover they can transfer their collages to the easel and build up three-dimensional, dripping-wet constructions in color; they clap to the rhythms they hear in a story; and they turn themselves into turtles creeping on the floor. They discover that paint will adhere not only to paper but to wood, cardboard, stones; they find stories emergent in their drawings; and they learn that there is a relationship between the "high" they can hear in music and the "high" of their own reaching. Other abstractions such as "round" and "square" are experienced as concrete objects, and as the block towers rise, beautiful in symmetry and intricate balance, their builders watch with surprise: such airy constructions, rising from the noisy flat blocks, and theirs, the work of their own hands.

Young children so exposed to interwoven sensory experiences find it natural to think in terms of interwoven concepts, as poets do. Some of their inventions reveal misconceptions, to be sure, but when a child reaches for clarity and meaning by pulling down from his store of words those that carry for him relevant associations, he is involved in an important integrating process. A four-year-old's definition of a cove is ingenious and convincing: "A cove is a cozy nest of rocks." Another four-year-old's description to her mother of a cake baked in school borrows a word which is singularly apt in this context: "It had eggs, flour, milk, and affectionate sugar." A three-year-old remarks to an adult who is singing off key, "That's not the right size, is it?" Finally, a five-year-old reveals her grasp of a common element in song and in painting: the teacher asks, after the children have been singing "Deck the Halls," "Do you know what this means—'Fa la la la la, la la la la'?" "Why yes," replies our child. "It's just like when you paint a design."

So it is that preschool children, in the midst of the melee of activity, are learning what language will do. They are finding words for new thoughts, putting together meanings, enlarging understanding. And their freedom to talk as they work and play with each other implies full opportunity to try themselves out, as well as to listen to and learn from others. Many times a day there are questions, mistakes, and ideas to puzzle over. But the teacher can always help with clarification. Four-year-old David, for instance, on a warm October day remarks that it is "Indian summer." A child who is standing near overhears this and turns it over in his mind. A little later he asks the teacher, "What did David say about that hot Indian?"

It has often been said that children in the elementary years can be expected to write only as well as they speak. The foundations are laid in the preschool. Through use of materials that broaden for them the possibilities of expression, through use of language that is fumbling yet inventive, unformed yet steadily taking shape, the children are learning to become thinkers, writers, intelligent communicators.

Exposure to books

Children learn from each other and from their teachers, but the books they are exposed to are also of strategic importance. The children are hearing stories read aloud every day, sometimes two or three times a day. That is, they are encountering ideas, people, and places that extend knowledge and illumine what is already familiar and emotions that stretch their understanding and teach them more about who they are and what they might become. They are learning, too, what a "story" is and what story-making involves and they are delighting in those stories and picture books that are small works of art. At the same time, of course, they are hearing language as others who are more skillful know how to use it. They are encountering words they want to master and phrases they cannot let go of—phrases that will eventually become their own: "Now dash away! dash away! dash away all!" "Caps! Caps for sale! Fifty cents a cap!" "Jack and Jill went up the hill."

Teachers know that for better or for worse, it is the exposure in childhood to styles, textures, and qualities in language that will leave its mark, as the writer—young or old—tries to discover in what ways he himself can make words work. And it is partly for this reason that teachers read aloud to children all through the elementary grades, knowing that in this way they can open up a great deal that might otherwise remain unavailable. In fact, this is one of the great challenges of teaching—to locate those varied stories, styles, ideas, and voices that are appropriate to bring to a given group of children. The field is wide open; no one is in a position to say yes or no to any choice before it has had a trial.

The beginnings are in the preschool. "Jack and Jill"—yes, of course. But who is to say that Thomas Nashe cannot also please the four-year-old with his "Cuckoo, jug-jug, pu-we, to-witta-woo!"?[9] Who is to say that the four-year-old is incapable of feeling at least some of the mysterious impact of Blake's

Tyger! Tyger! burning bright
In the forests of the night, . . .[10]

[9]Thomas Nashe, "Spring," in *Oxford Book of Poetry for Children*, compiled by Edward Blishen, illustrated by Brian Wildsmith (Franklin Watts, Inc., 1963), p. 102.
[10]William Blake, "The Tyger," *ibid.*, p. 111.

Prologue to the elementary years

Children grow, and leave behind them their preschool occupations and interests. And yet there are continuities. The seven-year-old or ten-year-old who seems to his teacher to be a very creative child no doubt lives and works and learns in an environment that is not too different from the one that nurtured creativity in him at four. The objects and activities that engage him differ, of course, and there are shifts in the nature of his relationships; shifts in directions and urgencies; as well as cognitive changes in his ways of thinking about himself and the world; but first principles remain the same.

Our overview of the preschool years has attempted to highlight these first principles, has attempted to say: here are some of the conditions surrounding these children that are important for them now and always; here are drives and capacities to respect and nurture. Individuality is strengthened, we have said:

- where children are encouraged to speak out honestly, to say what it is they see and feel, and to use their own eyes and ears;

- where emotional and sensory responsiveness are kept alive and rhythm, movement, and play are sources of vitality;

- where children have an opportunity to investigate, to manipulate and transform, and to use the old in new ways, unhampered by rigid expectations;

- where there is encouragement to probe critically, to search for ways of ordering and integrating, to face problems and find solutions, to become discoverers through taking action;

- where, above all, there is opportunity for complete involvement in work and play, in interactions with others, and in learning about both the outer and inner worlds.

For a teacher, this implies the responsibility to know about each child in her group and what it is that will strengthen his growth—how much support, how much independence, and how much structure and freedom from structure must be provided to encourage disciplined attention to work. It also implies the need to know about the children's interests or potential interests, the areas of learning that should be opened up to them, and ways of making these areas rich, vital, and wholly accessible. It also implies responsibility for boldness and inventiveness on the teacher's part as she finds ways to demonstrate to children that for herself, as well as for them, there are always "more pages possible."

More specifically in relation to creative expression, we have pointed out the importance to children of the opportunity to talk freely with themselves and with the teacher if they are to acquire mastery of language. It is through the tug and pull involved in trying themselves out in verbal interchange that understanding grows, and the ability to formulate and express ideas. Indeed, it is only when children are free to discuss their concerns openly that the classroom can become a place where it makes any sense to speak of the "engagement with life" and "involvement" that must underlie creative work.

We have suggested, also, that exposure to books read aloud is crucial if children are to have a broad knowledge of the ways in which words can be put to work and made to act powerfully on the mind and emotions; crucial, also, if children are to learn to love books—fact or fiction—and to turn to them as to other experiences that extend the self.

We have suggested that the expression of ideas and feelings in words is not unrelated to expression in the other arts and can be enriched by opportunities to draw and paint, model with clay, dance, pantomime, act, and sing. This means, especially, that the spontaneous dramatic play of the preschool years—that first experience with symbolic representation in dramatic form—should develop into improvisations and play-making, often interwoven with music, color and design, in the years that follow. Indeed, this fundamental form of expression, in which a role is fully lived and recreated through gesture, words, and movement, remains the child's principal way of learning and communicating what he knows all through the school years.

We have done little more than hint at the power young children have at their fingertips because they think concretely. True, the ability to handle abstractions and generalizations grows as children mature and paves the way to intellectual competence. But those who lose touch with the sharp sensory equipment they are born with—who forget how to observe and how to feel the impact of their own impressions—have lost one of the basic tools that the writer of any age must use in his efforts to perceive and clarify reality.

We have said that when children are writing their own stories or poems, they are often involved in one of the most important integrating experiences they will ever have. Self-expression is more often than not discovery of self, involving the attempt to organize—and thus know and control—feeling and to become clear about ideas that are taking shape. It is while the writer or artist is at work that he finds out who he is and what he has to say. It is while he works that he comes upon thoughts that surprise him and lead him on to still other unsuspected thoughts and help him enlarge his capacities for knowing, seeing, and understanding. As Gardner Murphy has said in *Human Potentialities,* "Once he has written the poem, he is a different man: he sees with different eyes."

In fact, the teacher, when she is discouraged about finding time for creative writing in the day's full schedule or when she doubts the relevance and importance of the children's small writing efforts, could do no better than ponder these additional words of Gardner Murphy in which the child's world can be seen as a part of the man's world, and the implications of all those small efforts become clear:

Man's interaction with the things of this world through the methods of the arts and through the methods of science will produce more and more that is new in man as the centuries pass. The very process of interaction with that which was previously unknown produces new content, new stuff, new realities, new things to understand and to love, as well as new instruments of observation, new ways of knowing, new modes of esthetic apprehension. These, too, will change the nature of man, not simply by enriching that which lies under the threshold of his immediate nature but by broadening the doorway through which he passes, so that he may see more of the vista he approaches and may as he does so become always a larger man.[11]

[11]From Gardner Murphy, *Human Potentialities* (Basic Books, Inc., Publishers and George Allen & Unwin Ltd., 1958), pp. 324–325. © 1958 by Basic Books, Inc., Publishers, New York. Reprinted courtesy of the publishers.

References

BAUMGARTNER, MARGERY. *Developing Children's Personalities Through Use of Language.* Unpublished Master's thesis. New York: Bank Street College of Education, 1958.

BLAKE, WILLIAM. "The Tyger," in *Oxford Book of Poetry for Children,* compiled by Edward Blishen, illustrated by Brian Wildsmith. New York: Franklin Watts, Inc., 1963.

BRONOWSKI, J. *Science and Human Values,* Revised edition. New York: Harper & Row, 1965.

JAFFE, ELSA BARTLETT. "Selecting Preschool Language Programs," in *Language in Early Childhood Education,* Courtney B. Cazden, Editor. Washington, D.C.: National Association for the Education of Young Children, 1972.

MURPHY, GARDNER. *Human Potentialities.* New York: Basic Books, Inc., Publishers and London: George Allen & Unwin Ltd., 1958.

NASHE, THOMAS. "Spring," in *Oxford Book of Poetry for Children,* compiled by Edward Blishen, illustrated by Brian Wildsmith. New York: Franklin Watts, Inc., 1963.

SCHWARTZ, MARILYN CHANDLER. *Children's Original Stories Seen as an Expressive Medium and Their Implications for Teaching.* Unpublished Master's thesis. New York: Bank Street College of Education, 1960.

SLOBODKINA, ESPHYR. *Caps for Sale.* New York: William R. Scott, Inc., 1947.

Prerequisite to creativity: the school setting

Chapter two

Children can be expected to write well when they are fully involved. This we have said again and again. Implied is a school climate that fosters involvement. Indeed, the theme of this book has its essence in this statement. Writing and thinking that enlarge a child spring from his absorption in what he has been experiencing and from the challenge he feels at all times—from himself, his teachers, classmates, and others encountered in his life—to open up questions, know and respect his own feelings, think out answers, discover, explore. Implicit is a school—though school never carries the whole burden—that offers rich opportunities for studies related to the genuine concerns of growing young people and that values at its center the individuality of its children.

Here are a few scenes that will introduce us to school settings where teachers are trying in a variety of ways to offer such challenges.

Engagement in a rich curriculum

In a classroom of six- and seven-year-olds in New York City stands an amazing construction. On a table the size of a ping-pong table, about four feet from the floor, a three-dimensional map of Manhattan is in the making. Streets, buildings, and traffic lights are all there, made by the children out of cardboard, wood, clay, paper, wire, and other odds and ends, brightly painted and artistically conceived. But the city of

New York has a vast underground substructure, and this the children are attempting to represent on the underside of the table. Pipes and tubes (some of them cardboard rolls) have been wired in place in positions and proportions roughly corresponding to the reality under the New York streets. An explanatory chart lettered by the teacher hangs on a stand nearby. This "experience chart" is the result of discussion and study. The children helped to determine its form and content, and many of them can read it:

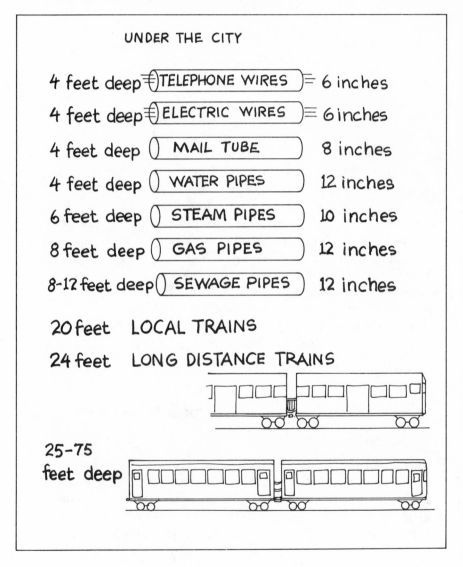

UNDER THE CITY

4 feet deep ⊜(TELEPHONE WIRES)⊜ 6 inches

4 feet deep ⊜(ELECTRIC WIRES)⊜ 6 inches

4 feet deep ()(MAIL TUBE) 8 inches

4 feet deep ()(WATER PIPES) 12 inches

6 feet deep ()(STEAM PIPES) 10 inches

8 feet deep ()(GAS PIPES) 12 inches

8-12 feet deep ()(SEWAGE PIPES) 12 inches

20 feet   LOCAL TRAINS

24 feet   LONG DISTANCE TRAINS

25-75
feet deep

How do the children know all this? Through weeks of discussion and research involving trips, subway rides, and walks out into the city to look down where excavations reveal the web of underground pipes. Pictures have helped, and books, and the resourceful teacher who located authorities who could give information.

In this classroom, obviously, there is a stress on an attitude of inquiry about the world that is immediately around. The children are grasping new concepts about their city—its geographical plan, its people and how they use the city, its needs, and its organization.

In another classroom in the same school, where the children are seven and eight years old, a study of New York City as it used to be in the days of the Dutch settlement is under way. The children in this class have already learned something about the Indians who inhabited the region before the coming of the Dutch; they know, also, a little about the league of Iroquois nations; they understand, in a rudimentary way, the Indians' dependence on nature and the reasons behind their banding together to form a government. For these children to move on to a study of the Dutch in America and their constant struggle for survival is a step that is easy for them to take and right for them and their need to learn through making, doing, and reliving roles.

An authentic Dutch kitchen is taking shape in one corner of their room. In the carpenter shop the children have constructed a double door, a small cradle, a churn; and a table and benches have been put together in the Dutch way, with pegs rather than nails. The children have gouged out wood to make bowls; they have dipped candles. Since there is no actual fireplace in the classroom, a large fireplace, including its decorative blue tiles, has been painted on a huge piece of paper stretched from floor to ceiling. The children are collecting pewter dishes from parents and friends, and a few pieces now stand on a shelf. A knitted blanket on the cradle has been made by the children. Practically every child in the class has learned to knit and has been responsible for at least part of a square for the blanket.

The children are planning scenes for a play that will be the culmination of their weeks of study, learning, constructing, cooking, sewing, and spontaneously playing in their Dutch room. The scenes will include a goodbye to the family in Holland, arrival of the family in the New World when the home is ready, conversations around the table about the new life, and some excitement when the "children" are sent out to play, wander beyond the wall, and fail to return when expected.

(They had taken refuge in a cave when a storm blew up and were trapped inside by a fallen tree until two Indian children rescued them.)

How have these children learned what they know about life in New Amsterdam? They have been out to museums, to the Van Cortlandt Mansion, and to a grist mill. They have read books and studied pictures; they have written stories; and their teacher has read aloud to them voluminously.

Their involvement in this learning is evident. Here is one small instance: The teacher is reading aloud from *Amsterdam Days and Ways* by Dorothy Hults. The children sit in a large circle, some of them knitting as they listen. They are hearing about the difficulties in New Amsterdam at a time when the governor was not listening to his advisors. The teacher stops for a few minutes and talks with the children about advisors. What are they? Do we have them in our government? Must their advice be taken? After brief discussion, the reading is resumed. When the teacher comes to the point where there is an announcement that Peter Stuyvesant will soon be the new governor, the children—all of them—spontaneously drop their knitting and break into clapping. Stuyvesant has become their hero. By this time of year they have learned a good deal about him, and it is a learning with a strong component of emotional involvement.

Make use of the arts

In the large music room cymbals are crashing, gongs are ringing, and the nine-year-olds are moving about in slow, stylized, controlled dance movements as they chant:

> Beware of the Jackal,
> Beware of the Jackal,
> Beware of the Jackal-Head, Anubis.
> Be careful,
> Be careful,
> Be careful.

The open door of the adjoining art studio reveals a collection of striking papier-mâché masks of Egyptian gods and goddesses—the work of this fourth-grade group.

The children stop their chanting, discuss with their music teacher what they are doing, and try again. They are oblivious to visitors. Girls and boys alike appear to be involved in a matter of high seriousness.

For weeks they have been learning about Ancient Egypt, and in the creation of this dance drama they are calling upon all their new knowledge and skills. And more. They are building their play around a theme that has personal significance to them. The Jackal-Head, Anubis, they have learned, is the Egyptian god who weighed good deeds against bad and fed to the monster in the underworld those whose bad deeds pulled the scale down. In the play they are composing, a little boy—in a dream—just manages to escape from Anubis, who wants to punish him for his carelessness in wasting precious water. This theme, of course, has evolved from study and discussion of beliefs about gods and goddesses and about good and evil. Whether the children realize it or not, in their dance drama they are dealing on a symbolic level with one of their own growing central concerns. What is fair? What is right? What is wrong?

The teacher of this group could point out, also, that in their study of Egypt the children are dealing with numerous other aspects of learning that have special appeal to nine-year-olds. Indeed, that is why the school staff in its curriculum discussion decided upon Egypt for these particular children. The study of hieroglyphics—so like their own secret codes—has fascinated them, and so have studies of the calendar, and Egyptian mathematics, and ways of making measurements for the pyramids. With the children's growing ability to grasp what a time-line is, they have developed some appreciation of the differences between ancient art forms and ours and have gone to museums to look at murals, sketch musical instruments and other objects, and learn how archaeologists date these objects through careful observation. In their play the costumes, painted backdrops, chants, and dance steps will reflect some of this new knowledge, while the symbolism and ritual will charge the knowledge with a power to emotionally stir the children.

The arts have an integral place in addition to times when a play is in the making. Is there any reason why children who are listening to poetry, for instance, cannot shift freely from listening to rhythmical moving and gesturing, right in the classroom? Watch these second- and fourth-graders who have been brought together to listen to portions of the record *Façade*, in which Edith Sitwell reads poems set to music by William Walton, producing an abstract effect of mood rather than specific meaning. The teacher, it is important to say, knows all of these children well. Though she is the second-graders' classroom teacher, she frequently goes into other rooms for poetry sessions with the older children. First she plays the "Lullaby for Jumbo" and elicits the children's questions and reactions, knowing that poetry of this kind will undoubtedly baffle them at first. "What impressions did you get?" she asks.

"The elephant was moving in a sort of jungle. No one was there."

"Someone walking through a graveyard."

"Kind of like you were listening to a ghost story on the radio."

"The person reading it was trying to make her voice go with the music."

"The only words I caught were 'grey leaves.' "

The teacher then reads the poem aloud and asks the children what they think its meaning might be. There are gropings to put impressions into words:

"Each person gets his own impression."

"It has some ideas mixed in with she doesn't really know what it means."

"Why does she say the red flowers make the elephant seem still moldier?"

At about this point the teacher reminds the children that there are different kinds of poems; some have a definite meaning, some don't.

"You remember the fish poem we heard last week? That had a clear meaning, didn't it?" ("The Fish, the Man, and the Spirit," by James Henry Leigh Hunt). The record is played again, and the children seem to be moving toward an understanding that if they can let themselves respond to the music and sound that may be enough.

"I think I saw a movie that used that music."

The teacher, without comment, then plays the ghostly "Four in the Morning," on the *Façade* record. The children sit quietly and listen. A few begin to make motions with their arms. Soon all catch the spirit and with their arms and hands express what this voice and this music seem to say to them. In a moment four or five children are out of their seats and moving around in wraithlike movements. Now eight or ten children are up and moving—not all in the group, for there is no compulsion about this. The room is full of tables and chairs, but they are not serious impediments. With beautifully controlled motions the children glide around, saying in gesture what they could not say in words, in response to the poem and the music.

Encourage honest thinking

The children we have just seen groping to understand the *Façade* record were indeed using their own ideas. Their comments reveal their honest impressions and questions. There is not a trace of a response that is given with the aim of pleasing the teacher or appearing to understand more than is really understood. This can only happen in the context of an atmosphere and relationships that encourage children to believe that their ideas and feelings have validity and that through use of their ideas they can grow and learn.

How does the teacher we have just seen work with a group of sixth-graders and encourage them to move in their own directions? We might find her playing a Yeats record and afterwards asking the children, "What did you notice?"—drawing from them and learning from them, rather than expounding to them. And here is a small group reading their own poems aloud, something they love to do. After Jane has read hers, Carl suggests, "Martha ought to read that one. She has a slow voice, like the poem." No slights intended. This is something the children in this class have discovered on their own—that voices have different qualities and so do the voices of poems. They look forward to the challenge of matching these voices.

Another teacher, this one in a class of nine- and ten-year-olds, is trying to help the children become active readers. She has given them some questions to think about and answer in conjunction with their reading of biographies. One of these questions is: "Has reading about this person in any way changed your ideas about either what you would like to do when you grow up or what kind of person you would like to be?" Here again are children who obviously have learned to give honest responses and who are trying to put down their true reactions, with no fear that they will be penalized if they do not claim to have been changed by their reading.

I, Juan De Pareja
by Elizabeth Borton de Treviño

"This book didn't change my opinion because one of the things I wanted to be is an artist and so is Juan De Pareja."

The Story of John J. Audubon
by Joan Howard

"Reading this book has not changed any ideas of what I'd like to be or what kind of person I'd like to be either."

The True Story of Captain Scott at the South Pole
by Will Holwood

"I don't think this book has changed my mind about what I'd like to be. Exploring doesn't have anything to do with architecture and it hasn't convinced me that I'd rather be an explorer than an architect."

Genghis Khan and the Mongol Horde
by Harold Lamb

"This book has not changed my ideas about what I want to be at all. I want to be the exact opposite of Genghis Khan. I want to save lives, not destroy them. I want to build cities, not destroy them. And most of all, I want to be a better father."

Even much younger children can be encouraged to state their own opinions, search out their reasons, value their own ideas. Here is a second-grade room where the children post their writing papers on a bulletin board. In this week's collection of papers the children are trying to come to terms with a question that has stirred them all. Their teacher has just been reading aloud to them E. B. White's Stuart Little, and now they have all seen the TV version of the story on their TV sets at home. Which is best? "All right," the teacher has said to them, "your assignment for your writing paper is to say which you prefer *and why.*" Note that she did not take what might be thought of as a teacher's stance and attempt to influence the children to prefer the book. What she was trying to do was show them that they should respect their own opinions if they could back them up with good reasons. Here are some of the papers:

"I like it better on TV. Because in the book there was hardly any pictures."

"I like Stuart Little better in the book because it told more, I think."

"I think it is better when you can read it yourself. Then you can have your own feelings."

"I liked the part when he was the teacher. I like when someone reads it because they don't skip parts."

"I liked Stuart in the book and on T.V. because they showed better pictures on T.V. And I like him read because it sounds funnier. But on T.V. they skipped parts and it didn't sound as funny. It still was pretty funny. I didn't like it read because the pictures were too small."

Discuss, share ideas

How are children to know what constitutes a good reason? How are they helped to dig down under thoughtless words and arrive at ideas that are sound? How are they to discover what they really think or are capable of thinking? They often discover through discussion, purposely led by the teacher to jolt the children into an attitude of examining, searching, and listening to others.

For instance, a sixth-grade teacher diverts her class from a loose mouthing of slogans about "their" candidates at a presidential election time, and in a social studies discussion insists that the children think about and focus on the qualities a good president should have.

A fourth-grade teacher, reading over the character sketches the children are writing for their book reports, comes across a repeated use of the word "brave." She challenges the children: "Is there only one kind of bravery? Is there a difference between 'moral' and 'physical' bravery? Is it all right sometimes not to be 'brave'?"

And in a fifth grade, where a study of the settlement of Jamestown is in progress, the teacher suggests one morning that they all think of themselves—22 children and two adults—as about to found a colony. How do they go about it? Should they have a dictator or a king or a "congress"? How would they all like having a dictator? What would this mean? The children tackle these questions with vigorous argument, strongly felt, and the whole study takes on a new life.

In a class of six- and seven-year-olds, the children have heard the classic *Story About Ping* by Marjorie Flack and Kurt Wiese, about the little riverboat duck who gets spanked for being the last duck to return to the boat in the evening. The following excerpts from a long tape indicate not only how fully the children can throw themselves into a discussion on a theme as vital as spanking, but also how the experience encourages them to try to formulate their opinions, no matter how difficult the process. As can readily be seen, the children's expression is often awkward and a little unclear. It seems very evident that children of this age need such opportunities to help them develop their language and thought.

(Deleted portions indicate either that the children were not coming through on the tape or that the discussion digressed from the "spanking" theme.)

Teacher: Now, in the evening Ping was always careful, very, very careful not to be last. Because what happened to the duck who was last?

Child: They got a spanking.

Teacher:	Now what about that? What do you think about that? About a duck getting spanked.
Child:	I think it wouldn't be nice to do. It's mean. Like I said yesterday, it's cruelness to animals. It really is. I think so.
Betty:	Cruelness, it's not cruelness!
Teacher:	No, what she's saying, have you ever heard that expression, "cruelty to animals"? That's what she means.
Child:	Yes, that's my opinion.
Teacher:	Charlotte.
Charlotte:	Well I don't think that's cruelty to animals because they don't give spankings hard.
Teacher:	How do you know that, Charlotte?
Charlotte:	Well, I don't think they spank hard.
Child:	They don't.
Child:	I think they do but . . .
Child:	It's almost torture, I think, about, that they don't get killed by it.
Jerry:	But there has to be one duck, like Cathy said yesterday, you know they couldn't all be first. I mean they're all second or all third. There has to be one duck that's last. So really, you know, maybe that duck couldn't get ahead. Maybe he was looking under for a fish and he saw that he couldn't catch up.
Teacher:	Who'd like to answer and talk about what Jerry said, just what Jerry said here? Paul.
Paul:	Well, um, oh never mind.
Teacher:	Charlotte.
Charlotte:	Well, maybe the boat was close to shore and all the bridges were out and they had to go pretty far from the boat so they may not be desperate. I mean they can't all be right next to the boat.
Teacher:	Danny.
Danny:	Well, I don't think that they should really spank him on the head. You could train him.
Child:	Well, I'm sort of agreeable with Danny. Like uh, like uh, if one's last you don't know if he's going

to toddle off at the last minute but I think you should sort of just pick him up and walk up with him.

* * * *

Teacher: Betty, do you think spanking helps the ducks learn to get on the boat in time?
Betty: Yes.
Child: Well, I guess that's what the Chinese believe.
Teacher: What do you believe, John?
John: I would say that's right. Like you could, but I mean you could have a wider plank at least so they could get on 'cause someone has to be last it can't be everyone first.

* * * *

Teacher: Would you like to hear the story?
Children: Yes.

(Story is read.)

Teacher: Why do you think Ping decided to go get that spanking? Why do you think he decided?
Child: Well, he wanted to be back with his mother.
Teacher: Was it worth it to Ping do you think?
Children: Yes.
Jonathan: Well, he thought maybe he wasn't going to be as fortunate as he was the last time.
Child: That he, that maybe a nice little boy would find him, this man who wanted duck dinner found him and just ate him instead of his having a chance of getting away.

* * * *

One feels that this duck discussion could profitably continue for a long time, but let us move on to a third-grade classroom now. Here two experience charts on the wall give evidence of a series of discussions that have helped children formulate some very basic ideas:

How does a language start?
Could we make one up?

What kinds of words
would we need?
These are some of our ideas: (this line in red)
Babies make lots of sounds.
They point to things
Grown-ups say the names
for the things.

Babies also ask grown-ups
to do things. They
imitate the sounds and
the action for it. They
learn the words from grown-ups.
We decided that our language   (these two lines
would need   in red)
DOING WORDS
NAMING WORDS
DESCRIBING WORDS
We decided that our first
words should be for
things that can help us live.

In a first-grade room two girls are overheard talking together before
the start of school in the morning—a reminder that "discussing" is
essentially a matter of sharing and discovering ideas. It belongs in
school in a hundred settings and is not something to be relegated just
to a time of formal group discussion. These two children stand near a
low table. One of the two girls is moving her hands above the table as
though feeling the air. Excitedly she says to the other, "The sky is air,
and air is around us, so this is the sky right here!"

Test it, try it—
even in the primary grades

In a class of seven- and eight-year-olds, the children are attempting to
read aloud stories they composed in picture writing in conjunction

with their Indian study. The papers have been exchanged, and it is found that children cannot make out stories they did not write. Then, when the authors try to read their own stories, even they stumble along. "There were some words I couldn't draw in pictures." In discussion with the teacher the children arrive at the idea that people need to agree on common symbols they all understand. In short, this is what a dictionary is all about, and it is a tremendous discovery for youngsters to make, one that probably could not have been made without the opportunity for experimentation.

In a second-grade classroom the children are all up and moving slowly about the room with what appears to be a controlled aimlessness. "Why can't you float?" the teacher asks. "What holds you to the ground?" Several of the children know that the answer is "gravity." This small experiment is related, of course, to the children's current questions about space and the floating of astronauts. It is only one small part of a study that is making use of books, pictures, films, and science experiments. The globe in the front of the room illustrates another way in which the teacher is attempting to help the children understand gravity. Small paper figures of people standing at various points have been attached to the globe to illustrate that gravity holds them, even though they may appear to be standing at right angles, or with their heads pointing down toward the South Pole.

Later on, as these children work on their play about astronauts, the teacher again asks them to move about the room. "Try to jump the way you would if you were on the moon, and let's see if you can make some really high jumps." Of course the jumping is not very successful, but it must be said that the inventive teacher's sound effects on the piano help wonderfully to create the illusion of height and distance.

In a first-grade classroom, small bunches of green bananas have been placed or hung in a variety of locations—on the shelf above the radiator, on a corner of the easel, on the top of a high cupboard, and on a shelf in the dark supply cabinet. Thermometers are propped near the bananas, and on a large rough chart of their own making the children are recording their observations. Which bananas are ripening the best, and at what temperatures? All of this relates to a recent trip to a market and its banana-ripening room. Again, children are learning through actually trying, testing, experimenting.

Encourage playfulness

It is chiefly in the primary grades that one can easily see signs of the playfulness that has a place in encouraging children to be inventive.

On a large playground the first-grade children are scattered far and wide. It is now time for them to come together to return to their room. How does the teacher assemble them? This particular teacher merely stands where she is and begins a light bouncing movement on her feet, calling out rhythmically, "Duck! Duck! Duck! Duck!" The children instantly run to her and cluster around. Obviously this is a signal they all understand, a gamelike signal. It is the language they themselves speak; and they trust and love the teacher who knows how and when to use it with them.

And here are first-graders who have been writing about a recent snowfall. On a little boy's paper we read:

When you get up from your bed
You go to your window
And you see the snow.
You say "Yippee!"

"Yippee" is probably not in every dictionary, but this child's teacher might say that it ought to be, if children are gong to learn that writing means putting *themselves* down on paper.

In a third-grade classroom the schedule for the day has been written on the chalkboard at the front of the room—a standard procedure, of course, in almost every school in the country. But this schedule is unique. Its heading is "Plizard Schedule." A visitor soon discovers other "Plizard" labels in the room. A child explains, "It's just a game we have." Anyone who knows the pleasure third-graders take in words and codes can easily reconstruct what may have been the genesis of this invention. And not only have the children in this room settled for "Plizard" as a playful sign and symbol that belongs only to them, but they are also daily dictating and adding to a continuing story about a mouselike character they have named "Plousey." It is hard to point to what may be the most important element here—the encouragement to the children to play imaginatively in their own way or the trust the children are experiencing in a teacher who can sanction this play.

Develop approaches to literature

In a fifth grade in Harlem, where most of the children have been struggling with reading on a second- or third-grade level, we find the class coming to life as a student teacher reads aloud to them the opening pages of Claude Brown's thoroughly adult book, *Manchild in the Promised Land*. In these opening pages the children see and hear a boy like themselves, a boy who has not been shielded from the violence of ghetto life. They listen, as they would not and could not listen to, say, Kenneth Grahame's *The Wind in the Willows*, standard fare for many children of this age. And not only do they listen. The student teacher helps them discover that they themselves can read these first pages.

In a sixth-grade class the children are studying the Middle Ages and a gifted student teacher has been introducing Chaucer through discussions, books read aloud, records, and examination of a beautiful edition in Middle English script. How does she help the children realize the essence of Chaucer's style? One way is through the introduction of a comparison with Bob Dylan, a singer/songwriter whom the children all know though they may not completely like or understand him. Certainly this is an ingenious way to help children come to some understanding of what goes into an author's style. Listen to some of the comments:

"Chaucer says it right out."

"Dylan—well, something could mean a lot of things; you're not supposed to know."

"Chaucer writes in the language of the people."

"Dylan writes his own personal language."

"Chaucer writes what he sees."

"Dylan writes what he feels."

The children are exploring what for them is a whole new realm in literature and are doing so through the exercise of their own insights.

In a rural school where the second-graders are making somewhat slow progress with their reading, the teacher has recognized that part of the difficulty lies in the children's inability to relate printed words to actual experiences, events, objects. Her attack on the problem, which we need not describe in detail here, is many-pronged. What is relevant for us at this point is her decision to read a great deal of poetry aloud to the children—poetry in which images are clearly linked to the words. After she has read, she asks the children to draw what they have seen in the poems. Not only is she helping the children with their reading, but she is also delighting them with the world of print and giving them access to poetry they can understand and love. She chooses, among other poems, Gelett Burgess' well-known "Purple Cow" and Elizabeth Madox Roberts' clear and brief three lines entitled "The People":

The ants are walking under the ground
And the pigeons are flying over the steeple,
And in between are the people.[1]

Needless to say, the bulletin boards in this room are bright with purple cows and with pictures revealing the attempts of seven-year-olds to order their perceptions of the three planes where ants and pigeons and people dwell.

Experiences outside the classroom

In these classrooms we have seen teachers and children engaged in activities that demand explorations, that lead in many different ways to rich involvement, and that may lay foundations for good creative

[1]From Elizabeth Madox Roberts, Under the Tree (The Viking Press, 1922), p. 67. Copyright 1922 by B. W. Huebach, Inc., Copyright © renewed 1950 by Ivor S. Roberts. All rights reserved. Reprinted by permission of Viking Penguin Inc.

efforts. The examples we have given are only a few among many. We have placed special emphasis on social studies and the arts, believing they are of central importance. However, certainly children zestfully attack many other types of challenge. Any teacher who has seen children so caught up in a math lesson that they want to give up some of their outdoor play time in order to continue knows this; or children excited over discovering ways of organizing research notes; or a sixth-grader plodding on alone in the attempt to construct a telescope; or first-graders involved in a camera project—photographing the back of each child in the same jacket—a project that is helping them discover clues to the ways they habitually identify people by posture.

I could add that some of the most important experiences children have, in connection with learning in school, are those that go on outside the school. I am referring here not only to the trips children take to explore their cities and museums; not only to the outdoor walks to sketch in the park or on the street when snow has fallen gloriously on the garbage cans; I am also thinking of those rare opportunities a few schools now offer their upper-elementary-grade children to go off and live in another environment for a week or so—on a farm, or at the beach.

On the Oregon coast, Camp Westwind is available to schoolchildren in the spring season. Here they may live with their teachers and counselors, studying sea life, geology, astronomy, forestry, enjoying the beach and the ocean. One group of fifth- and sixth-graders from an Oregon public school 90 miles inland recently spent a week at this camp. Twice a day, in scheduled writing periods, they jotted down impressions in a wide variety of forms—notes, diaries, or descriptions in poetry or prose. Here are some selections from their *Writings from Outdoor School.*[2]

At Camp

When I get to Outdoor School
I intend to find a door to another

[2]Poems reprinted by permission from *Writings from Outdoor School* by Grades Five and Six, Seth Lewelling School, Milwaukie, Oregon, North Clackamas School District. Patricia Heringer, Peter Hinds, Gerald Scovil, Janet Witter, teachers, May 1966. "The Waves" reprinted from *Somebody Turned on a Tap in These Kids,* edited by Nancy Larrick (Delacorte Press, 1971). Copyright © 1971 by Nancy Larrick Crosby. Reprinted by permission of the publisher.

world. This door will be the surface
of the ocean. When I open the door I
will find animals and plants, that
may think what ugly creatures we are.

Boy

Tide Pools

As the waves pound against distant
rocks the tide pool stays calm, dead,
and silent—but life is there. The seaweed,
limp in the water, floats as if death had
strangled life out of it, but as dead as
it may seem, life is still glowing inside.
Even the water is full of life, plankton,
and although they are microscopic, they are
alive.

Boy

Foggy Day

We saw the sea gulls playing in the wet
sand and thought we'd like to join them.
The day was a normal beach-like day with cold
and smoky fog above the mountain peaks.
Feel the cold wind on the sandy beach!
With wet tennis shoes we walk with a
feeling of the seashore, all bundled and covered
as the winds blow.

Girl

The Waves

As the waves come rolling
and roaring upon the beach
like hands grasping for food,
over my feet, over my knees,
I feel as if by some magic force

I'm standing back, back and away,
even though I'm standing still
as a statue.

Girl

Sand

The feel of sand in my hand is soothing.
Sometimes it feels as if you're trying to
grasp into eternity and nothingness. Other
times it feels as if your time is ever
so slowly slipping away, out of your reach.

Girl

These children are alive, extending their perceptions, looking both inward and outward in new ways. And they are celebrating their joy. As they write, their experiences crowd up into their words and take on fresh dimensions. Indeed, in offering these writings from the Outdoor School, I see no better way to make the point: the prerequisite is the setting. Good writing springs from involvement in experiences that excite feeling.

But before we turn to examine more closely the writings of children throughout the grades, there is still something to say. There are doubts to consider.

"Isn't it true," many teachers might object, "that some children just don't write, no matter how rich a program you develop?" This is certainly true; there may have been individuals even at Camp Westwind who could not put down any truly vital responses on paper. Some children write much more easily than others; some children become very blocked for personal reasons; some children are just not as interested in writing as they are in other forms of expression; and it is especially true that the best writing of children often seems to flow from experiences unrelated to classroom work, however exciting this work may be. Here, for instance, is a paper handed in to a teacher by a third-grade girl who lived across the street from the school in one room with her family of six:

The Dancing Fairy

There once was a fairy who loved to dance but she could not, because she only had room enough to do one step. And she called that step the lonely step because she had to do it over and over again in the same place. Her mother knew how she loved to dance. So one day her mother bought a new house where she could do more than one step and when the fairy came home she cried with joy, "Thank you mother," and she began to dance and dance and dance and dance.

What is important here is the fact that the teacher has created an atmosphere in which the child feels free to write this personal story.

If school has meaning as a workshop in which children find the stimulus to write, it is because of the atmosphere that has been established; the excitement that has been generated upon looking at and learning about many aspects of living; the exhilarating exchanges between children and teachers and among the children themselves; and the growing confidence that comes from being encouraged to explore one's own feelings and to search, and dare, and invent. Sometimes the children's writing will relate directly to school experiences; often it will not. But is school to be divorced from the whole stream of living?

I have seen a school—an experimental storefront school for primary children in East Harlem—where the doors were kept, almost literally, open to life. Here the children were free to find involvement in ways not often possible for children in our schools. On one of the days when I was visiting, the first-graders had brought in from the street an emaciated stray dog who seemed near collapse. He was made comfortable on old cushions on the floor; children brought him water and laid dog biscuits and cookies—their own midmorning snack cookies—beside him. From time to time children left their work to kneel beside him and pet him and listen to his breathing. Would he live, they wondered? A boy made a leash and several children, of their own accord and without a teacher along, took the dog out to the street when they judged he might need to go. During the morning the work of the children proceeded—at the carpenter bench, the easels, the story corner—yet the dog was at the center of this school day, drawing a flow of compassion from the children.

Toward the end of the morning some of the children were given the task of cleaning up their basement playroom, which they had left in disorder the day before. They swept the floor and arranged their usual ring of chairs at one end of the room for a "club" meeting. The room was neat. Suddenly an idea came to someone—the dog, bring him down here to rest. First his cushions were placed on the floor in the center of the circle of chairs; then the dog was brought down and covered with a blanket. Five or six children drifted to the circle. Suddenly a boy who had been repairing an old table lamp came dashing down the cellar stairs. The lamp now had a new base—a piece of birch limb—and a new shade—an empty gallon paint can. The boy plugged in his light and set the lamp on the floor beside the dog. Another child ran to switch off the ceiling light. The children sat down quietly in the semidarkness, and there they were, giving their dog what they could—physical comfort, loving attention, and something they could not have defined but were led to by a universal human need: they had devised an almost ritual situation; they had found the magical power of darkness, a small light, a circle. Who told them? Who directed them? Who thought of all this? They themselves were the initiators, and on this day they were probably experiencing more of "life" than any other first-graders in the city. Whether they later wrote or dictated something about the dog (who was taken to a veterinarian and recovered) is not the issue here. What they enacted in the darkened cellar was more appropriate than any merely verbal expression could have been. After all, where are we placing our values—on a collection of papers written by children or on a totality of meaningful experiences and interactions that may produce "new things to understand and to love, as well as new instruments of observation, new ways of knowing, new modes of esthetic apprehension"?

References

BROWN, CLAUDE. *Manchild in the Promised Land.* New York: Macmillan, 1965.

DE TREVIÑO, ELIZABETH BORTON. *I, Juan de Pareja.* New York: Bell Books, 1965.

FLACK, MARJORIE, and KURT WIESE. *The Story About Ping*. New York: Viking, 1933.

GRAHAME, KENNETH. *The Wind in the Willows*. Illustrated by Ernest H. Shepard. New York: Charles Scribner's Sons, 1908, 1935.

HOLWOOD, WILL. *The True Story of Captain Scott at the South Pole*. Chicago: Children's Press, 1964.

HOWARD, JOAN. *The Story of John J. Audubon*. New York: Grosset and Dunlap, 1954.

HULTS, DOROTHY. *New Amsterdam Days and Ways: The Dutch Settlers of New York*. Illustrated by Jane Niebrugge. New York: Harcourt Brace Jovanovich, 1963.

LAMB, HAROLD. *Genghis Khan and the Mongol Horde* (World Landmark Series No. 12). New York: Random House, 1954.

ROBERTS, ELIZABETH MADOX. *Under the Tree*. New York: Viking, 1922.

Seth Lewelling School, Grades Five and Six. Patricia Heringer, Peter Hinds, Gerald Scovil, Janet Witter, teachers. *Writings from Outdoor School*. Milwaukie, Oregon, North Clackamas School District, May 1966.

SITWELL, DAME EDITH. *Façade*. Music by William Walton. Columbia ML5241.

WHITE, E. B. *Stuart Little*. Pictures by Garth Williams. New York: Harper, 1945.

The sixes and sevens: beginning to write

Chapter three

When I use the term "beginners," I am purposely avoiding the labels "first-graders" and "second-graders." As we know, some children are ready for writing at six or even earlier and others at seven or later. Those schools that are using the ungraded primary approach or making open classrooms available give recognition to this fact. My concern in this chapter is with the work of children who are at the beginning stages. Whether the ages are six or seven is not crucial.

Nor am I making distinctions between writing and creative writing. Any formulation of his ideas, any sentence or two that a young child attempts to put down on paper—when he is not actually copying the teacher's words from the chalkboard—is creative if the child is thinking for himself.

Dictation

It cannot be overemphasized that children who are just beginning to write need the experience of talking as a solid underpinning—talking with friends, dictating stories, discussing. If they are going to learn eventually to write easily, then they must learn to put themselves and their voices into the words they speak. And they must hear the words of others—their classmates and the clear and interesting words of the teacher as she talks with them and reads aloud. Certainly in any program with beginners, the spoken word comes first, the actual writing later. In fact, dictation continues long after the children are learning to write their first stories.

The following story was dictated by a seven-year-old boy:

Our Trip

The ferry boat ride! I loved that! The windy place where I almost fell off the boat! It was real funny because my hair kept blowing in my eyes. Then I ran back to the warm place. When we came to the dock, I hated that crashing noise. It sounded like giants stamping—like a giant octopus. Don't you know that noise? No one could miss it—no one in New York, no one on the boat.

This story has the immediacy of the experience itself. It is full of noise and wind, and it vividly reflects the child talking, feeling, laughing, gesturing.

Group dictation

The children in a six-sevens group in a New York City school had a fall picnic in the park under the George Washington Bridge—a dramatic spot, of course, for New York City children. The huge span stretched above them, and below it stood the little red lighthouse, known to them all through the much-loved story *The Little Red Lighthouse and the Great Grey Bridge* by Hildegard H. Swift.

Later, back in the classroom, the children recalled the trip in discussion with the teacher, and she jotted down their impressions. Still later, as the class develops the idea of painting a large mural of the bridge and lighthouse and river, the teacher uses the dictated record of impressions to help remind the children of what they saw and what they might want to put into the mural. Though she knows that few of the children can read them, she excerpts descriptive sentences and phrases from their discussion, prints them separately on long thin strips of oak tag, some lettered in red, some in blue, some in black—just for variety and attractiveness—and posts them where they can be seen.

In the end, a bright mural covers the wall at one end of the room. Above it are three of the children's descriptions:

> "There were hills behind the bridge and silver speckles on the grass."

> "There was water surrounding the rocks."

> "The net was hanging under the bridge out over the lighthouse. The workmen were painting and fixing and sparks were coming out."

And on the wall at the side of the mural are posted the remaining excerpts:

> "The bridge is like a dot-to-dot picture to trace over."

> "It's like a string with lights on it."

> "There were boats in the river and fish in the river and waves came after the boats."

> "The fence around the Little Red Lighthouse. . ."

> "The Little Red Lighthouse is under the bridge. . ."

> "The things that hold up the bridge are standards and cables. . ."

> "There were lights on the bridge. . ."

> "We cooked at the fireplace."

> "We listened for sounds."

The story of the trip is told in words, as well as in color and design, the two approaches complementing and enriching each other. And not only is the teacher helping the children see how words can work; she is helping them learn that there are several closely related ways to relive, learn from, and sharpen their experiences. Perhaps she is also showing them that their very simply stated descriptions of sights and sounds and actions make for good writing; in fact, she is demonstrating to them that they are quite capable of all that is required of them at this stage. There are evidences, too, that she is exploring vocabulary with the children, helping them discover and use the correct words for what they are describing—interesting words like "surrounding" and "standards" and "cables." Finally, there is ample evidence that the teacher is not satisfied with anything less than correct English usage herself. Although this is a project with children who are only beginners, why shouldn't she use quotation marks around each child's sentence and supply the dots at the end to indicate when she is excerpting from a child's contribution? Her explanations of these practices can only fascinate the children and give them a taste of excitement over the learnings that lie ahead of them.

Another teacher helps her children pull together their thoughts and questions by dictating an experience chart related to their study of space and the sun and planets. (To see these children in action, turn back to page 54.) The discussion that resulted in this chart took place following a filmstrip which in itself had helped the children clarify some of their concepts:

> The sun is a star.
> It is far, far away.
> It is burning hot.
> It is so hot that nothing can live there.
> We cannot go to the sun.
> A spaceship cannot go to the sun.
>> But the sun can help us live on earth.
> It gives us light and heat.
> It helps plants to grow.
> Without the sun the earth would be
>> dark and cold.[1]

[1]Elizabeth Stone, *A Study of Science and Language Arts Curriculum in a Second Grade Class* (unpublished Master's thesis, Bank Street College of Education, 1968), p. 45. Reprinted by permission of the author.

Strictly speaking, this is not the work of the children themselves. The teacher guided it with her questions and reminders and helped determine its form. But such guidance, indeed, is generally the role of the teacher when young children are dictating a story, a recall of an experience, or even a poem around a central idea. What is important about this piece of writing is the encouragement it has given the children to express themselves clearly and simply, to work a little at organizing their ideas, and to see that writing can have this clarifying, organizing function.

At this early stage, teachers sometimes offer children a framework, a pattern for them to follow in their thinking. This limitation can help them focus their thoughts and gives them the plea ure of working within a form. After all, children of six and seven are still young enough to delight in simple language patterns that emphasize repetition and contrasts.

Here is a teacher who is helping her large class recall a trip to a busy industrial area in New York City, where they had seen boats, bridges, and derricks. "Close your eyes," she says to them, "and try to get pictures in your mind. Think about things we saw that went slowly, and things that went high in the air." This, of course, is not intended as a rigid prescription and the children do not follow it rigidly. Yet it helps them to highlight and remember aspects of the trip they might otherwise not have recalled. It seems obvious, too, that in asking them to think about things that went slowly, the teacher is setting a tone for them—intentionally or not—a tone that leads them into a slow rhythm. Or is it the contribution of the first little boy that sets the tone? Here are the beginnings of this group discussion:

Boy: The boats are going very slowly
        The bridge goes up, up, up
        The cars are rumbling
        And the bridge goes down.

Boy: The escalator goes slowly, slowly up
        The other goes down.

Boy: I saw the boats go up and down the canal
        I saw the drawbridge go up, up, up
        And we walked across.

Girl: The boats on the river go Toot-Toot
        The drawbridges go up, up, up

And way down, down, down
The derrick moves back and forth and sideways
Picking up mouthfuls as it goes and dumps them
    into the hole in the building.

Exercises in observation

Children of these ages delight in the challenge of finding similes and metaphors to clarify their observations. Give a six-year-old an opportunity to tell how a caterpillar feels to the touch, or how soft is soft, and he will not only feel like a discoverer, but like a successful one, because you are asking him to use his native equipment. He can still see and touch and smell and hear more sharply and with more individuality than most of us who are older; he is free of our clichés. In fact, it is a teacher's responsibility to give her beginners full opportunity to discuss their new experiences in terms of what they have vividly sensed. In no other way can these experiences retain their reality for the children and become a part of their learning. If a teacher—or student teacher—can sit down with a small group and let them do no more than exercise themselves in finding similes and analogies that can clarify their concepts, she will see from their responses that she is giving them a genuine taste of the joy of thinking and the joy of writing.

Here a group of children watch a snowfall that is whirling and driving like a blizzard:

• It looks like salt in the air!

• When it blows it looks like white streaks whizzing through the air!

• It looks like a lot of little pieces of chalk.

• It looks like a whole bunch of white prickly porgies flying through the air.

• It looks like specks of paper.

• It looks like white bullets whizzing through the air.

Perhaps only the child who offered "prickly porgies" knew what they were, but no matter. This was his idea, his interest. Let the other children learn from him.

Another group of children tell how it felt to play outside on a very cold day. Perhaps they were influenced and helped by the fact that earlier their teacher had been reading them Betty Miles' vividly descriptive book, *A Day of Winter*, yet the children are not actually copying what they have heard. Instead, they are talking about their own freezing hands and lips and noses and toes.

- Cold hands, skinny with lines.

- Nails hard from the cold.

- Lips ice dry.

- Wind that fights us.

- Noses that feel sticky like glue.

- Toes brick stiff.

- Cold tears, happy winter tears.

- So cold it hurts to breathe.[2]

What things are soft, round, quiet? Fast, slow, dark, and heavy? These are just a few of the concepts that sixes and sevens enjoy defining—and not only sixes and sevens, of course. Children all through the elementary grades, as well as adult writers, find this a stimulating exercise. Here are a few examples from various primary groups in various schools, illustrating how responsive children are to this kind of challenge, how imaginatively they can call upon their own experiences:

Soft

- As soft as the inside of a turtle might be.

- As soft as a newborn baby's cheek.

- Your heart beating and cotton are the softest things I know.

[2]From *Somebody Turned on a Tap in These Kids*, edited by Nancy Larrick (Delacorte Press, 1971). Copyright © 1971 by Nancy Larrick Crosby. Reprinted by permission of the publisher.

Quiet

- As quiet as a shock.

- As quiet as a flea going to a dog.

Black

- As black as a closed drawer.

Round

- The world feels round if you have long enough arms to stretch around it.

A small group of eight children sit with their teacher beneath a clock. How soft is this ticking? What does it sound like?

- The clock is saying, "It's two minutes after one o'clock."

- It goes tick-tock, choo choo, like a train.

- It sounds like a cat's slow purring.

- It reminds me of a soft hand knocking on a door.

- It sounds like somebody clicking with their tongue,
  Or clicking for a horse to make him go.

- It sounds like rain falling.

- It sounds like popcorn popping.

- It sounds like soft little choppings with an axe.

- It sounds like cutting cardboard with scissors,
  Or like shaking a piggy bank,
  Or like tapping a pencil, lightly,
  Or turning on and off a light.

The same teacher, with another small group, guides the dictation of the following "Observations On An Apple." Obviously the children held the apples in their hands, felt them, cut them into quarters, looked at them, thought about them, and finally, of course, ate them. It is clear that the teacher must have asked the children to touch, look, smell, and listen, all along the way.

Some Observations On An Apple

- I am holding an apple.
- It feels like a hard ball.
- It feels nice and smooth.
- It feels fresh.
- Two sides feel round and fat.
- Two sides feel "in" in the middle.

- The apple skin has a bunch of red spots, like freckles.
- The apple skin feels squeaky.
- It feels snappy and slidy.
- It has dents in it
- And five bumps on the bottom.
- It looks like there is a little opened-up star on the bottom of it.

- A quarter of an apple looks like a little boat.

- Inside the apple is slidy like an ice-skating rink.
- Outside it smells sweet and sugary.
- It smells cool sometimes.
- It smells warm sometimes.
- It smells in-between cool and warm sometimes.

- An apple sounds crunchy and munchy like a carrot when you eat it.
- An apple tastes like it should taste.

- You can make apple pie out of an apple.

- You can make applesauce and apple juice

- And apple crisp and apple cider

- And apple butter and apple jelly

- And apple omelet
  Out of an apple.

An apple starts big.
But, when you eat it,
It grows smaller and smaller
Until the last bit is gone,
And then,
            there's
                ZERO!

A vivid sensory experience for all of us comes when we rise from a chair and discover a foot asleep. Any such vivid experience can be presented to a group of children as a writing—or thinking—challenge:

- It feels like a thousand ants running all over the bottom of my foot.

- It feels like needles and pins.

- It feels like thousands of little toothpicks sticking into my foot.

- It feels like cracker crumbs.

- It feels like sawdust all over your foot.

- It feels like salt and pepper sprinkled all over your foot.

- Like cat's claws digging into you.

- And like shavings on your foot.

- It feels like prickles all over you.

- It feels like a procupine scratching a little bit.

- When you try to stand up, it feels like shavings going up and down.

- It feels like hairs all over your feet.

- It feels like pouring a lot of sand all over your leg.

Later—two months later, in fact—a child who had been involved in this group dictation came up to the teacher with another idea to add to the story: "It feels like thumbtacks pricking in the side and bottom of your foot." This gives evidence that children—some of them, at least—do remember these dictation sessions, are stimulated by them, and may carry away with them ideas to make use of on their own.

Individual dictation

"Wonderful for the children, but so hard to manage." This is the usual complaint. Yet, as aides, special teachers, and student teachers become increasingly available, teachers can hope more and more to give individual children a chance to write through dictation.

In a class of beginners, the children were encouraged to put together picture books consisting of their own drawings arranged in such a way as to tell a story. The children then sat down with an adult who wrote the story on a large sheet of paper as it was dictated and later helped the children excerpt those portions that they—or she—could write in beneath or beside the pictures. The result was that a surprising amount of adventure and information found its way into stories of just a few words. A number of these stories were about space and space trips, since this class, like one we have seen earlier, was involved in a space study. The block-building area of their floor was full of constructions of fascinating complexity—launching pads, rockets, helicopters; and the walls were crowded with drawings and collages related to the project. It is true that children as young as six cannot learn very much about space, but there are certain clarifications that can and probably should be attempted. The whole subject can easily become an overly exciting and possibly disturbing mishmash of fact and science fiction. The tendency to combine fact and fantasy is clear in the following story from this class. It was as illuminating for the teacher as it was satisfying for the child:

Here is a rocket. It is going into space.
The rocket is going to Mars.
Here is the rocket in space.
The rocket is on Mars. Here are the Martians. Here are their houses.
    The Martians show the spacemen around.
The Martians say goodbye to the spacemen. The rocket goes to
    Venus.
The rocket lands on Venus. They see a lost man chasing bugs. He
    shows them around. They fall into the holes of the bugs' houses.
    They dig themselves out. The man on Venus takes them back to
    earth.
The capsule goes off.
The capsule splashes down into the water.
Lots of helicopters come. The aircraft carrier comes.
The aircraft carrier comes to the dock.
The President gave the spacemen a lift to the spaceman's house.
They arrive at the spaceman's house. The spaceman asked the
    President to stay for dinner. He said Yes.

The End.

In another school a little girl and a student teacher sit down together. The child has asked to tell a story about a tiny yellow plastic gun she holds in her hands—a toy she brought to school on this particular day. The story will be about the gun and a grasshopper, she says, because a grasshopper is just the right size for the gun. And the name of the book will be:

Mr. Grasshopper's Book

Once upon a time there was a grasshopper. He lived in a thicket. Every day he went out to catch food with his little gun. And when he came back he had a little fire in the thicket. And it was a flea.

This was all there was time for. The child seemed to be enjoying the miniature images she was creating, as well as the word "thicket," which was not entirely clear to her but was fun to say, one of those words that can build in a child a love of language and its mysterious ways of stirring the imagination. Perhaps someone had been reading to her Aileen Fisher's collection of poems, *Cricket in a Thicket*.

The following day the student teacher, feeling that more of this story surely should be forthcoming, urged the child to continue. This is what was dictated:

And after supper he went to bed.
After he went to bed, he ate breakfast.
And then he went to play.
And then he went to work in his little house.
Then he went to play in his little friend's house.
And then he went for a walk.
THE END
hop-joke, hop-joke, candy.

With the exception of the "joke" at the end, the story has lost all its quality. It is no longer the grasshopper's story. The thicket has vanished. This result suggests that though young children may sometimes want to go back to the thoughts of the previous day, they often do not. But in her completely original "joke" ending, the child, perhaps taking a restless leap, finds her way back into her own story world. What does this little joke mean? Where does it come from? The student teacher could only explain that the child seemed to enjoy the sounds of the words. Perhaps there is no reason to explain it further. It is better just to enjoy the startle and freshness. What an idea—end a story with a little string of sounding words, as though they constituted a signature or a formula as proper and potent for the conclusion of a story as "Once upon a time" is for the beginning!

Similarly, one is glad to find a story like the following, dictated in the fall of the year by a seven-year-old boy who did not yet have the facility to write it himself. Superficially, perhaps, it resembles thousands of accounts children write or dictate about experiences that have had special meaning for them—summer experiences, farm experiences:

Gruffy and the Steer

My grandfather owns a farm. There are steer down the road. They live near the silo. A silo keeps hay in it. A silo is tall and round like a tin can.

Some of the steer are black, and some are brown. Their noses run a lot. They take the grass from my hand. The steer are shy. They are very friendly.

Gruffy is my dog. He chases the steer. He barks and he growls but he is afraid of them and he runs away when they just take one step forward.

The reason this story is unlike thousands of others may be that our writer is a child who has retained—through nature, encouragement, or both—the ability to observe small sensory details that make a scene live when it is put into words. He notices colors, the runny noses of the steer, the one step that scares the dog; and he can describe a silo in a splendid concrete image. This makes for writing that has exactly those qualities a teacher hopes all her children will develop as they learn to master the fundamentals: simplicity, clarity, honesty, and sharpness of observation. And not only is this writing alive; better yet—the child behind it must be a live one. We know he is a lucky one—lucky to have a farm to go to, where new sights and sounds keep him alert and observant.

Also lucky is the little boy who dictated and then wrote—with his teacher's help—the following account about his work in the school carpentry shop. Left entirely to himself to write, he might have floundered completely over the vocabulary he needed. But he knows and uses interesting words in his speaking vocabulary. With help and practice, he can learn to write as he speaks:

My Aircraft Carrier

I started an aircraft carrier. I might make some airplanes for it. It will have a neat conning tower. The conning tower is for radar and sonar. People can look down from the tower and see if the deck is clear. And they say to the pilot, "The runway is clear."

Another type of story many children love to dictate is the imaginative tale full of adventures and mishaps, symbolically representing some of the ups and downs of their own inner lives—stories that have an important releasing and organizing function, as we have pointed out earlier. A teacher who can find ways to encourage such dictation is doing her children a service. Of course, stories of this kind are handwritten by children as soon as they can manage a flow with their pencils. Since this is the case and we will soon look at many of these handwritten stories, the dictated variety will not be included at this point. It is time to turn to the question, "How do children write 'creatively' when they are taking their first slow steps with their handwriting?"

Writing begins

Getting the ideas down

The foundation is laid when a child can handle his letters and knows that he may try to put words together whether or not he can spell them correctly, when he is encouraged to feel that anything he may want to write about is acceptable, when he knows that he may move at his own pace, and when he realizes that it is, after all, not so hard to write down his ideas.

Some teachers give their beginners crayons and large sheets of paper and ask them to sit down on the floor to use them. "Just go ahead and write your story. Spell your words as you think they might be spelled, or just put the first letter of the word down and leave room for the rest. Then come up and read the story to me, and I'll write in for you the letters you didn't know."

Or a teacher might show her children in the beginning that a story can be a very simple statement. Here is the teacher we have already seen at work with her class on the George Washington Bridge project. In the fall of one year, with another group, she took a trip to a farm. The children had been particularly delighted to walk in the bed of a dried-up stream. Later, in school, the word "stream" came up in discussion and was, of course, interesting to the children. The teacher suggested that they think of two sentences using this word, explaining briefly what "sentences" were. Then she wrote on the chalkboard as children dictated:

The stream was dried up.
We walked in the stream.

Each one of these sentences, she pointed out, was a small story, wasn't it? The children then got to work copying these stories on their papers, and those who were burning to go ahead and were able to do so, wrote more. Result: a thrilling sense of accomplishment.

This teacher, after such beginnings, has a daily writing period, when children are encouraged to write about anything they wish—perhaps something they've done or seen, the weather, trips they've taken, or the arrival of new student teachers. Before writing, the children take turns telling aloud what they think they might write, so that all can hear a variety of ideas and be encouraged to feel that variety is important and no one kind of story is expected of them. Needless to say, the children are helped with new words, keep word lists, and have a spelling period when they study their new words.

By February of the year, children who begin in this way are producing stories they want to read aloud to the class. After all, writing is to be read and shared. In connection with these readings, the teacher encourages discussion that is positively oriented, so that no child will feel crushed by criticism. She may ask, "What feeling do you get from this story? How do you think he may go on to finish it?" (Some of the stories become so long that often a child works on them over two or three writing periods.) By this time of the year, too, the children are posting their stories—after correcting their mistakes—on a low bulletin board. Each child has his own space and thumbtacks his stories there, one on top of the other until he has a small collection for himself, as well as for others to look at from time to time. The importance of the opportunity to share their stories with each other cannot be overstressed. Particularly important for the children's sense of accomplishment, as well as for their motivation, is sharing by reading aloud. As the teacher describes it, "The simplest one-line sentence has a special glow when the child reads it himself to the class, or the teacher reads it to the class with even more expression than the beginning reader might be able to muster. My children consider this the highlight of the morning work period and they sign up on the board to insure that they will get a turn."[3]

What are these stories like by April? Here is a sampling. Some are short and still written on large sheets; others cover many small pages. Almost all are decorated with drawings. Their writers, from a six-sevens group, are more seven than six at this time of the year.

April 7

Yesterday my gerbils had six babies. I think the babies are absolutely disgusting. But when they get fur like their mommy and daddy and still are little they will be cute!

April 15

Today is a good day, because this morning I was looking at my Gerbils and what do you think I saw? The baby Gerbils had a little golden fur! I think they are going to be cute!

Girl

April 1

I like flowers I suppose
But I would like them a little
more if I lived around them.

Boy

April 7

Once there was a boy named John. And he wanted a bicycle so he looked in a toy store. And he had 5 dollars. And he asked how much money it was. The man in the store said it was 10 dollars.

April 9

So he went home to ask for five more dollars. But his mother said no   so he asked his father and said yes so his father gave him 5 dollars. And so he got the bicycle.

Boy

[3]Quoted from a personal communication from Pearl Zeitz with her permission.

April 14

Once upon a time there was a girl named Nina. She said I want a party. Her mother said no.
yes yes said the girl
No no said her mother. Why not
said the girl   because   said her mother
Go to the movies said her mother. Why said
the girl   I want you to   said her mother.
I don't want   said the girl

Girl

April 1

It is April 1
It was March 31 yesterday
The months will go on and on
          forever.

Boy

March 31

Eric is coming to my house today. We are going to play catch.

Boy

April 14

Once upon a time there was a cat. He went out to hunt. Then he saw a lion. He ran away. The lion was right behind him. The cat got home safely, because he ran up a tree and hid in the tree. The lion couldn't climb. So the lion went away   then the cat went home.

The end

Boy (Same as above)

March 30

I was out of school for five days sick with a sore throat. The doctor gave me a shot. I screamed and my mother laughed! The Doctor said he was sorry to have to give me a shot. After a while I began to cry because it hurt! Then she sang me a lullaby to make me to go to sleep to have my nap. After a while I told my mother I wish there was a medicine without a shot.

Girl

April 13

The big day is here. The rocket hit the moon.
A moon man came out. Watch out! John
A moon man! Kill him   I can't. Look
at that thing! help!

Boy

April 5

Once upon a time there was a girl whose name was Julie. She was six years old. One day her mother said, "Julie please help me set the table we're having a guest tonight. She said yes. She put down on the table salt, and pepper, spoons, and cups. And then her friend came. They were talking and talking. It was fun for them.

Then after dinner her mother came and took her home. And when she came home her dress tore! And that was the only dress she had! And her mother did not know how to sew! And they had no money! One day she went to school in her under-pants! All the children laughed. Then when it was sewing time she took her dress that was tore and sewed it. Then when she was finished she put it on. Then all the children said, where did you get that dress! She said I sewed it. Then when it was going home time her mother came for her And her mother gave her a kiss! for doing a good job on the dress.

Girl

What may strike the reader first of all is the variety in these writings. They range all the way from small observations and daily concerns involving relationships with children at school and parents at home to imaginative stories—even the beginnings of one small exciting space story, finished by the child later on. It is clear that the children are writing as individuals, using varied ideas and developing their writing skills on their own levels. Some have moved ahead of others in ability both to express themselves and to handle the technical skills; yet all are able to manage adequately, and it is interesting to see that even those who leave out periods and commas are moving toward an understanding of the need for them, by sometimes leaving spaces between the words where there are natural pauses.

If the writings of this group of children move along with what may seem to be surprising fluency, it must be remembered that in their classroom these children learn to use words through rich language experiences including discussion, reading, hearing stories read aloud, and daily writing. Certainly many teachers, as well as writers, are convinced that the best way to learn to write is to write. Mastery of sentence structure is slowly built up, and more important still, ideas often make their appearance in the course of the writing; they are generated in the very process.

Look at the story on page 85 about the little girl named Julie. It begins rather flatly with the table-setting episode and the visit with a friend. Then it moves into the exciting fantasy of the poor girl who through her own effort finds her way out of her troubles. The two parts of the story seem to bear little relationship to each other, and one might say that the first part is the more honest of the two. Yet the imaginative fling into the second part leads the writer into the necessity of constructing a real story based on the elements of conflict, suspense, and resolution—not only a valuable experience for her, but perhaps important also as symbolic expression of something goading her, troubling her, in relation to her own mother. The important point is this: Would she have written the second part at all if she had not put pencil to paper and begun with Julie setting the table? Possibly not.

Let us look a little further at the ways in which young children discover ideas and even work on some of the elements of writing when they are encouraged to move ahead on their own initiative. The children whose writings follow obviously have already developed a good deal of writing skill.

Children discover as they write

In the following story, the child gives his own name (we use "Gordon") to the "best chef." His story, like the Julie story above, seems to be in two parts:

Henry was a giant.
He was sixty feet tall.
He lived in Ireland.
One day a farmer came to Henry's house.
He said that there was a present for him.
Henry was glad it was a boat.
Henry went to the beach.
Henry was glad the boat floated.
Henry started the motor.
The president wrote Henry a letter.
The mysterious Cake Brothers were back.
All the chefs in town were afraid.
The mysterious Cake Brothers planned to hit at the best chef. His
 name was Gordon.
 Henry was walking down the street.
 He saw the mysterious Cake Brothers.
 He ran after the mysterious Cake Brothers.
They hid behind some garbage cans. They started shooting guns.
 Henry got a garbage can top. The Mysterious Cake Brothers
 kept on shooting the guns. Henry grabbed a garbage can top. The
 bullets started bouncing back.
 The mysterious Cake Brothers ran.
Henry caught them.
Henry brought them to the police station.
The police were glad that the Mysterious Cake Brothers were back
 in jail, and Henry got a reward.

What appears to happen here is that the writer first has to find his main character and get him into some sort of action before a real plot can emerge. Henry on the beach receiving a present of a boat is scarcely the Henry who is fighting the Mysterious Cake Brothers— just as Julie setting the table was very different from the child who had no dress to wear to school. This suggests that a teacher might help a child get started—if he is complaining of having no ideas—by asking him what kind of character he would like to write about. Does he have someone in mind—a boy, a girl, an animal, a giant?

When Gordon finally moves ahead he may be using props straight out of TV or stories he has heard, but no matter—as he writes he is living through action of gigantic proportions, possibly just what he needs at this time.

Regarding the next story, it is impossible to know whether the little girl intended in advance to write a story built upon the idea of search for characters who, one after another, cannot be located. It seems more likely that as she wrote she enjoyed these losses and findings, and continued to add them, discovering great satisfaction in them. As anyone knows who plays peekaboo with an infant, the loss-and-return plot is the most basic—and the most humanly necessary—of all plots; and there are many times when a child of six or seven or even older needs the reassurance he can build up for himself through creating images of safe return. See how this story becomes more the child's own as she proceeds. The family of bunnies living in a tree is gradually transformed into a more human family, living where there are stores and closets and beds. As the ideas take shape, they work for the child, helping her achieve her ends.

Once there was a bunny. She lived in a tree. One day she had some babies. Their names were Jean, Danny, Mike, and Mary. They all lived in the tree.

One day Mary went out to play. She went out in the woods. She got lost. She began to cry because she was standing right next to a wolf. Her mommy was looking for her, and she was looking and looking for Mary. And she began to cry.

Then she said to Jean, Danny, and Mike, "Go out and find Mary." They did. They found her.

When they got home where was their mommy? They were surprised that their mommy was not there.

So they began to find their mommy.

They looked and looked. Then they went out to the store. They looked all over. They did not find her. Then they went home. Then Jean looked in the closet.

There was their mommy.

They all cried because they were so happy. But then they

looked back. Where was Danny? Danny was not there, so they looked in his bed.

There he was.

Then they all went out to dinner.

Images of strength

The imaginative story in the hands of six- or seven-year-old children becomes one of their most important tools. Earlier, in the preschool years, they spontaneously dramatized as they played, in order to grasp hold of the realities around them. Now, with words under their control, they bound ahead, imagining scene after scene in which they are the doers, the testers, the champions, or the ones who leap over hurdles toward new achievements. With their sharp instrument, the pencil, they can create violence to exorcise violent feelings; they can slash down their fears; they can use the pencil as a magnet to bring comforting images close; or the pencil can be a compass to help them discover where they stand, organize their approach, and set out with a new feeling of control.

We have already seen Gordon's giant catching the Mysterious Cake Brothers and defending himself against their bullets with a garbage-can top. Note that Gordon himself, the "best chef," does not enter this conflict; perhaps he does not yet feel equal to it. Lucky that he can call in a giant to fight his battle! On page 84 we saw another little boy creating conflict in a story, with this difference: the weaker, smaller adversary wins. Here is the story again:

Once upon a time there was a cat. He went out to hunt. Then he saw a lion. He ran away. The lion was right behind him. The cat got home safely, because he ran up a tree and hid in the tree. The lion couldn't climb. So the lion went away   then the cat went home.

The end

The small cat, through his wit and his skill, escapes the lion. It is as though the child himself is beginning to feel and to trust his own power. It is no accident that at this time, according to his teacher, the boy was beginning to make real progress in his writing. Up until this period he had been writing only short sentences like the one of March 31 (page 84):

> Eric is coming to my house today. We are going to play catch.

But now he begins to write story after story, grabbing up his pencil whenever he has a chance, no longer afraid of the lion.

And here is a beginner in the same school who is finding an outlet for his aggressiveness in writing these five lines about a crocodile, allowing himself to enjoy symbolically some of the raging strength he does indeed possess, but he knows he must control in school:

> The crocodile was mean.
> He ate whole boats.
> You better watch out for him.
> He opens his big jaw
>   and he crunches them to bits.

Images of growth

In all these ways children shield and fortify themselves. But the image of physical strength in a violent face-to-face encounter with an adversary is not the only one that reassures and serves as armor. Many of our beginners' stories seem to spring from a need to sum up growth, to say to oneself: "See how far I have come, how much self-reliance I have now, how I am leaving my babyhood behind." The story is one of the arrows the child shoots ahead, one of those signs of an effort to fortify identity, shape it, assert it toward maturity. In the "sneaky baby" story presented in our introduction (page 6), we have already seen a beautiful example of a story that represents for its author a symbolic statement of conflict whose resolution is glimpsed ahead.

In the following rabbit story by a boy in the same class, we have a similar affirmation of growth toward maturity. Note how the baby rabbit is first referred to as a female ("for herself") but later becomes "he"—perhaps a reflection of the boy's wish to visualize for himself the time when he will not be scared, will be old enough to find a house for himself, and will not be coming back, even to a father who wants him. (Of course, it is possible that other meanings could be found in this story, particularly by someone who knows the child very well. A teacher can rarely be sure that she knows how to interpret all of a story's threads of meaning. But is it necessary for her to do so? In writing the story the child is serving his own purposes.)

Once upon a time a rabbit got married. She found a house for her babies to live in. It was warm.

She got four more babies. The father was happy. One of the babies was old enough to find a house for herself to live in the woods.

The woods were dark. The baby rabbit was not scared. The deep, deep woods seemed cold. The father wanted the baby back. The mother said, "He's not coming back."

The baby did not come back. The father went in the woods to look for the baby. But he did not find the baby.

In the following story by a girl we have a horse for a symbol. When the beloved stallion is lost, another will be found to give her needed protection. One can only marvel at the succinctness of this conceptualization of a little girl growing up:

Once there was a little girl. She got a white stallion for her birthday. She rode over many mountains.

One day her horse got sick and died. But she got a horse that she loved more.

It was a brown horse.

And she loved it.

One day she was walking in the woods and she got lost in the woods.

It was a dark and scary woods.

She called to her horse, and her

horse came and took her home.

Even in stories that are realistic and not symbolic, young children often look ahead, asserting their strength, their growth. The story that follows was written after the teacher had been reading aloud to her class of seven- and eight-year-olds Fred Gipson's greatly loved dog story, *Old Yeller.* "Did you ever have to lose a pet, the way these children had to lose Old Yeller?" the teacher asked. "You could write about that."

My turtle died in the country.
I cried all summer. I didn't have a happy summer. I didn't even know how to swim.
Oh well I am 7 now.

Girl

At the bottom of the page she drew a happy-looking little figure, something like this:

Getting rid of the ghosts

Ghosts pop up in most young children's stories at some time or other. They are convenient symbols for fears and may represent for some children threatening presences believed only yesterday to be real. They are evidently intriguing presences, even though now known to be imaginary; "ghost" can mean "danger," "punishment," "mystery," "horror"—and to draw close, to step as far as one dares, is exciting and even necessary in the proving of bravery and strength.

The following three stories are all from the same first-year class. Possibly the ghost idea caught on as the children read or heard each other's stories. Yet the three are very different, each one representing an individual child's own way of using the symbol for his own purposes.

In our first story, by a little boy, the ghosts do not seem to enter "our" world at all. They stay near their own spooky house and spook around only with their friends. A teacher might ask herself: Has the child resolved a good deal of his fear, or is he holding it at arm's length?

The Spooky Ghosts

Once upon a time there were three ghosts. In the night they really spooked! They saw their friends and said "Boo! boo! boo!" And once in a while they went back to their spooky house.

In the next story the child brings the ghost right into her house at night and deals with it. After first trying the unsuccessful reasoning approach, and even making the ghost himself a little afraid, she screams and calls for help, then turns the ghost into a "friendly" ghost, and finally takes the most mature step of all in deciding that she must be dreaming.

About a Ghost Who Spooked Every House

Once there was a ghost who went to a house in the night. It was dark. He was afraid. He went in the house. He was playing because every one was sleeping. "Boo," said the ghost. "Boo." It is night. "Is it night?"

"I don't know," said a girl. "When is it going to be morning?" she asked.

"In a little while," said the ghost.

"I want it to be now!" the girl said.

"Well, it isn't," the ghost said.

"I say it is morning. Anyway, who are you?" said the girl.

"I am a ghost," said the ghost.

"I don't believe in ghosts," the girl said.

"Well, turn on the lights and see me," said the ghost.

"Silly, you can't see ghosts," the girl said.

"Well, you can see me," the ghost said.

"I s-s-ee-ee-ee-y-y-ou," the girl said, "And mommy, help me!"

"I am friendly," the ghost said.

"Oh, I must be dreaming!"

Our third child also looks first at reason. The parents in the story represent the rational approach and affirm that there are no ghosts. But this is not enough for our boy. He must somehow deal with the ghosts himself. He lets them appear and kill off his father and then even kill off himself. Is this revenge on his father, followed by punishment, or does the child simply enjoy the sense of power he gets in disposing of the whole ghostly business through killing?

The Boy Who Believed in Ghosts

Once there was a boy and he believed in ghosts. One day when he woke up, he asked his mother if there was such a thing as ghosts. She said, "No."

That night he asked his father the same thing. He said, "No." "But I think a ghost is hearing all this." "Nonsense," said his parents, "go to bed."

The next morning the boy had a spooky feeling and that night some ghosts came in. His mother fainted. His father is a policeman but a ghost killed him. The boy got out of the house, but another ghost killed him.

Monsters and outer space

The monster, of course, is also a ghost, perhaps the twentieth-century child's favorite ghost. More horrible than a white-robed apparition and probably more destructive in its powers, the monster is the symbol of fright today for children who can use such a symbol.

Furthermore, he lives in those black planetary realms that represent the mysterious and threatening "unknown," inconceivably distant, strange, and full of danger, and perhaps made doubly threatening by the fact that astronauts today are actually exposing themselves to the dangers out in space. What once could be seen through the safe, transparent walls of imagination must now be glimpsed bare, as possible reality. As a result, the modern child throws all of his fear and awe—both projected and reality-based—into his conceptions of monsters and the worlds they inhabit. And the scenes he can create for himself—often, of course, with the help of TV and the comics—are as horrendous as were ever dreamed of in old tales of dragons and devils, ogres and giants.

What do our six- and seven-year-olds make of the monsters? Some of them, who look at TV hour after hour, may need to learn that the monsters they see there are not real. Others, who do not quite believe in them, still may like to frighten themselves with the images—for fright is titillating. Here a little second-grade girl talks to a teacher about what she might see if she went up into space. The teacher could not take down every word that came pouring from the child, but noted her pleasurable excitement as she spoke:

The Martians live in Mars. They look like spacemen. They like to go to other planets. They go on a space ship. People do not like to see the Martians, because they get scared. They look like monsters. They have ugly faces, because they make faces. They have big teeth. They have big fingernails. And they kill people with their claws—their long fingernails. I have seen a monster. I saw it on TV.

Another little girl, a first-grader, describes a situation up on the moon. Is there an element here of fright that is more painful than enjoyable? If so, the child is perhaps dealing with some of it in the act of writing:

The Red Moon

One night on a rocket there was a little girl. She was alone. She landed on the moon. It was red. The girl was scared and she was frightened. She wanted to go back, but her rocket was gone. It vanished.

Am I going to be here for the rest of my life? A moon monster said, "Yes," and went away. "Oh-oh-oh- oh-oh-oh-, oh no."

Fortunately, many young children who find monsters and the frights they may symbolize too much to face and handle at this stage of their lives can invent protective devices. We have already encountered a ghost (p. 93) who asserted that he was "friendly." Likewise monsters who are "friendly" or "good" appear in our stories by sixes and sevens. The author of the following is the same little boy who later in the year wrote "The Sneaky Baby" (p. 6). It is clear that he is not ready to even look at the "bad monster" here, but under the protection of the "good monster" he makes his way home as fast as he can.

The Friendly Monster

Chapter I   The Rocket

One day there were two boys. One day the two boys were in the house and one of the boys saw a rocket. He said, "Look Tony, there's a rocket in the garden. Let's go out and see it. Look at it, let's go inside. Look at this control. Push it. Look, we're going up. Look we're going up. Look we stopped. Let's get out."

Chapter II   The Monster

"O.K. Look at that monster."
"Don't be afraid of me. I'm a good monster."
"Good."
"Come with me. I will show you the bad monster."
"No, no, it's bad enough here."
"I like it here. Why don't you?"
"Can we go home?"
"Yes, if you think you have room for me.
"O.K. we will, good."

Other children attack the monsters, striking out at what threatens them and proving their powers. A first-grade boy, talking with the teacher about monsters and space, tells her:

. . . Then I kill him. I kill the monster with karate. I hit him with a big knife. The monster looked like a baby. . . .

Does he mean as easy as a baby to overcome, or is he symbolizing in this way a baby at home?

We have seen that some young children are interested in the science, as well as the science fiction, aspects of space. Their stories reflect not fright but a sense of fun in the play of imagination, as in this one by a first-grade boy:

The Whale Who Went to the Moon

Once a whale went into a rocket. It was a big, big, big rocket. Then the count down went on. In two weeks he was on the moon. How do you think he liked it? Well, don't ask me, ask him.

When the whale came back, he liked it on the moon. He found a secret lake. He jumped into the lake. But he never got to the water. Why? Because there was no water. It was a crater. But he didn't hurt himself because there was no gravity.

A teacher learns about her children as she sees what they are inventing and coping with in their imaginative stories. And the children, whether they consciously realize it or not, are indeed coping and discovering their own resources and feelings as they face the challenges of this time of their lives: they must find out who they are in relation to their classmates and teacher; who they are as they grow from dependent infancy into childhood; how they measure up; and what skills will serve them. All these concerns, of course, are carried with them every day, all day, on the current of living, in school and out. They are part of the involvement in learning that no child can escape and that no school can afford to ignore as it plans for its children.

A new perspective emerges

As children grow from five to six to seven, from less mature to more mature, the play of imagination veers, broadens, and flows in new directions. With growth comes the ability to step outside of self and look around with the eyes of the other, to see the world from a vantage point removed from the ego center. When a teacher finds a story like the following among her children's papers, she is seeing the evidence of this new development:

If I was little
Crayons would be huge.
Flowers would be trees.

A dog's bark would be thunder.
A cat's mew
Would be like a siren.

Girl

In my own experience as a teacher of six-year-olds, I discovered the evidence one October morning as we all sat around the block buildings in our room, discussing the work of the morning. We were looking at the Empire State Building, the roads, bridges, tracks, and trains. Suddenly Caroline, who had built the Empire State, said that she wished she were only as high as the little wooden doll workman, who was standing there by the building. "Then I could go climbing up the crisscross blocks to the top." Instantly the other children broke in and carried on this imaginative play, seeing themselves as miniature people walking about in their block city: "It would look like a real city!" "We could drive the trains around!" Then they examined the long table in our classroom ("a skating rink!") and the crossbars under the chairs ("our jungle gym!"). So began a year of searching out opportunities to look at the world from a fresh perspective. Stories were written by our goldfish; even a river was made to speak and describe his tired feelings after the heavy boats had sailed over him all day. As the teacher, I recognized the children's zest as they created these stories, and I gave them encouragement to stretch their perceptions in the new ways they were discovering, sometimes suggesting topics myself. For instance, when we were in the midst of our study of boats and had even been to a navy yard to see a ship in dry dock, I said to the group one day: "Suppose a whale out in the ocean suddenly saw a great ocean liner sailing along beside him, and he had never seen one before—what would he think?" (Whales, too, were of great interest to the children just at that time.) The idea proved to have tremendous appeal, and the story the children dictated revealed the lively movement of their imaginations under the spur of this challenge to take a familiar object and examine it from a new point of view. The children's ability to think around this topic so freshly was related not only to their natural playfulness, but also to the knowledge they could bring to bear as they considered the whale and the liner side-by-side:

A Whale Sees An Ocean Liner

One day a whale in the ocean suddenly saw a great ocean liner
come sailing along beside him.
"How big is this!
It's too big for me!
It's even bigger than I am,
And I'm the biggest fish in the ocean!"
said the big whale, so big as big can be.
"I am so big that no little fish could eat me up.
And I am much bigger than the little rowboats around in the sea.
But this is bigger than me, much!
I cannot do anything with it!
I think it can eat me up!"

"What a great big animal, with three spouts coming out of those
great huge barrels.
I've never seen a fish with three spouts coming out!
Those great big barrels—I could crawl down one!
What are those things in back that grind the water?
I wonder what that can be.
That must be the tail of the fish!
This big whale, it looks so funny with a point.
And what are all these eyes!
I've never seen a whale with so many eyes in my life!
I'll bet that big Mr. Whale could see all around!
He could see East, West, South, and could even see me right now.
It makes me feel scary and shaky if he could see me right now.
I think I'd better dive down and look from way under the water.
Oh my goodness! What has happened!
How big is this monstrous whale!
He even has a point on the bottom!"
"I go up again and I see thousands of eyes looking out of those other
eyes."

"This whale moves faster than me.
What kind of a whale is this!
This whale has such a big tummy that he can hardly breathe.

99

This thing—how can it smell the salty water?
I can smell the salty water."

"Goodbye! I'm going away. You're going too fast for me!"[4]

In another school, two seven-year-old boys write what purports to be a "news report" issued from the block city the children in the class have constructed on a large floor area. This city, the fruit of a great deal of social studies exploration, stands there with its high buildings, streets, traffic lights, docks—a miniature replica of a portion of the island of Manhattan. On the day of the "news report," the two large box turtles kept as pets in this classroom were found walking about in the "city." What an opportunity for the children to scale themselves down in size and look at the catastrophe from the standpoint of the inhabitants of the city!

The Giant Turtle Report

New York has never had
Giant Turtles roaming the
streets before.

There are two giant turtles reported. One of the turtles was in the water. They broke the main heliport. Fish boats from the Fulton Fish Market are not going out for fish because they think the turtles will invade the boats. The turtles have eaten up lots of fish. They're terrors to the sidewalk. Helicopters have been circling the turtles. The turtles walk around like big elephants. The turtles have knocked down buildings. They're heading toward the Sanitation Department. Please do not go out of your homes.

Here are some more second-graders whose teacher has encouraged social studies writing in a highly imaginative vein: If the people of the past were suddenly brought into the present, what would they think? This is just the question for children who are ready at a moment's notice to try on the skins of others, look about, and discover that there are new ways to see the world.

The story below grew out of a brief study of early man undertaken

[4]Excerpt from Claudia Lewis, "Tell It From Your Mouth," in *Childhood Education*, Vol. 26, No. 13, Nov. 1949, p. 113. Reprinted by permission of the publisher.

by the teacher because this particular class of mature sevens seemed to be highly interested in the subject and ready to take a small plunge into the past. That the writer of the story was enjoying the fantasy of it all seems evident; equally evident is the fact that she was making a little comparative study—on the level of a child turning eight—demanding that she think about housing, the use of fire, the meaning of money, and the functions of supermarkets. These are big terms for a second-grader, but they are related to ideas very much within her grasp and are appropriate and exciting to her when approached through the framework of a story.

When I have shown this story and the two that follow to teachers, I have often heard the comment: "These children must be geniuses! My second-graders could never do anything like this!"

Geniuses? Most likely not. True, they were very able children, and the school they attended offered rich opportunities for involvement in learning and development of individuality. If other second- or third-graders are not writing like this, or at least somewhat in this vein, we might ask why they aren't. Do we know what our children could do and could become if we were able to give them in school all the opportunities we believe in? Do they have time for writing? Do they have their teacher's encouragement? Do they have an inviting physical setting?

A New Stone Age Man in the United States

I am a New Stone Age Man. One day with my friend, I was walking in the forest, when suddenly out of the sky there came a giant silver bird. We stared at it in amazement for a few seconds and then a man dressed in a thick brown suit came out of a trap door in the bird's belly. He stared at us and said, "I am going to take you back to the United States with me."

So he, and another man in the same kind of suit, picked us up and carried us into the belly of the silver bird. When we got in the bird, there were things you sat on called seats. Then, in the front of the plane, some magic signs flashed on and off that looked as if they had fire (they said: "Fasten your seat belt") but of course we didn't know what to do. Then a lady came over and fastened our seat belts for us (she was called a stewardess).

When we got out of the bird, which I soon found out was a plane, the man who brought us there took us into a colored thing with hard black dirt on the bottom. We soon found out that these were called "cars." When we got out of the car, we had to walk on hard, grey stuff called "pavement." While we were walking on the pavement, the man said we must go to the supermarket. "What is a supermarket?" my friend asked. "It is a place where you trade food for money." "What is money?" I said. "It is something used for trading, to make it easier," said the man.

When we got into the supermarket, I discovered it was a big stone cave with lots of strange light from suns in the ceiling. We went to one part of the big cave where I saw more meat ready to eat, all sliced and trimmed, than I had ever seen before. The man picked up some meat and took it to the front of the place where he gave another man some green stuff and then walked out with the meat wrapped in something brown, which was called paper.

After that he took us into the car and we drove to a place that looked like a lot of caves standing on top of each other. (This is called an apartment house and many families live there, each in a separate series of caves all on the same level.) We walked up the stairs to his apartment. When we got through the entrance, we went into a room called a kitchen, which is where food is cooked and kept. But instead of using flint to make a fire, he pressed a button on a shiny white and black thing called a stove, and lots of little flames shot up. Then I saw something called a refrigerator, a big, white, very cold box, in which food is stored and kept cold. Suddenly, I heard a ringing noise. The man ran to pick up a little black doll with no face that rings when somebody wants to talk to you (I still don't understand how this works).

We ate some food and then the man's woman took a round, shiny black plate and put it in a box of wood with many strange things in it. There was music, stranger than anything I ever heard. I fell asleep and when I woke up there I was, resting in my hammock in my straw hut.

The End

Girl

The same teacher, another year, again departed from the usual second-grade study of the immediate environment and spent some time on the explorers, recognizing her children's interest and believing that a teacher today must experiment with subject matter and concepts that may have been inappropriate a few years ago.

Actually, the Christopher Columbus story below reveals the child author's firm grounding in the present as well as her interest in the past. That she was enjoying the chance to review and use newly acquired knowledge about the importation of spices seems evident. That she could create such a beautiful, amusing amalgam of fact and fantasy is due to her own imaginative talent, no doubt, plus the stimulus inherent in the very suggestion: What would the explorers think and feel if they came back today?

When Christopher Columbus Came to My House

When Christopher Columbus came to my house, he looked at the door and just stood there, waiting for some one to come. He thought to himself: "Maybe I should push that black dot," (which was a bell,) so he did. Some one came to the door. It was me.

I said: "Who are you?" and I stared at him because he was wearing such funny clothes.

He said: "I am Christopher Columbus. Who else?"

I said: "I am on my way to the grocery store to buy some spices. Would you like to come with me?"

This time he was staring at me because he was <u>still</u> looking for spices. He said: "How can you get spices so quickly, when it took me <u>many</u> <u>months</u> and I still did <u>not</u> get them!"

I said: "I will show you," and I took him to the grocery store. On the way there, he said: "What are those octopuses over there?" and he pointed to the street.

I said: "Those aren't octopuses. Those are cars."

In the grocery store he was very impatient to find out how we got spices. So I said: "All I know is that I get them from the grocery man. We will have to ask him where he gets them."

I asked the grocery man.

He said: "I buy them from a man who specializes in selling foods and spices to stores like this one. He is called a wholesale man."

Columbus asked: "Where does the wholesale man get them?"

The grocery man answered: "He gets them from factories and importers."

Christopher asked: "What are factories and importers?"

I said: "Factories are places where they make things."

The grocery man said: "That's right. And they get the stuff to make spices mostly from foreign countries. The people who buy spice stuff in foreign countries and ship it here are called importers."

Christopher asked: "What foreign countries?" because he was very curious.

The grocery man said: "These are some of the countries: India, the East Indies, Africa, China, Japan, the British West Indies, Malta, Mexico, Costa Rica, Chile, and other places."

Columbus said: "India! Wasn't that the place I was trying to find? And I just <u>don't</u> think I got there."

So I took him home. Before he went back to his ship, I gave him a present. Guess what it was? It was a nice <u>BIG</u> bag of <u>spices</u>!

In the child's last paragraph above we can sense her wish to do something nice for Christopher Columbus, who had been so thwarted in his search for spices. And no wonder. This technique of writing from a "new perspective"—putting oneself inside another very different person—can encourage a stirring of feeling, a thoughtful identification.

In the following story about the visit of Leif Ericson to New York, the little boy who is writing it seems to enjoy inventing baffling experiences for Leif to encounter, yet he is more and more experiencing the feelings of Leif in all these awkward situations. In the end he takes the explorer back to his boat so he will not be laughed at any more.

Leif Ericson Visits New York

Moving down the river, the Hudson River, was a dragon ship powered by 60 slaves pulling oars. The leader of the ship was named Leif Ericson.

When he reached shore, he jumped off the ship and saw a big ferry (The Staten Island). The man in the booth laughed and let him on the ferry. The man in the booth called up the Daily News and told them to bring their best photographers to take some pictures, because he had never seen anyone dressed the way Leif was.

When Leif was on the ferry he looked up in the captain's cabin and said, "What's that?" He was so surprised that he didn't see any slaves rowing. Instead he saw a man in a suit in front of a steering wheel.

Finally the ferry reached Manhattan. When I saw him I said, "Who are you?"—then he said "I am Leif Ericson!"

I took him to the car and he said "What's that?" I said "A car of course." You see he never saw a car before.

So I put him in the car and drove him to the Museum of Natural History. I showed him fossils of his father, Eric the Red!

Then I took him home for dinner. He said "Do you have any dried antelope?" I shook my head no. "Do you have any grizzly bear?" I shook my head no. "Do you have any whale blubber?" I shook my head no. "What do you have?" he said. "Meat loaf with bacon and sauce," I said. "What's that?" he said. "It's chopped meat—cow," I said. "I'll take some."

So he took it and ate it and then I took him for a subway ride.

He stepped up to the turnstile and tried to go into the turnstile with two shark's teeth. But they wouldn't go in.

So he called the man in the booth. When the man came, he said, "Where did you get those crazy clothes?" Because he had never seen a coat or suit before in his life. He was dressed in a skirt and had on a helmet with horns, on his head.

After the subway, I took him to the horse races at Yonkers.

The people were surprised to see a man in a skirt and a metal helmet with horns.

So I took him back to the ferry. He went back to the dragon ship and he ordered the slaves to row. He did not like being laughed at.

Writing ability evolves

As soon as children have enough ability to read simple story material that a teacher can write for them, they enjoy completing an unfinished story; for some children this may be just what they need to help them discover their ideas and acquire confidence in themselves as writers. Here is the beginning of a dinosaur story one second-grade teacher prepared for her class at a time when their interest in dinosaurs was high:

Many millions of years ago, a boy dinosaur named Danny lived in a great forest. Danny, his mother and his father and his sister loved to eat the tender green leaves and the juicy berries that grew in the forest. Danny and his sister splashed about in a lake.

One day, Danny asked his mother if he could take a walk, by himself. "Yes," said his mother. "But be careful and don't get lost."

All the children in the class tackled this, most of them apparently delighted with the chance to carry the story on. Even those children whose writing and spelling skills were fairly minimal plunged in and managed to say what they wanted to say. When the children read their stories aloud later, not one of them stumbled over what he had written; to each the meaning was perfectly clear. This is the way children learn to write, propelled by the desire plus the feeling of freedom to put down whatever they can, imperfect though it may be. Here is a sampling indicating the range of skills (these are the first, uncorrected drafts):

So Danny set out alone once and a while he stopped for a drink. He was suddenly interrupted by a loud roar. What's that? thought Danny   suddenly a meat-eating Allosaurus came out of the foliage and shrubbery. Danny was scared suddenly its' claw went toward its' own head and he pulled it off   then Danny saw it was his father in disguise. Lets go home said father and they did.

Boy

I will not. Then he start into the forest. Sundy a grate big dinosaur came. Danny sied   helo in a squy vos. The way dinosaur do. The big dinosaur said what is your name? my name is Danny   he said. What is your name?   my name is big dinosaur.   i like you they both sied. and they both went home to—Danny house.

Girl

Danny was off! On the way Danny got hugry. He saw some berries. He aet three bushis. Then he got sleepy. So he dosed off. He was awaken by a grate roor. It was tranasous Rex. He ran home as fast as he could go. Mother! Mother! he called. What! seid mother. I was sleeping and a tranasous came. ho seid mother   its O.K. becaus you didn't get hert.

Boy

O.K. said Danny   I will be careful. I will not get lost. He went of into the woods and there he saw a bear but since he was much bigger then the bear he wasn't afraid at all. He just went on walking in the woods and there he saw that same bear. but since he was much bigger than the bear he was not afraid and he just went on walking in the woods but that bear just wouldn't leave him alone. By that time Danny had gotten very mad and he didn't like it one bit and so he started home. When he got home he told his mother about what happend but his mother didn't believe one bit of what he said and Danny said but it's true but his mothe would not believe it. and so he told his father but his father wouldn't belive it and Danny said but it's true but his father just wouldn't believe it. Danny said then come into the woods with me and I will show you there is a bear and they went with Danny. When they got into the woods Danny said the bear should be around here so they looked for the bear but they couldn't find him so his father said so there realy wasn't any bear and his mother said so you lied and for that you will get no supper and Danny started to cry and he said but I did see a bear mabie he just went away and his mother and father said mabie that true you will get supper and when they started to go home the bear came out from his hidind place but they never saw that bear again.

The end.

Girl

In all cases in the above stories there are dangers or conflicts, but in the end safety, comfort, resolution. The happy ending is a necessity.

In another school a teacher discovered this necessity when she read aloud to her seven-year-olds E. B. White's *Stuart Little*. The children were dissatisfied with the open ending, in which the reader is left to decide for himself whether Stuart, the little mouse boy, will ever find his bird friend, Margalo. Open endings are undoubtedly more suitable for older children, who can feel sustained by broad vistas and have less need for literal closures.

In this case, the teacher suggested that the children write their own endings for *Stuart Little*. As we look at some of these stories we can again see the variety to be expected when children are working ahead at their own rates and levels. Some of the children could write without assistance, except in the spelling of certain words; others asked to dictate the whole story; still others, who began to write by themselves, became so caught up in the imaginative flow and so frustrated by the slow writing process that they asked to finish by dictating.

The first one below, written by the child himself, shows that he is really visualizing the scenes and images of the story:

And then he got up and got into his little car and drove to the direction north to find Margalo. He got off the next exit in to another town. At last he found Margalo sitting on a tree.

Boy

One can also expect to find minimal statements embodying nothing more than the essential facts:

I think the end of Stuart Little is that he found Margalo and he and Margalo go home and live happily ever after.

Girl

Perhaps if this little girl had dictated after she had completed her succinct summary she might have found story details and images flowing up into her thoughts, as in the case of the child whose story follows. This long story, begun by the child with her pencil and then abandoned in favor of dictation, reveals a true storyteller at work.

Obviously the teacher, who encouraged dictation for those who wanted it, believed that the children would profit in the long run from the chance to tell rather than write.

One day when Stuart was walking and looking up at a tree he heard a footstep. Before he knew what was happening a net was over him and he was going into the back of a truck with lots of other animals like cats dogs and birds. The first two days he didn't know where he was going or anything but the third day another animal was caught and dumped into the truck and Stuart saw a sign that said welcome to New York! He rode for two more days, and then he was carried into a pet shop across the street from his house. When he was in a cage with a few other mice he had a chance to look around. Then he looked at the bird section. First he saw a parakeet that was orange and pink and a couple of other birds, and last of all a brown bird. At first he couldn't believe it. Was it? It was. It was really Margalo. Then Margalo looked at him. When the storekeeper went to another corner of the room Margalo said, "Stuart, Stuart, is it really you?"

"Yes, it is. Is that really you, Margalo? Then the store door opened. It was the Littles. They said, "Do you have any nice small animal that we could buy?" The storekeeper said "Yes, we have a few nice birds and mice." "Can we see them" said Mrs. Little. "Sure," said the storekeeper. First they went to the birds. When they got to the last bird, George said, "Could it be Margalo?" Right away Mr. Little said "Of course not." Mrs. Little said "Well I think it is." Then they heard from the mice corner, "George." Then they looked over and they knew it was Stuart. Then George said to Stuart, "Is that really Margalo?" "Yes," said Stuart.

Before Stuart or anybody else quite knew what was happening, Stuart was on Mrs. Little's shoulder and Margalo was on George's shoulder and Stuart was telling his story as they went back home.

Girl

Finally, let us look at an unusual story by a boy who had a gift with words—a gift fostered both at home and at school by adults who recognized his abilities and exposed him fully to poetry and stories read aloud. No one said to him, "Write a poem," when he sat down to invent a new ending for *Stuart Little*. But his story does have poetic feeling and rhythm. That is, the content of these moments of the story—sad thoughts about Margalo, and then surprise and joy—seemed to the child to call for a heightened language. Some of his words and rhythms he may be pulling a little inexpertly out of the poetic vocabulary he has been exposed to: "in the very month of May . . . which and where of them to go to. . . ." But by hearing, borrowing, and trying, a child finds his way.

> As Stuart was riding along the road in the very month of May thinking about Margalo and his family and thinking which and where of them to go to, and just as he was going to burst out crying, he heard a sweet voice, and to his surprise, it was Margalo!
> She told him the whole story,
> She told him that she had seen him.
> She had felt sorry when she saw him.
> So she came down from hiding in the tree
>   and then they went home.

With this story that clearly says we should read poetry to children to give them a poetic grasp and to help them in their first efforts, we turn now to poetry and the forms it takes in the hands of our sixes and sevens.

The beginnings of poetry

Children who arrive at our school doorsteps at age five or six all come from environments that have exposed them to playful verses and jingles. The lucky ones know Mother Goose; almost all of them have learned without effort the catchy TV commercials; and many of them have picked up chants from the games on the street:

> Bluebells, cockle shells,
> Eevy, ivy, over . . .

One potato, two potato,
three potato, four . . .

It is no wonder that when these young children first begin to write what they call a "poem," it is usually something that has the playful character of a nonsense rhyme. Here one boy works his way through several rhyming forms:

There once was a cat,
She lived in a hat
Whenever she sat
She sat like a rat.

There once was a bear
He had long hair
In summer he was hot
And in winter he was not.

There once was a mouse.
She lived in a house.
She wasn't so good as she really should.
She never was bad,
She never was good,
She just understood.

When a teacher reads such an effort, she should feel pleased to see the child experimenting and discovering rhyming words so success-fully, though she knows very well that poetry is more than this and hopes the boy will eventually move through this phase.

One teacher tried to help her beginners—who were second-graders—make the most of the nonsense jingles they were writing by suggesting recitation of them with musical accompaniment, some-what in the manner of Carl Orff's work with children.[5]

The instruments that were available and that could be easily han-dled by the children were bells, gongs, and a wooden xylophone. As

[5]See Carl Orff and Gunild Keetman, Music for Children. Angel 3582. (Phonograph record.)

the teacher and children discussed the possibilities of combining the music and poetry the following plan emerged: The rhymes could be recited by two or even three children in unison; the "orchestra" could tap out a suggestive rhythm immediately following each poem; and this could make a program that other children in the primary grades would enjoy seeing and hearing.

Visualize the large classroom, its tables pushed to the walls. The children are seated on the floor in the center of the room, with those children who are going to rise in pairs and threes seated near each other. The four or five children of the orchestra are on the floor in one corner with their instruments beside them. The visitors from the other classes occupy chairs at one end of the room.

The program begins: Two girls stand and recite rapidly, delicately, and rhythmically:

Do you know
What I like to do?
I like to go
To the zoo
With you.

Girl

The orchestra then taps out a few notes, not attempting to follow the rhythm of the poem exactly, but suggesting its brevity, sound quality, and speed. The children sit down; two or three more rise for the next poem, and so on, until all have had their turns. The poems are recited with such an easy mastery that the word "recitation" seems entirely wrong to use here, suggesting something more artificial than actually was the case. The children were caught up in accented rhythms that came to them very naturally and gave them, as well as the listeners, great pleasure.

Here are a few more of the poems, just as they were written. Note that not all of the children have discovered how to line out a poem so that its rhymes fall in the conventional positions, but this was no impediment to them whatever. As they spoke their poems, the rhymes and rhythms were vividly felt. Children gradually learn the lining system with their teacher's help.

I went to lake and saw a
drake   I said hello and
he said   NO
I went to the pond and saw
a duck   I said hi   and
he said   Quck

Girl

I had a hat that I use for a rack
and I use my rack for a coat
and I use the mat for a hat
What do you think of that?

Girl

One day in May
I saw a Monguydoddltoodleliay
He was black, and he
said   tickle-tack.

Boy

The angel is like
A swan
A swan   a swan   a swan

Girl

A long time ago
Indians were everywhere you
    looked in the plains
    and in the woods.
And now everywhere
You look there are houses
    and houses.

Boy[6]

[6]From *Somebody Turned on a Tap in These Kids*, edited by Nancy Larrick (Delacorte Press, 1971). Copyright © 1971 by Nancy Larrick Crosby. Reprinted by permission of the publisher.

The last poem above shows that its author is already moving away from the concept of poetry as jingle. He has an idea to express that has arrested him, a new awareness, a new way of looking at the familiar world. And this new awareness seems to him to call for poetic expression. He is absolutely right, of course. Though poetry is hard to define, the boy has indeed made a discovery about it. As the poet John Hall Wheelock says, "A poem is what happens when a poet re-discovers, for himself, the reality we have lost sight of because, to use Shelley's metaphor, it has been overlaid by the veil of familiarity."[7]

We can see other beginners also moving toward discovery as they play with the sounds of words or invent expansive forms based on repetition. Here a little girl dictates a paragraph about Halloween, finding suggestive rhyming words on a level far removed from the jingle or limerick. Actually, she may have felt that she was making a poem, even though the end result was not lined on the page in conventional poetic form:

Halloween

Black cats, ghosts and goblins are
halloween fun! Creaky houses are fun
too, oh boo! Halloween. Trick or treat
is said so much   hush   hush! Scary
costumes are worn so much. Witches,
pitches, little ditches!

Here are six-year-olds who have been encouraged to write "name poems." This exercise brought forth a flow of feelings, as well as a flow of sounding, descriptive words:

Cathi

Cathi is like a candy cane and like a cuckoo
bird and like a copper color crayon and like
a clown in a circus and like a castle in
a kingdom.

Girl

[7]John Hall Wheelock, *What Is Poetry?* (Charles Scribner's Sons, 1963), p. 27.

Julie

Julie is like a soft sweet muffin.
Julie is like a soft sweet star.
Julie is such a soft sweet name
  Oh I just love it, my dear.

July was born in July, in July,
Julie was born in July, in July,
  Oh I just love July.

Girl

Laurie

Laurie is as bright as the sun shining in the blue.
Laurie is the moon, sitting in the stars.

Girl

In the Julie poem our writer not only discovers soft, sweet words, but also repeats them, out of the felt necessity to give her emotions room and break through the bounds of ordinary speech. Also breaking through the bounds are these two children who may be using repetition and pattern to help them express their feelings about snow, as well as to make a picture of the way snow falls and piles up.

It is snowing.
The sun is coming up.
The ice is on the roads.
The snow is on the ground.
I like snow.
It is snowing.
It is snowing.
It is snowing.
It is snowing.
I like snow.

Boy

Snow, snow
To my nose.
Snow, snow
I pose.
Snow, snow
To my toes.
Snow, snow
To my face.
Snow, snow
To my legs.
Snow, snow
To my knees.
Snow, snow
To my arms.

Girl

"I pose," writes the little girl above—simply because she needs a rhyme. Fortunately she abandons the rhyming attempt as she proceeds, since it hinders her from saying what she really wants to say. This need for a rhyme is stimulating to children, and often it helps them explore words. However, it just as often trips them up and leads them into artificiality. In the example below, the child begins successfully, finding simple and right rhyming words. But in the last line she meets her defeat:

Snow is fluffy
Snow is white
Snow falls
All night.
When I wake up
In the morning
The snow is on the street
It is hard to buy some wheat.

Girl

There is no reason to try to cut children off from all rhyming attempts. But how does one show them that a simple, unrhymed piece of observation like the following is also a poem?

Snow is soft like cotton.
Snow is a white blanket to houses.
Snow is quiet.

Girl

The teacher can, of course, say to children, "Poetry doesn't always have to rhyme." But the really convincing way to show them this is to read aloud good poetry that does not rhyme; poetry that surprises and reveals, and is built on rhythms that follow the contours of the thought.

One teacher read to her class of very young beginners—five- and six-year-olds—the book of haiku poems, *In A Spring Garden*, compiled by Richard Lewis and illustrated by Ezra Jack Keats. These poems are very direct, simple observations in brief, unrhymed poetic statements. The children seemed to particularly enjoy the poems about insects, animals, and other creatures, such as frogs and toads. They loved the suggestions that a frog might have a staring match with a person, and that a chicken's vigorous scratchings might be its way of trying to say something. Of course, the book's striking colors were a great attraction.

Seeing the children's pleasure in these poems, the teacher suggested that they, too, could write some short observations about the ways of animals they knew; draw a picture first, then write or dictate something about the animal or creature in the picture. She made no mention of the word "haiku." After all, the haiku poem, as it has developed over centuries in the hands of Japanese poets, is a very delicate, sophisticated, and complex instrument for the registering of meaning and mood. Fifth- and sixth-graders can begin to understand it and master it for themselves. Younger children can enjoy the poems on a more superficial level, seeing in them just what this teacher encouraged her children to see. When she asked them to write in the manner of the *Spring Garden* poems, she was hoping for nothing more than close observation, expressed very simply—an excellent basic exercise, and no labels of "haiku" or "poetry" necessary. The children's writings indicate that there had been some discussion of ways the animals move, perhaps to give the children a focus or a springboard (these writings are from both boys and girls):

The cat walks softly. He walks smoothly and jumps smoothly. He can even walk down the stairs smoothly. He can jump over the swing easily.

A robin takes small steps and goes fast. His wings flop up and down when he flies. He folds his wings down when he isn't flying.

This is a pigeon.
It moves in a wobbly way.
In the air it moves smooth.

My goldfish.
They move softly
Through the water.

This is a turtle. They walk very slow.
They do not talk.

Twitchy nose rabbit. He curls his paws in front of him.

The second-grade teacher who read *Stuart Little* to her children was very knowledgeable about poetry and throughout the year read aloud a great variety of poems, old and new, rhymed and unrhymed. She believed in children's capacity to appreciate and by no means restricted the readings to poetry written especially for children. In the spring of the year, when the children were discussing weather and its changes, the following poem by e. e. cummings, printed in the style of an experience chart, was displayed in the front of the room:

in Just-
spring   when the world is mud-
luscious the little
lame balloonman

whistles   far   and wee

and eddieandbill come
running from marbles and
piracies and it's
spring

when the world is puddle-wonderful

the queer
old balloonman whistles
far   and   wee
and bettyandisbel come dancing

from hop-scotch and jump-rope and

it's
spring
and
     the

        goat-footed

balloonMan   whistles
far
and
wee[8]

In such an environment, it is not surprising that a little girl brought up to her teacher one day the following spring poem written during a writing period.

The Time

The time
   When the sky
     is blue
     and the
   daffodils are blooming.
   That is the time.
   Yes that is the time.

[8] E. E. Cummings, I from "Chansons Innocentes" in *Tulips and Chimneys* (New York: Liveright Publishing Corporation and England: MacGibbon & Kee Ltd/Granada Publishing Ltd. 1923), pp. 21–22. Copyright 1923, 1925 and renewed 1951, 1953 by E. E. Cummings. Copyright © 1973, 1976 by Nancy T. Andrews. Copyright © 1973, 1976 by George James Firmage. Reprinted by permission of the publishers.

This was followed, a few days later, by an outbreak of spring poems in the class. Another girl wrote the following:

Who Told You?

Who told the birds to
        fly south?
Was there a special call?
Who told the bears
        to hibernate?
Was it the cold wind?
Or was it the raindrops?
Who told you?

On the next day, still another little girl wrote:

Look at the grass
        in Spring.
Feel the wind
        blowing in Spring
Can you hear the
        Special call?

And on the third day a boy delighted the class with:

The Hard Mystery

Where do they go?
Where does the rain travel?
Does it go into the gravel?
This is a mystery
        to you and me
                in history.

These children, writing with so much freedom and beauty, were influenced by the atmosphere of this classroom where they were encouraged to think, question, and discuss as they learned about the phenomena of the weather and the seasons. They were also influenced by the enthusiasms of their teacher, by the words and patterns of e. e. cummings, and by each other as they listened to each other's poems.

It should be added that the poems—along with some of the other nature writings of the class—were collected under the title *Nature Stories and Poems*. The teacher typed and rexographed them and made them into booklets, one for each child, with bright covers to be decorated by the children themselves. Furthermore, the poem "Who Told You?" was set to music by the children with the help of the music teacher. Nothing very complicated, of course. The teacher simply asked the children to try to hum tunes for the phrases. He then picked these up without altering them very much, as the final result shows. Of course some help was necessary in rounding out the whole to make a song.

WHO TOLD YOU?

Poem by N___ T_____
Music by Group F

Who told you? Who told the birds to fly south?

Was there a special call? Who told the bears to hibernate?

Was it the cold wind? Or was it the raindrops? Who told you?

The simple system of musical notation was used to help these young children take their first steps in reading music. The song was included in the booklet of *Nature Stories and Poems*, and actually most of the children did learn to sing it. This whole spring festival culminated in a very short program of readings of poems and singing of "Who Told You?" for the pleasure of children in the other primary grades.

Because this second-grade teacher had so much success in introducing her children to poetry and stimulating their own understanding and writing, I want to look a little further at her work, emphasizing particularly the effects on children of exposure to good poetry.

Another year, with another class, the teacher read aloud Edna St. Vincent Millay's "Afternoon On A Hill":

I will be the gladdest thing
    Under the sun!
I will touch a hundred flowers
    And not pick one.
I will look at cliffs and clouds
    With quiet eyes,
Watch the wind bow down the grass,
    And the grass rise.
And when lights begin to show
    Up from the town,
I will mark which must be mine,
    And then start down![9]

The reader is urged to refer to this teacher's own account of the reading, in order to sense the children's receptiveness and her trust that children can and will find their own way to an understanding of poetry.[10] Let me only say here that right after the reading, without any comments on the teacher's part, the little boy asked to say something:

"When I was in the country, I went up Oxbow Road.
Oxbow Road leads to a mountain.
When I looked down from the mountain,
I felt like a king.
The trees and the grass
Are like my people."

[9]Edna St. Vincent Millay, Collected Poems (New York: Harper & Row, 1956), p. 7. Copyright © 1917 by Edna St. Vincent Millay. Copyright © 1945 by Norma Millay Ellis. Reprinted by permission of Norma Millay Ellis.

[10]Excerpt from "Please Don't Tell the Children" by Elaine Wickens reprinted from Young Children, Vol. 23, No. 1 (Nov. 1967), pp. 15–18. Copyright © 1967, National Association for the Education of Young Children, 1834 Connecticut Avenue, N.W., Washington, D.C. 20009.

Hearing this, a child commented, "That is just like the poem." Another child added, "Mark said a poem."

Children who hear a great deal of poetry will learn what poetry is and will find encouragement to try their own poems. Needless to say, the more a teacher can expose children to poetry of various styles and voices, the more likely it is that the children will find their own voices and will feel free to experiment in directions that appeal to them. This is our hope. We are not in the classroom to teach young children what poetry is, but to encourage them to find out and to try their own new, young, contemporary ideas, even to teach us something about ways of charging words with poetic sound and sense.

Young children today can enjoy Edna St. Vincent Millay—who wrote for another generation—but let's not forget the rock singers in our midst, who present a new kind of balladry that is enormously appealing to children. It is not surprising that a seven-year-old girl wrote (dictated, at home) the following, with a seven-year-old playmate. Visualize the two girls sitting with their small toy guitars and singing.

The Hamsters

Here we come a-crawling down the street
Get the softest pets from everyone we meet.
Hey Hey! with the Hamsters!
People say we're hanging around
But we're too busy squeaking to bite anybody in town.
We're just trying to be naughty in the most squeaking way.
We're in the rodent family
And we've got something to say:
Hey Hey! with the Hamsters!
You never know where we'll be found—
We're just liable to be dropping in
In your home or town.

This ballad will perhaps lead the children to other ballad experiments. In fact, here one of the two Hamster girls is trying a poem—we might call this a ballad, too—directly influenced by spirituals she has heard on the radio as well as by the Edna St. Vincent Millay poem. So we have come full circle. The influences intermingle; our child makes of them something on her own:

It Was A Day for Peace

It was a day
The sun was shining out
From the hills
It was the lightest day of my life.
I could see the whole world
It was a miracle that day
The skies were full of sun
That day, Oh Lord, that day.
That day was full of sun
That day, oh Lord,
It was a miracle for me.
Good night.

This child is already quite a poet, with a love of language and perhaps a special gift for poetic expression. Not all of our children will move this far by age seven, or in this direction. We can be sure, however, that all of them do come to us equipped with a love of rhythm and an ability to create what the poets call "images" in similes and metaphors.

Here are a group of children aged six to eight, most of them Spanish-speaking and "woefully inarticulate" in English, according to their teacher. Yet see how easily they can be stirred to find concrete images to express their feelings—with the teacher's help. It was one of those first spring days, unseasonably warm, delicious. The children had just come in from their noon recess. The teacher, herself enjoying the day, thought the children might like to talk about it and began by asking them to "tell about the day." Most of the children did not respond. A few said that it felt like spring or was a nice day. Obviously this was not the way to reach the children. The teacher then remembered that she had better refer to specific sensations: "If you had to say how today looks, would you say it looks red or blue?" "Do you feel more like wearing boots or sneakers?" "Is it a day for braids and ties or for loose hair and loose ties?" As the children began to catch on and felt the freedom to say whatever came to their minds, the teacher began to write their responses on the chalkboard, and could hardly keep up with the flow. Here are some of the images—imaginative, playful, and concrete:

How did the day feel? Like China cups, like balloons, like your heart is warming up, like a deer feels, like your head is too heavy today, like spring mixed up with the sun . . .

How did the day smell? Like peppermint, like flowers are going to grow where you're standing, like the trees are having leaves. . . .

How did the day taste? Like ice cream, like French fries, like cherry soda, like clouds, like if you took a big bite of the world, you'd have too much air in your stomach and fly away like a balloon. . . .[11]

There are many other ways to help children move toward the imaginative thinking that is part of the poetic experience. A teacher discovers these as she works with her children and uses her own imagination, trying this and that and venturing suggestions that she believes may open up new thoughts for them.

A teacher of second-graders, asking her children for images descriptive of such concepts as "black," "softness," "whiteness," "deepness," and "light," included a startlingly different one— "walls." To help the children think in this new vein, she first described "hands" for them, as many kinds as she could think of. This is what the children did with "walls."[12]

I saw walls of weaved fingers and nails and even walls of cockle shells, and once I saw walls of steel and bronze and things like brick. I saw walls of gold and silver and flowers with lots of petals.

Boy

[11]Reprinted from *Horn Book Reflections*, Elinor Whitney Field. Copyright © 1966 by The Horn Book, Inc., pp. 327–328.
[12]Claudia Lewis, "Our Native Use of Words" from *Dimensions of Language Experience*, edited by Charlotte B. Winsor (New York: Agathon Press, 1975), pp. 146–147. © 1975 by Agathon Press. Reprinted by permission of the publisher.

There could be brick walls, walls of woven fish scales, wood walls, red marble walls, earthenware walls with cracks, brown cavern walls, walls of books sewn together, walls of strong sunlight, walls of fire, mirror walls shining in the sun, plaster walls and walls of beast skins.

Boy

I saw dim and trim rays
  big and fat,
  bright and light rays.
I saw big and small walls
  shelled and belled walls,
  pigged and cowed walls,
  babooned and broomed walls.

Girl

These children are already seeing with the artist's eye. Their images belong to our time, suggesting perhaps fantastic backdrops for ballet and theater experiments, or the collages and designs that hang in modern museums. The arts are meeting here—color, visions, language, ideas, rhythms; and the children, so easily grasping at these resources, are racing ahead with them into their own century.

Teachers need to discover both how to give such children enough free rein and how to learn from them and move forward with them, keeping an eye on the nature of their own visions and constantly trying to rip apart the "veils of familiarity."

References

CUMMINGS, E. E., *Tulips and Chimneys*, New York: Liveright Publishing Corporation and England: MacGibbon & Kee Ltd/Granada Publishing Ltd., 1923.

GIPSON, FRED. *Old Yeller*, drawings by Carl Burger. New York: Harper, 1956.

FISHER, AILEEN. *Cricket in a Thicket*, New York: Charles Scribner's Sons, 1963.

LEWIS, RICHARD. *In A Spring Garden*, pictures by Ezra Jack Keats. New York: Dial Press, 1965.

MILES, BETTY. *A Day of Winter*, illus. by Remy Charlip. New York: Knopf, 1961.

MILLAY, EDNA ST. VINCENT. *Collected Poems*, New York: Harper, 1956.

STONE, ELIZABETH. *A Study of Science and Language Arts Curriculum in a Second Grade Class:* Unpublished Master's Thesis. New York: Bank Street College of Education, 1968.

SWIFT, HILDEGARD H., and LYND WARD. *The Little Red Lighthouse and the Great Grey Bridge*, New York: Harcourt Brace, 1942.

WHEELOCK, JOHN HALL. *What Is Poetry?* New York: Charles Scribner's Sons, 1963.

WHITE, E. B. *Stuart Little*, pictures by Garth Williams. New York: Harper, 1945.

The eights and nines: growing into the middle years

Chapter four

Three stories tell us a good deal about these children who are turning eight and moving toward nine, leaving early childhood behind them.

The Once Upon A Time Story

Once upon a time Aunt Addie was one year old. She had blue eyes and blonde hair. Once upon a time Aunt Addie was ten. She played in the garden with her brothers and held out her apron to catch the grapes they dropped from the trellis. Once upon a time Aunt Addie was twenty-five. She went to work every day and helped her blind brother. At this time my grand-father was born. Once upon a time Aunt Addie was sixty. At this time my mother was born. Now Aunt Addie is ninety-three. She knits mittens for us. Once upon a time Aunt Addie will be no more, but I will always remember her.

Girl

Time past and its relation to time present; self in relation to other generations—these are now becoming clear; the child here is even beginning to predict the inevitable losses of the future. Such a child, achieving perspective on herself and her place in time, is ready for studies that will take her back into history.

Parents Are A Nuisance

Parents are a nuisance I really don't
    know why
They spank me for no reason and make me
    want to cry.

Parents are a nuisance they make you stay
    in bed
Especially when you're sick with a cold in
    the head.

But when I think about how much they really
    love me and help to make me grow up kind
    and keep all naughty things off my mind
I really love them too.
But as you know parents are a nuisance
    anyway.

Girl

Parents are loved, of course, yet the pull and tug away from them—to prove one's independence and freedom from earlier needs—is strongly felt. No wonder the book *Pippi Longstocking* by Astrid Lindgren, about an extraordinary all-powerful child who lives alone without parents, is one of the stories most loved by children who have reached this stage.

The Indian Boy

One day an Indian boy named Little Chief who was walking in the forest saw a bear. Little Chief was going to kill him, "But," he said "No, I won't; he has a family of his own." Little Chief went on. He went deeper and deeper in the forest. Soon he got too deep and he saw a fox and wolf. They were hungry. Every second they got closer and closer. Little Chief got more and more scared. He asked himself, "Should I kill them? Yes or no?" He said, "Yes, I have to. I will." BANG! BANG! BANG! "I killed them," said Little Chief. My mom and dad will be proud of me," said Little Chief. When he got home with the fox and wolf his mom said, "We can have them for dinner." "Oh, goody!!" said Little Chief.

When his father got home he said to Little Chief, "You are brave and I am very proud of you, my boy." They all sat down for dinner and ate.

Girl

"See how capable we really are," the child is saying in this story. "There will be very difficult decisions to make, but we can make them." Perhaps it is no accident that the decision here involves the question of killing. Eight- or nine-year-olds are beginning to look at the problems that confound us all; in fact, many of them bring feelings to the question of the killing of animals that we have long since hidden beneath a calloused acceptance. The story also says, "Yes, we want our parents to be proud of us—but proud because we are responsible and almost grown up, not because we are their precious little children."

Reflections of the new independence

Language play

New sense of competence, new perspectives, new eagerness to master skills—it is no wonder that these can lead the children into a great deal of experimentation with language. Words are becoming new tools, not only for serious work but for the fun of demonstrating cleverness to others and to oneself. Class newspapers are filled with riddles, jokes, simple crossword puzzles, and often with tongue-twister poems that say, "Look at what I can do! I bet I can trip you up!" Numerous rhymes like the following appear among the children's papers:

I want to see my daddy a minute,
My didy a sinute,
My midy a dinute.
I want to see my daddy a minute to sing
    him a little song
To sing him a little,
To ling him a tittle,
To sit him a lingle long
(I think my daddy would like it because it's
    very short, long.)

Girl

There was a man
Who had a wish fish dish.
So when he said,
"I wish for fish,"
Three fish came
On his wish fish dish.

Boy

Let me point out parenthetically that the author of this last rhyme did not understand how to line out his poem in the readable way just presented (and worked out by the teacher). The child wrote:

There was a man
Who had a wish
fish dish. So
when he said I
wish for fish three
fish came on
his wish fish
dish.

One might ask: Was the teacher's conception of the proper lining the only acceptable one? Are there some virtues in the child's own form, such as a hint that rhyme in a poem can hide internally in the lines?

Allied to this pleasure in tongue-twisting rhymes is the fun the children take in the invention of silly names for characters in stories—generally, of course, silly characters whose foolish behavior only demonstrates how superior the authors feel. These names can sweep through a class, the characters appearing again and again in stories by various children. Sometimes names from favorite books are borrowed or given new twists, as the reader will recognize below in these two stories from one class. The first borrows an idea from *Mrs. Piggle Wiggle* by Betty MacDonald, and the second from *Mr. Popper's Penguins* by Richard and Florence Atwater:

Those Bad Table Manners

Once there was a boy whose name was Henry. Henry had bad table manners. His table manners were so bad that his Mother told him to eat in the kitchen. His Mother called Mrs. Miggle Giggle. "Hello," said Mrs. Carter, "Henry has very bad table manners," said Mrs. Carter. "Oh! I have the cure," said Mrs. Miggle Giggle. "Send Henry over for it," said Mrs. Miggle Giggle. When Henry came back his Mother gave him some bad table manner cure. After that he ate beautifully.

Boy

Mr. Popper's Penguins

Once upon a time there was a man whose name was Andre Popper. Mr. Popper had 1000 penguins in his back yard fighting with each other.

He took the 1000 penguins on one leash to the park and started fighting. One's name was Nicklepot who got a black eye. The one he was fighting with was named Pencilpus who got a black eye also. The other day the penguins said that it is no use to fight when we are brother and sister. So now let's not fight any more and be good to each other.

Two Girls

The following story about learning to speak English comes from another class. The author, who undoubtedly identifies with the Queen ant, is having a fine time with the idea of teaching an ignorant dinosaur. She is enjoying not only the nonsense, but also the know-how, and unwittingly reveals some of her new skill and her growing understanding of the complexity and fascination of the process of learning the sounds of a language.

Andy the Dinosaur

Andy was a very sad dinosaur because he couldn't roar properly. He always said honk instead of roar! Andy was once walking in a big bunch of leaves and trees when he came upon a big heavy rock. He was still very little so he didn't know about insects yet. And I think most of you know that ants live under flat rocks. But he was very strong so he lifted up the rock and he saw a whole family of ants. Honk!!! he said. "What do you mean, Honk??" asked the Queen ant, who had never heard a dinosaur going honk!! before. Honk!!! said Andy again. "Don't you know how to speak English?" asked the Queen. "Honk," said Andy shaking his head no. "Well, I'll say you don't," said the Queen ant. "Would you like me to teach it to you?" "Honk!!!! Honk!!!!" said Andy shaking his head yes. "Now, let's start the lesson. "Say roar." "Honk!!" said Andy. "No! No! No! No! You're all wrong. Go ro-ar!!" "Hork!!!" "Well, at least you changed your sound instead of honk. Now say roar!!" "As loud and clear as you can." ROAR!!!! "You did it! You did it! You did it!" The Queen was so happy she danced a couple of steps of the Scottish jig, and Andy did the same thing. Do you want to learn English? "Rob Rie can do that," said Andy. "Andy!" "Andy!" said the Queen ant. "You just did it." "Rie rid?" asked Andy. "You sure did," said the Queen ant. "Rank you, rank you, for teaching ree." "You're welcome." "Come again some day and I'll teach you some more."

Girl

Finally, in this poem, look at the rhyme mastery, the sense of fun, and the skill in coining a new word:

My Pug, Rosy

I have a little pug
That drinks out of a mug

And can eat a little bug
She always bites the rug.

Her name is Rosy
And she is always nosey.

She is a very funny dog
And eats like a hog.

I think she is <u>adorable</u>
And I like her <u>a-more-able!!</u>

Girl

All of these poems, stories, and tongue twisters have come from classes where children wrote freely and frequently. It seems obvious that the children were pursuing their interests, using their inventiveness, and learning along the way. This does not mean that such learning could not be, or was not, augmented and consolidated through word study initiated by the teacher. At this time, when the children are reveling in what they can do with words, they welcome the study of homonyms, antonyms, similes. They are interested in dictionaries, foreign languages, the derivation of words. We have already seen, on pages 52–53, how one third-grade teacher led her children into sophisticated discussion about the origins of language. In this same classroom another year a large "Homonym Tree" took shape on the bulletin board, and it was a thing of beauty as well as a functional resource for the children. On the branches of the large tree, cut from colored paper, the children tacked their pairs of homonyms—bright paper fruits with the words printed on them. The tree grew in color and fullness as the children discovered new pairs of words.

Certainly it is a mistake to think of creative writing as something set apart from all the various language explorations that can challenge the children to think and work in new ways with words. Ever since Sylvia Ashton-Warner demonstrated her success with the Maoris, teachers have been discovering more and more that, especially for children who are behind in achievement, an interesting and important word—even one taken from a Batman card—learned, talked about, and dramatized, can unlock understanding and lead to increased ability to read and write.[1] Indeed, poets know that a poem

[1]See Sylvia Ashton-Warner, *Teacher* (Simon and Schuster, 1963).

often begins with a single word that drops into consciousness trailing with it provocative sounds and associations.[2] Likewise, teachers reading poetry with their children know that understanding of a poem is often reached through mutual exploration of the words themselves and their meanings and effects.

An eight-year-old's fascination with words, or rather with their component letters, is well demonstrated in the following piece of writing about a "house." The student teacher in this third grade had suggested to the children that it might be fun for them to think about houses and describe one they would like to live in—either a real-life house related to their social studies or an imaginary, fantastic house. She suggested also that they think about who they would like to have living with them in this house. Most of the children launched at once into fantasy, and one little girl wrote this unique story, vividly illustrating it by making her letters into pictures of the objects they symbolized, such as B for bed, O for round pool, C for chair, T for table, and so on.

> If I could have a house I have a house of letters.
> Not the kind of letters you say dear someone, but the kind you write like a, b, c, d, e, and so on.
> Life in that kind of a house is crazy. If you look through the a you are over the Z and under the L and beside the N and the S.
> You could eat any letter you want, because each letter's a food.
> You sleep on B, and swim in O, and sit on C and put your food on T, and feel g, and see E, and talk to P.
>
> Girl

New directions in imaginative writing

Do eight-year-olds continue to write in the symbolic vein that came so naturally to them at six and seven? Are there still witches, giants, and crocodiles, created out of emotional necessity? Yes, though with differences to be expected of children who are a little older.

[2]See Herbert Read, "What is Poetry? An Afterthought," in *This Way, Delight: A Book of Poetry for the Young.* Selected by Herbert Read. Illustrated by Juliet Kepes (Pantheon, 1956).

The seven-year-old boy on p. 90, angry and needing an outlet, became a crocodile with crunching jaws. But an eight-year-old boy, propelled no doubt by a similar need to crash out against others, handles a much more elaborated construct. His imaginary "house," bristling with symbols of power, was created during the same writing session that produced the preceding "alphabet house."

> I would live in a house boat ten stores high with a two storei swimming pool and my own shootting galleri and each time I shot down Bob [a classmate] I would get 1,000 points and I have a bed made out of red hair and the covers out of toranosauris rex.

Witches are killed off very easily by eight-year-olds, and spooks are exposed. In the following stories, which all come from the same class, the children are demonstrating that though scary apparitions are still fun to write about—especially around Halloween—they are not to be taken seriously:

> One day the bad old witch went to get someone to eat. She saw some children and their names were Eddie, David, and Leila. They all had knives, and when the bad witch came they killed her.
>
> *Boy*

> One sunny day Tony got out of bed and he got dressed. Then he went to a spooky house. And Tony went into the house. And all of a sudden the door slammed shut. Then he went upstairs. Then a ghost came out of the wall. And that was really Peter in a costume. Then he saw Frankenstein and that was really Dennis and then Dennis, Peter, and Tony went out a window and went home.
>
> *Boy*

> The Haunted Tree House
>
> One night while Dick and Jane were asleep they heard a noise. When it was morning Dick and Jane ate breakfast and got

dressed. Then they ran out of the house and went into the tree house. But when they got in the tree house some things were gone. That night they heard the noise again and some things were gone. Night after night they heard noise and some things were gone. Then that night they didn't go to sleep so they knew who was taking things away. It was a mother bird and her youngsters. And Dick and Jane started to laugh.

Girl

Down with haunts, spooks, and witches, these children say. They aren't real. As for the monsters, friendly or unfriendly, that loomed large in the younger children's stories, they are fading out of the picture for many eight-year-olds. Space and time are now arenas for science-fiction adventures, not entirely within the realm of the conceivable, yet built on factual knowledge and filled with powerful protagonists who are the children themselves.

Professor Poodleschnoofer

One day Professor Poodleschnoofer who is a scientist made a time machine and his son wanted to try it. And his son's name was Tommy. So Professor Poodleschnoofer said "O.K. but I am going too!" So they went inside it. Tommy said he wanted to go to the age of Dinosaurs and then he wanted to go to see Cro-Magnon man. So they went.

When they arrived they saw a Triceratops fighting an Allosaurus. The Allosaurus lost the fight, but the Triceratops did not know what Professor Poodleschnoofer was so he started to chase them so they ran to the time machine. But it was not there. So they looked and looked. Then Tom slipped and the Dinosaur almost got him but Tommy kicked the Dinosaur and the Dinosaur went away.

Then they saw the time machine so they went inside it and they went home. But when they were home Tom said "I want to go to see Cro-Magnon Man." But the Professor said "Not now but maybe the next day."

Two Boys.

In the next story there are monsters, but they are only vehicles for language play in the ego-bolstering eight-year-old manner:

The Googolers

Once upon a time there were Monsters called the Googolers. They lived on a far away planet called Sumpcanbogeny and do you know how they talk? This is how they talk: Goolgo Blink um Zumarakaroshbe co ZYX-wamaounaeiounon and the longest word they had is this—Nakumbonoyoxoaaa-camunpyroksodolodaZaYay
and they look like this

That is the story of the GooGolers

Boy

Rockets, outer space, and other planets even enter into some of the "house" stories written on the day of the "alphabet house" and the "houseboat ten stores high." Note that the dangerous intruders in these stories are not monsters, but robbers, and the defenses erected against them come straight from the electronic future:

I would live in a city on a nother planet. It would be in the year one zillon. The city would be ruled by me. And I would make a door that had an electrical eye and If a robber comes a phazzer would shoot out of the eye. There would be a electrical force shield around the city. I would have some robbot body guards. I would also have a flying saucer. I would live with my bum little brothers.

Boy

My House!

My house would be made out of glass. It would be in outer space. I would have my own little rocket ship. There would be many secret passages. I would be president. Oh I forgot to tell you my sister and I would live there.

Boy

These stories, crammed with power symbols, are as important in the fantasies of eights turning nine as Henry the Giant was at an earlier age. But the symbols have changed because the children have changed, their concepts have broadened, and the imagery that now appeals to them is more reality-based. These eights and nines are increasingly ready to throw off bunny disguises and appear as themselves—enormously strong and blown-up selves—traveling into space, shooting down annoying classmates, kicking dinosaurs aside, ruling the planets, and protecting themselves with electrical eyes. As they play with these symbols they are working at that major task of schoolchildren—the fortifying of belief in themselves and confidence in their development as boys and girls.

Assignments given for writing topics are often failures because they do not reach the inner concerns of the children. Our house assignment may have loosened an imaginative flow for several reasons. First, it was just concrete enough. An imaginary house is something that can be constructed from the ground up in fabulous proportions! Second, the assignment invited the child to put himself at the center of the situation and to include feelings about others.

The assignment itself, however, was not the sole reason for its success. These children were experienced writers—experienced in writing stories and poems of their own devising. They were in a school that encouraged all forms of expression and open interchange. Furthermore, many of the children had been exposed to this atmosphere since their nursery school days. Even before they could write, they dictated and dramatized.

The school situation, I have said, is the prerequisite. Yet even with a class of children in a school where there have been fewer opportunities for creative work, there is still much that the teacher can do. She will find her third-graders more than eager to say things that are important to them. They need time to write, the stimulus of an interesting program, and a teacher who can appreciate their need to project themselves into their stories. Her choices of assignments or suggestions for topics—when she feels she must give them—are crucial.

Here is another "house" story from a third grade. In this case the assignment did not encourage pure make-believe. It was based on a social studies investigation of types of homes, from caves to tepees. The children were asked to choose a home they might like to have lived in, describe what life was like in that home, and think about why the people who lived there made this particular kind of home. The story below can well lead us to ponder again just why an assignment based on the idea of house or home is such a fruitful one. The child chooses a cave, and his use of the first person shows us how vividly he is putting himself into the situation:

The Cave

When I was a little cave baby I ate food to grow up. My father hunted animals for food. My mother took care of me. Each day I grew bigger and bigger. Then I was a cave boy. I helped my father hunt for food. My father made spears out of wood. He cut a straight piece of wood and then he got some leather and tied a sharp thing to the wood. When we came home each day with the food we made a fire and cooked it. We made tools too. We made them out of stones and rocks. Each day we played with our friends. We always had fun because we could make things out of mud, stones, or rocks, and sometimes we could build a house out of mud. I grew bigger and bigger. Then my father died and just my mother took care of me. When my mother died, I was like my father already.

Boy

The boy has made the assignment a point of departure for writing his own story. Its importance to him is made clear in this comment by his teacher:

"He relates his growth from baby to boy to man, his growth from dependence to independence, his growth to competence, security, strength, and maturity. The life he describes was filled with chances for growth and change, but he knew his parents would not desert him until he was mature enough."[3]

The boy's story reminds us that a child's piece of writing can serve him in a symbolic way whether or not the protagonists are fantasy figures. Children need to create symbols for their concerns, and they can find them in the real as well as in the imaginary world.

Moving toward reality

Stories about people

As we have already pointed out, a teacher of eights can expect to find her children writing an increasing number of real-life stories that are actually about themselves and other children. Here, for instance, is a story that is scarcely a story at all, in terms of plot or suspense. The adventure that it seems to promise comes to an end just as the story gets off the ground. But it is full of lively dialogue between two boys—dialogue straight from life and expertly handled. The child who wrote it is putting what he cares about into the story; he is having a wonderful daydream about driving a car and taking his friend off for a ride, and he seems to enjoy getting his two characters face-to-face and making them talk. Whether he knows it or not, he is in this way practicing some of the important elements of story writing. Perhaps the child has not moved away completely from the idea that a story should have something make-believe in it; hence the name "Yertle," which was the name of a box turtle who was a great pet in this classroom.

> Once there was a boy named Yertle. One morning Yertle was asleep. Then he awoke at 7:30. Then he went downstairs at

[3]Sophia Neaman, *Raise the Bridge: Discovery in Creative Writing* (unpublished Master's thesis, Bank Street College of Education, 1967), p. 63. Reprinted by permission of the author.

8:00 and ate breakfast. After breakfast he went downstairs to get his car to get his friend Stuart for a ride. Then he wondered what street he lives on. "Oh well I have to go back to the house to call him up." UN5-1865. "It's better to know his phone number because he will tell me what street he lives on." "Halo Stuart yes this is Yertle." "What do you want?" "Will you tell me your street number." "O.K. it's 107th Street." "Thanks Stuart." "Don't mention it." "Bye Stuart." "Now I'm back to my car let me see first the motor then I'm all set to go. Here I go to 107th street. There's his house down the block." "Oh Stuart," said Yertle, "I'm waiting for you." "So soon." "What's so bad about it?" "Nothing's wrong with it." "OK" said Stuart. "Come down. Where do you want to go?" "I want to go to N.J." "But where is N.J." said Yertle. "It's across the Hudson river" said Stuart. "But how can we cross?" said Yertle. "By a bridge said Stuart. "O.K. Stuart we're going, hold tight here we go."

A girl in the same class appears to be at about the same stage in her story-writing skills. She chooses a real-life situation and fills the scene with bits of fresh, realistic dialogue. However, she introduces both make-believe and magic—does she think it necessary?—and like the boy above has not yet discovered how to round out and conclude a story. Perhaps one should say she has not concerned herself with this aspect of story writing here. Obviously what she cares about is a series of interactions involving children and an adult, and one can only hope that as she continues to write she will become even more relentlessly truthful about what she sees in the small charged interchanges between people.

The Magic Toes

One day Betty Adams got up. "Mommy mommy," she said. "I have two magic toes." "Oh shut up, will you?" her mother asked. "No. I'm excited. Can't I be excited?" she said anxiously. "You'll not speak freshly to me. Do you understand?" her mother asked. "Yes Mom, I do," she said sadly. Ding! Dong! Who is it? mother said. "It's Lois," said Lois. "Hello," said mother." "How are you" she asked. "I'm fine" said Lois. "May I see Betty?" "Sure it's fine with me" said mother. "Betty, Lois is here" said mother. "Who is here?" said Betty. "Lois is," said mother. "Okay I'll be there in a minute," said Betty. "I have to get dressed!" "Okay" said Mother. "Did you eat your breakfast?" asked Mother. "No I didn't said Lois. "How would you like a cup of hot chocolate" asked Mother. "Mmm I sure would" said Lois. "Hi Lois" said Betty. "Hi. Marie is waiting outside, she doesn't want to come in. Well, I'm gonna let her have some hot chocolate too." "Marie, why don't you come in?" asked Betty. "I come in since it cold and I freezing and hungry" said Marie. "My mother is making hot chocolate for you and Lois," said Betty. "Mmm" said Marie.

"Marie, I have two magic toes" said Betty. "Two magic toes you're fooling us!" said Lois and Marie together. "Yes, I do" said Betty. I'll even show it to you." "Something smells around here" said mother. Betty ran out of the house crying. "Betty, Betty," screamed Marie. Come back and get your shoes!" "No. No." Betty said in a weak voice. I don't have time to my feet aren't cold because I have two magic toes" she said laughing.

Marie, Betty, Lois and Miss Adams lived happily ever after.

Should a teacher discuss with children shortcomings such as we have pointed out in the two stories above? Should she try to explain something about the importance of plot and resolution? It is possible that in doing so she could kill the children's drive to write in their own way. Older children—fourth- and fifth-graders—are much more ready to profit from pointers on such elements as suspense and resolution. However, a teacher can take cues from the children themselves. If an eight-year-old's story is read aloud and children in the class express a wish that more would happen or that the story would end in a different way, then this may be the time to discuss story content and endings that are satisfying. By and large, however, writing for eight-year-olds is a working process in which the children are finding ways to say what they need to say.

Here is an eight-year-old girl who has progressed to the stage of being able to produce a true story with conflict and resolution. Like the two stories above, this one is concerned with real-life interactions, and its major importance lies in this fact. True, any teacher would be pleased to see a child writing with such a good technical grasp, but more important than the technical skill is the girl's ability to take a good look at some of the uncomfortable events of her inner life and to expose them in a story. She has only begun to peel off the outer layers and has perhaps found too easy a solution to the problem she is dealing with. One can hope, however, that she has the potential to go deeper and to become—with time and experience—more and more open to the disturbing forces in her life.

The Present

"Dear, dear," thought Jane, "I'm invited to Carla's birthday party, it's even a slumber party and I haven't gotten her a present yet." Jane thought about it all day. She thought "What shall I do! What shall I do?" The teacher happened to call on Jane, but she was thinking so hard about the present that she didn't hear the teacher. The teacher (who's name was Mrs. Jones) had to say "Jane" five times before Jane heard. Jane almost jumped out of her seat when she heard the teacher's fifth "Jane."

"Ding ding" there was the bell for recess. Jane never wanted this time to come, because the teacher had been quite a bit annoyed when Jane didn't hear her soon enough, and had asked Jane to see her at recess.

Thank heavens all Mrs. Jones said to Jane was that she should have been paying more attention and never to do it again. The day was a long one with all Jane's problems. After a long time a bell rang to go home. "Ding ding." Jane slowly went to the back of the classroom. She opened her schoolbag to put her books in. Ew! it sure was a mess! She reached in to get all the papers out. She suddenly felt something strange. She crossed her fingers that it would be a present. She slowly lifted it out. It WAS a present!!! She quickly remembered that she had gotten it a week ago, put it into her schoolbag and forgotten completely about it. Jane put her books in her schoolbag and (of course with her present safely in her pocket) went zooming off to Carla's.

The next day everyone who was invited to Carla's party asked Jane "What was that funny look on you yesterday?"

"Nothing, just nothing" answered Jane.

Stories about animals

Eight-year-olds concentrate on more than relationships with their peers; their feelings flow in strong attachments to their pets and compassionate championing of creatures who seem to them to be in trouble. The affection that often cannot be overtly expressed to parents finds a degree of outlet in these new channels.

We have already read "My Pug, Rosy" on pages 136–137, a girl's loving description of her dog. Here is another, which doubtless will remind any teacher of many similar attempts by her own children. This is first-rate writing because it has simplicity and the child's genuine feelings very easily find expression through her direct observations of the puppy.

The Dog I Saw

Once I saw a dog that was three weeks old and he was determined to do everything. He was brown and white and he was very cute. He was so clumsy that he just fell flat on the ground. And they had to carry him back to the building. He was very playful and very gentle. He was very fluffy and he had very floppy ears. He was always trying to run away.

In the next story we are back in that half-fantasy, half-reality realm where special understanding can exist between young children and creatures of the barnyard or the forest. (No wonder E. B. White's *Charlotte's Web* is just right for many girls and boys at this stage.) In this story a robin is the hero who succeeds in making a rescue with a little boy's help when the adults in this scene prove to be slow to understand what is going on.

The Desert Town

Jane lived in 1850, in a town called Missia in Egypt. Down by the desert was a swamp, where she got her water and food. One day when she was getting the water she fell in. "Help!" No one heard. She sank farther. "Help! Help!" Then her friend the robin came. He quickly saw what was the matter and flew to Missia. It first tapped on the mother, then father, then big sister, no one came. Then it remembered little brother, and flew very fast. When it got there it tapped him on the head. He came with all his friends. When they got to the swamp they saw what had happened. Her brother said, "Get all the townspeople and a net." They all ran to the town. They came back with a net. They pulled her up with the net. When they pulled her up she was muddy. That night they had a big feast. Jane said, "Thank you very much." They always follow the robin now.

Girl

Finally, here is a direct expression of compassion:

At night the leaves
Fall off the trees
And the wind blows so strong.
The rain falls down so hard.
The poor old dog is still out in the rain
Without a coat at all.

Girl

Is the "poor old dog" real or imaginary? Possibly quite unreal, but does this matter? The child is discovering her feelings and using them.

The new perspective writings

We have already seen the younger children delighting in stretching their perspectives, producing stories told by whales or rivers or historical characters who suddenly find themselves in our midst. Eight-year-olds, able to feel what a "poor old dog" might feel and ready to begin structuring stories around interchanges with people, continue to thoroughly enjoy the attempt to see the world through the eyes of another creature or object, human or nonhuman. This approach of course can lend itself to purely humorous writing, as "The Little

Worm'' below. This story was dictated by a small group of children who had been cleaning out a window box in their classroom and discovered a worm looking out at them, or so it seemed. The children were with a student teacher, whose suggestion it was that the worm be made to talk. The result certainly indicates that suggestions can be very appropriate when the adult who makes them knows the children well and understands their particular brand of humor and the challenges that stimulate their imaginations. The "yellow and black giant worm" refers to a child's watercolor painting, thumbtacked on the wall in the classroom.

The Little Worm That's Squeezing Through
the Crack in the Window Box on the Windowsill

I am wandering through the crack in the window box. Everything looks peculiar. Everything is new. There is no soil. Where's my soil, anyhow? I feel so lonesome for it. It is so bright in this BIG WORLD! and I'm so small. It's so tight in here. It's not like in between two flowers. In the front and back end of me I'm very comfortable but in the middle I'm squeezed. My front end is having an adventure but the back end is in the same old place. I'm so unhappy. I don't know where I'm going. I'm so mixed up—it's too big out here and too cold. Everything's so different, so airy. There's so many creatures and giants. They are standing up. Are they plants? What are they doing. What's that thing clicking on the board and all that white stuff? What is that yellow and black giant worm up there? I've never seen worms with clothes on, and all these worms have clothes on.

In an entirely different vein a teacher challenges her children to experience the feelings of Indians when they first saw the great sailing ships of the white men approaching—and then, walking up the beach, the white men themselves. This, of course, was in connection with the children's study of the Indians of their region; and it is important to know that the teacher had been reading to the class M. R. Harrington's very engrossing *The Indians of New Jersey*. Without this background reading the children would not have visualized the situation as clearly as they did. Even so, some of the children were more able than others to identify in specific, human ways with the Indians.

The culmination is in the last story below, by a child who is well on the way toward mastery of dialogue, though she is still too young to admit anything but a comfortably happy ending. The immediacy the dialogue gives to her story is unmistakable and suggests that a teacher might well say to her children as they are preparing to write, "Make your people talk. Let's hear what you think they might actually say." Of course she does not want her children to feel that they must all write alike. The great virtue of the stories that follow is the variety of ideas and feelings expressed; the variety of styles of writing. The children are attacking the problem in their own ways.

I would feel as if many gods with hundreds of wings are coming to take our lives and burn us and show us their clouds and make us gods.

Boy

I was a little baby and some white men came to take me away. At least I thought so. The white wings were scary. Boy was I scared.

It was the scariest day of my life. I screamed my head off. Well the white men got the land.

The END

Girl

There was once an island. The Indians lived on it. There were palm trees on it. They lived in tepees. The tribe was named Lenapee Indians. One day something came toward the island. All the Indians did not know what to do. The women hid. The babies cried.

The boys got their bows and arrows. By that time you could see what the thing was. The women peeked out from behind the bushes. The babies screamed. The thing came nearer. They looked like white faced men. The white faced man said do not be afraid. We are friends. The Indians did not believe them. So they shot them. From that day on we do not know what happened.

Girl

"Mother mother I see some people."
"What, some people? Get up on the roof."
"How?"
"Here is a ladder."
"Allright."
"Let me see."
"Who are they?"
"They're—they're—
"They're white faced people on funny looking birds. I'm scared."
"I am too. But they have silver bodies."
"So they have silver bodies."
"Come on."
"Allright I will get Father."
"Why?"
"Because if they are dangerous father will have his gun ready."
"OK."
"Father   Father."
"What?"
"Come here some white faced people are coming. They're coming near us."
"Don't be afraid of us. We are your friends."
"It's night you can sleep with us. Goodnight."
"Goodnight."

Girl

Drawing the threads together

The children whose stories we have just read are those who later studied the Dutch in Manhattan. These are the children who built and furnished a Dutch "house" in the corner of their classroom and at the end of the year presented a play made up of short scenes from Dutch life. (See p. 43).

The previous year, this teacher's class also studied the Indians and the Dutch and prepared a play—a series of scenes—based on what they had learned about Dutch life in New Amsterdam. As the planning progressed for these scenes, the teacher decided to talk with the children about what an audience likes to see in a play. She pointed out the importance of suspense and helped the children realize that good ideas for a play are ideas that can be acted. Here is an example of a teacher offering some helpful techniques and not leaving the children alone to thrash around by themselves as they prepare to work on a common project. Also, in emphasizing that the audience must be kept in mind, she is introducing the children to an important idea relevant to the art of writing—one they will often need to be aware of as they grow older. As an exercise that might help them in constructing their play, she gave an assignment in story writing, asking them to keep suspense and action in mind. She did not restrict them to Dutch topics, yet most of the children, immersed as they were in the Dutch study, remained within the Dutch scene. How easily these eight-year-olds could leap into melodrama full of suspense and action is illustrated in the example below:

Once upon a time in New Amsterdam there once was a family called the Hendricks. There were two boys and a father in the family. The older son who was 12 had a name Tunis. The younger one whose name was Petrus was 9. Their father whose name was Nickulus was 36. The mother had died when the younger son was 7. One sunny day Petrus and Tunis were walking in the woods. A bullet came flying and hit Tunis in the shoulder. Tunis screamed. Petrus didn't know what to do. Then he remembered his mother had been killed by a bullet.

After that his father told him that by putting water in the place he got shot it would make him well. Tunis was getting worse by the second. Petrus raced for the spring. He finally found it and ran back to Tunis. He felt his heart. It was bearly beating. He poured the water on the place he got shot. Slowly but surely Tunis got better. Then they went home and lived happily ever after.

Boy

Some of the children were able to use this particular assignment as a vehicle for the expression of melodrama, as well as ideas and feelings that were very important to them. In the following story, conceived as a play, a child who loves to write is able to make use of

153
The eights and nines: growing into the middle years

some of the knowledge she has acquired during the year-long focus on the Indians and the Dutch (though obviously she still has something to learn about the true functions of Indian witch doctors). At the same time she builds her play around an ethical problem of real concern to her: should one tell the truth at all times? This is what an eight-year-old girl can make of an appropriately-based assignment that gives her scope for the use of imagination, knowledge, and emotion:

(Untitled)

Narrator: This is not a true story. But it is a "could be true" story. The cast is a Dutch girl, her little sister Mary, their mother and father, an Indian girl and an Indian witch doctor.

Once two sisters lived at the time that Kieft was governor. They lived in the country. They were expected to be very good kids. They went to school and they were studying nature and they liked it. That is, they liked studying. But they did not like the hard benches.

One morning, at about 5:30 A.M. they were talking.

Mary: Sarah, do you think we should go to the woods?

Sarah: Well, I'm going because I want to find out more than the class.

Mary: All right. If you promise to look out for me.

Sarah: O.K., if you promise not to waste my time.

Mary: Let's not waste time talking here. We can talk on the way!

Narrator: They are walking peacefully and talking.

Sarah: Mary, stop fooling! Remember what I said!

Mary: I'm glad we did this!

Sarah: It was my idea!

Narrator: They went on walking and talking and arguing! Then they came to the creek. Sarah and Mary waded around. Then they went in

	deeper water. They looked at the fish and trees and things. They were coming out of the creek. Sarah had what she thought was mud on, and around, her feet.
Sarah:	Mary, let's go into shallow water so I can wash off this mud!
Mary:	I'm getting tired of the creek too.
Sarah:	Here we are, back in clear water. But this mud will not come off!
Mary:	That is not mud. Those are worms!
Narrator:	Sarah tried to walk but she couldn't. Then she remembered the owl call that her Indian friend had taught her. Even though Kieft was governor, they were friends.
Sarah:	Hey! I remember the owl call that Red Feather taught me!
Narrator:	It was about 6:00 now. The mother and father were not up yet. So Sarah called the owl call. Her friend Red Feather came running.
Red Feather:	What is it? What is it?
Mary:	Sarah has worms on her feet.
Red Feather:	Stop crying, Sarah. My great-grandfather knows we are friends. He says that two friends cannot finish an Indian war. He will know what to do! But there is one thing I know. I will take these leaches off you.
Mary and Sarah:	What are they?
Red Feather:	They are leaches, or bloodsuckers. Doctors put them on sick people. But they are <u>harmless</u> even though blood will pour down.
Sarah:	Then what do you do?
Red Feather:	I will rub some herbs in it. Then I will put on a bandage.
Narrator:	She did this by putting the bandage on and then she took from her sack a prickly leaf and stuck it between the part around the foot and the flap that she had in her hand. She did this with the other foot too.
Mary:	Red Feather, Sarah and I are very, very grate-

	ful to you. But if we go home and tell Mother and Father about it they would be furious!
Sarah:	I don't want to invite ourselves, but would your great-grandfather—
Red Feather:	I never thought of that. Let's go!
Narrator:	So Red Feather and Mary helped Sarah to the Indian camp. When they got there they went to the witch doctor.
Witch Doctor:	Now, Red Feather, you know better than to bring these people to me!
Red Feather:	Great-grandfather, these are my friends. This one, Sarah, got leaches on her feet. I did the herbs and bandage.
Witch Doctor:	That is all you have to do! Now off with you!
Red Father:	But that is not all. They were supposed to go to school. But they wanted to find out about nature and they do not want their mother and father to know about it.
Sarah:	It is 7:00 now, but we did not go to bed till 4:00 last night!
Witch Doctor:	That is lucky. I like you two pretty much now. I have an idea now. Listen! You go home quietly and get your school books. Then tiptoe quietly back to the door. Come in, wake them up, tell them that you started for school early today and Sarah tripped and cut her ankles and you had to come home.
Sarah:	That's a lie and if we tell lies it is a _sin_ and we would be very very badly punished.
Witch Doctor:	I have thought about that. If I say a prayer on both of you it will not be a sin.
Narrator:	So they talked for a little while. The witch doctor nursed the bites. But then Sarah and Mary had to go.
Witch Doctor and Red Feather:	Bye-bye. Take good care and remember the plan!
Narrator:	Sarah and Mary were a little sad to go but

The eights and nines: growing into the middle years

	they had to. When they got home they tiptoed in and out. Then they came in again.
Sarah:	Mother and Father, we left for school early this morning and I tripped and cut my ankles so we had to come home.
Narrator:	Their mother and father believed them.
Mary:	Even though it's four hours later, I'm going to tell them the truth!
Sarah:	O.K., I think we should!

THE MORAL OF THIS PLAY IS: DON'T GO SOMEWHERE WHERE YOU ARE NOT SUPPOSED TO GO!

Other approaches

Another teacher whose children were studying the early days of the Dutch in New York not only encouraged story writing, letter writing to imagined Dutch relatives, and spontaneous dramatizations to help the children plan their play, but also introduced the children to the technique of writing up their research in clear, simple, interesting prose. Each child chose a topic to read about—such as Dutch houses, food, amusements, or schools—and was helped to formulate several questions he would need to answer. The writing task was to organize and present what had been learned, with an attempt to begin the first paragraph with what had seemed most interesting. The children bound together their photostated papers in booklets, one for each child, and took great pride in their accomplishment. Needless to say, the information gathered and shared in this way provided very useful background material as the children worked on their play.

The question might well be asked: "But is this creative writing?" Surely there is no reason to wholly exclude expository writing when we are thinking of the kinds of writing that lead children to invention, discovery, individual expression, and experimentation with uses of language. Producing an expository piece that is clear, strong, and pleasing in its structure can demand of the writer a good deal of trying and testing, pushing and pulling. A teacher errs with an assignment of this kind only if she leaves out the push and pull and hands over preorganized outlines to the children. She errs, too, if she places so much value on the writing up of research that the children rarely have opportunities to experiment with the many other forms of expression that appeal to them.

Here are excerpts from the booklet:

School in New Amsterdam

The schoolmaster taught and the children were afraid of him because he was very stern. The schoolmaster rang the bell to summon the children to school. School lasted from 8:00 a.m. to 11:00 a.m. Then the children went home for a large meal and came back from 1:00 p.m. to 4:00 p.m. There was school every day of the year, even summer, except on Sundays, market days and holidays.

The teacher's desk was on a high platform in front of the room and all of the children sat on hard wooden benches.

None of the children had their own books because printed books cost too much money. Instead they listened to the teacher recite and read and used hornbooks and slates.

If anyone whispered or looked out the window to see a robin building a nest, they were punished. Boys had to stand on a table with three heavy books on their heads. Girls had to sit on tacks.

(Comparative daily schedules follow, one from a school in New Amsterdam, the other from the writer's own school in New York City.)

Boy

The Fire Department

There was no fire department in New Amsterdam. Everybody helped. Everybody formed a fire brigade.

A fire brigade is when lots of people form a line together from a place with water to the fire. The people pass the buckets along. They hardly ever got the fire out because it took a long time. They had to make sure that the flames or sparks did not get on the other houses. When the cry of fire was raised all citizens would rush to the street corners or to the public buildings and snatch up buckets which were hanging there when needed. All haystacks had to be moved north of the wall.

Boy

The eights and nines: growing into the middle years

Note the challenge presented to the child in the above attempt to define a "fire brigade." A good deal of push and pull must have gone into this.

Dutch Houses

The first houses were just crude huts. Then in later times they changed into great mansions made of yellow brick, red brick and wood. Sometimes the brick was laid in fancy designs. The Dutch lived a happy life although they only had 2 or 3 rooms. The doors, known as Dutch doors, were split in two in order to look out and keep animals out. In the start almost all the houses had thatched roofs. They stopped this because the straw could catch fire. After that they used tile for their roofs. The roofs looked like steps. The rooms were small and neat. The most important room was the kitchen. On top of the fireplace was the family's best plates. This room was used for eating and sleeping. The second room, the parlor, was used for fancy purposes. Days in New Amsterdam when people had to stay indoors were not looked down on for the homes were delightfully delightful.

Girl

Among the many other forms of expression that appeal to eight-year-olds is the personal account of an event that has had dramatic impact. Most children, by the time they are eight or nine, have been exposed to at least one destructive storm that has felled trees or flooded the streets; we know that all are exposed occasionally to the assassinations of prominent figures; and children living along the eastern seaboard have had to cope with frightening power failures that have left them in darkness for many hours.

Following such crises, children come to school with the need to talk about them, write about them, relive them, in order to regain their equilibrium. But these accounts extend beyond their use as safety valves. They are often among the most creative pieces the children produce, personal, individual, and full of feeling. Each child has his own story to tell and needs no prompting to plunge in and tell it in his own way.

The following stories from one third-grade class, written after a blackout in New York City, demonstrate the variety that can be expected. A teacher might note with pleasure that the first boy found a playful way to symbolize the blackness. She might be even more pleased to see the personal handling of family life in the last two. The openness and honesty in these detailed revelations are to be prized. They indicate to the teacher that the children feel trustful in the atmosphere of her classroom and can really show themselves, a most encouraging sign to her as she evaluates the papers. E. B. White has said, "All writing is communication; creative writing is communication through revelation—it is the Self escaping into the open."[4]

The Night the Black Ghost Came

The night the black ghost came it was Nov. 9, 1965. When I was writing a secret code and the light was getting duller and duller. It was my friend, Black Smother. He smothered the light. Then he went away. It was still black. He didn't have any fun since 1960. But this is the second time he did it. We had to use candles. My brother and sister were watching T.V., but a few minutes later my father came. I told him I was watching T.V. He said, "Go right ahead." I turned it on and nothing came on. And I said, "So that's why you said that." If it would work, he wouldn't let me turn it on.

Boy

The Black Out

Yesterday, at five twenty-eight the lights went out. That night my brother was in the subway. My mother and I were scared stiff. My brother was there at the beginning of the black out. He said that candy was given out. I was shaking like a milk shake. He came home at nine-fifteen. I thought that the lights wouldn't go on but they did.

Girl

[4]William Strunk, Jr., *The Elements of Style*. With revisions, an Introduction, and a chapter on writing by E. B. White. 2nd Edition (The Macmillan Company, 1972), p. 60.

The eights and nines: growing into the middle years

When the Lights Went Out

Yesterday the lights went out. My Mother went out to see if anything else worked but nothing did. When she turned off the flashlight she hid behind the door and when my brother and my sister and I went out mother said, "Boo!" We were so scared that we ran so very fast. My Mother lit ten candles. So it was very light. After dinner Mother said, "It's time for bed. Where your clothes and your pajamas tonight." So we wore our clothes and pajamas to bed. We went to bed, kissed Mother, and went to sleep. In the middle of the night I woke up because I had to go to the bathroom and get a drink. I did. Then I went to sleep again.

Girl

The Night 4 Babies Cried

One weird night I just sat down to do my homework when in the living room where my mommy's friend Ethel said, "It's getting dim in here." I said, "The kitchin is too." My mother said, "Everything is." I said, "Ah oh here come the four kids. Mac my brother, Jimmy his friend, Joseph, Jimmy's brother, Manny another friend of Mac's, and last but not least Laurie, Manny's sister the youngest. They all ran in and said, "Boo-boo-mommy I'm scared aya-boo hu." When ever the doorbell rang everyone cried out "Don't answer it, I think it's a robber." But it was only a next door neighbor who wanted to know information about the lights and they told us something about it. Or else someone who's candles blew out and they couldn't find their way. Finally they cried themselves to sleep. But Jimmy's Father was in the hospital and his mother told Al (her husband) that it was pretty dark to get operated on. So he checked out of the hospital and picked up Jimmy and brought him home to bed with Joseph. In the morning the only one who would rather be in the dark was me.

Girl

The eights and nines: growing into the middle years

When is it poetry?

Words, rhymes, and repetitions

We have already seen eight-year-olds turning out tongue-twister nonsense rhymes and going beyond nonsense to coin new playful words:

> I think she is adorable
> And I like her a-more-able.

In the same vein, another third-grader invents a verb and puts together rhyming lines that suggest bicycling:

> Bicycling, bicycling
> Where are you going?
> I think you are going
>   To and Fro-ing.
> Going, going,
>   To and Fro-ing.
>
> *Girl*

Many of the children at this time are developing the concept that poetry calls not only for tricky words, but magical words as well, even beautiful words. Here a boy discovers the rhyme in "heard" and "bird" and seems to be trying to make a poem that catches some of the beauty of these words:

> *Birds*
>
> Birds fly in the blue sky
> Some fly low
> And some fly high.
>
> Seagulls fly over the sea
> And on the sea.
> They are heard
> By me.

The seagull is a beautiful bird
And on the sea
They are always heard.

A girl builds a poem about a cat around a concept and a phrase that
may have especially intrigued her: the "graceful paws" of the cat. Did
she know what a light and lovely poem she was writing? Perhaps not,
yet she must have taken some pleasure in the very act of calling up
these images of trees, snowflakes, whiteness, soundlessness:

The Cat

Its footprints cannot be heard as it
    creeps on the leaves.
No one hears them crunch.
Like a snowflake falling to the ground.
And now look as she jumps on the tree!
Did you hear her?
No you didn't . . . No one can hear her
With her gracefulness locked on every paw
    and the lightness in her body as she
    jumps from tree to tree.
With her white coat . . . so white . . . you might
    mistake it for a snowflake that had
    fallen.
It is the cat with her graceful paws.
You cannot hear her. No, no one can hear her.

A boy tries to express in a poem his love of the New York sky-
scrapers and subways. He has found one sentence he likes to use as a
repeated refrain. This repetition must have seemed poetic to him—a
way to put his feelings into words—and indeed it is poetic, even
though fumbling; the result is a poem perhaps more typical of a
child's early attempts than the cat poem above:

Buildings and Subways

I love buildings as a sight to be seen.
The way buildings go up is nice.

I love buildings as a sight to be seen.
For instance the Pan Am Building.
And the Empire State Building.

I love subways as a sight to be seen.
The way subways run is nice.
The way subways go up is nice.
I love buildings as a sight to be seen.
For instance the Pan Am Building
And the Empire State Building.
I love buildings as a sight to be seen.

Another third-grader writes a witch story and invents tricky, suggestive words for her witches to chant whenever they speak.[5] Upon their first appearance we hear:

Sprinkle specker
Prickle pelter
Take us to our
Special Shelter.

And again:

Powery powery
Pinker pot
Take us to
Our evil spot.

Finally, as they throw purple juices into a pot:

Brendel and shake,
Boil and bake.

This fortunate child knew the witch scenes from *Macbeth*—her mother had been reading them aloud to her at home. With "Double, double toil and trouble" sounding in her ears, it is no wonder that she could reach into the cauldron of words and pull out just the right magical ones for her witches.

[5]Claudia Lewis, "Language and Literature in Childhood" from *Elementary English*, May 1967, Vol. 44, p. 519. © 1967 by the National Council of Teachers of English. Reprinted by permission.

Another child, probably under the influence of our contemporary rock ballads, tries to construct what she calls a "made-up folk song." Here one can sense the child's groping effort toward musical expression as well as toward symbolism. She is in love with singing lines and rhymes, and moving thoughts that are just beyond her grasp:

My Made Up Folk Song

Once I had a little boat
That sailed upon the sea
Its summer color was black and white
I sang about it day and night.
Every day I said to myself
I'll go and get my father
In Vietnam across the sea
But my boat was too little.
I hated to think
That it would sink
Right to the bottom with me.
While my mother sat at home
She wept, for
Every night in the wilderness
Where my father suffered the war.
But my boat helped the most
Because it shone triumphantly in the sun
Until it smiled at you
Just as my father used to do.
Once I had a little boat
That sailed upon the sea
Its summer color was black and white
I sang about it every night.
The boat smiled back at me.

New ways of looking at the familiar

Even second-graders, as we pointed out in the last chapter, can begin to see the familiar world with eyes that bring new perspectives into play. Looking out at a row of houses on the street, a little boy suddenly realized that once, perhaps in this very place, "Indians were

everywhere you looked," and he put this thought—quite rightly—
into a poem (p. 113).

It is not surprising that as the children grow older such arresting
thoughts appear more often in their poems. Here a third-grade boy
makes quite a discovery about the presence of his shadow, and his
poem—written in a form of his own—reflects his excited feeling:

Me and my Shadow

Everywhere I go my shadow is
here!
I am not alone because the sun
is here!
And my shadow   my shadow and me,
I am never alone even when
asleep if the sun shines on me.

A girl compares the movements of birds with the movements of
airplanes and seems to be reaching for a poetic quality in the words
she uses:

Birds Flying South

The wingèd beasts of the air
    that fly in V's and other shapes
go and come back. How gently they move.
    They seem to put the breeze in the back of
                              their wings—
Not like the machines that fly among them.[6]

How are the children to be led to such conceptions of poetry? How
are they to be taught to write in this way? It is not so much a matter of
leading and teaching as it is of exposing the children to the teacher's
broadly-based enthusiasms, exposing them to a wide variety of poems
read aloud and accustoming them to an atmosphere of discussion and
discovery. True, all of the third-graders whose poems we have looked

[6]From *Somebody Turned on a Tap in These Kids*, edited by Nancy Larrick (Delacorte Press, 1971). Copyright © 1971 by Nancy Larrick Crosby. Reprinted by permission of the publisher.

at here were children who had rich exposures both at home and school.

Let us turn to the work of a teacher who started from scratch with children who had no ease in writing when they entered her third grade. For some of them, English was a second language.

Sensitive observation

This teacher began not with poetry writing but with the attempt to encourage the children to become sensitive observers; and the first thing she asked of them was to talk about what they observed. If, for instance, a heavy rain suddenly began to fall and a child exclaimed, "Oh, it's raining!" she would ask the children to stop what they were doing, look out at the rain, and describe—if they could—what it was like. As the children became comfortable with this approach, she began to ask them for one-word responses. "Give us just one word that seems right for this rain!"

By Christmas the children were dropping their clichés and finding fresh, expressive words. The teacher felt the time had come to begin with written responses. In early January she asked them to write, in unconnected form, a series of single-word reactions to their Christmas vacations. The results were indeed poems of a sort. One boy wrote:

Vacation

fun
Movies
snow
ice cold
Toys
Games
Visit
enjoy
Wow!

Since the children found this writing fun and by no means an overwhelming task, the teacher continued to ask throughout the year for similar one-word lines, while she at the same time encouraged other types of writing and expression. She continued to stress oral expression to give the children freedom with words and ideas. One exercise they particularly enjoyed developed after hearing Dr. Seuss' *And to Think That I Saw It on Mulberry Street*, a story in which a child builds up a fantastically tall tale based on simple observation of a horse-drawn cart on the street. The children in this class could not have written down their own tall tales, but they could tell them. Dividing into groups of four and five, they built up their imaginative stories, became extremely involved, and enjoyed the experience.

Meanwhile, the teacher continued to encourage the children to become good observers, to look, listen, touch, and tell in their own ways. She found *The Quiet Story* by Rhoda Levine useful in setting a listening mood. In her own words: "I read this book to my class in soft, quiet tones. I then asked them to be silent. After a few moments of silence we began to discuss what happens when you're quiet. They noticed how much more keenly they heard and saw their environment. Then I reread the book. I asked them to imagine themselves in a familiar place—school, livingroom, bedroom, playground—either with a friend or alone, and to write about what it would be like if they were perfectly quiet."[7]

Here are examples of the "quiet mood" writings that resulted:

When I am in school and it's quiet I hear sounds and I start to think a lot. I hear when the train is coming and the machine is running. And after that then I start to think how they work.

Girl

When I was in the closet
I was very very quiet.
I heard all sorts of things
Like I heard my self
breathing and I heard trucks
and motor cycles outside.
I heard things I can't even
explain.
I kept quiet.

Boy

[7]Quoted from a personal communication from Jane Drucker with her permission.

By the spring of the year the children could easily focus on their sense reactions and write down their responses. In fact, they often wrote spontaneously, without any teacher direction. Neither the teacher nor the children called it poetry, but here are the sensory observations, moods, and metaphors that lead to poetry. They constitute that imaginative thrust that can free a thought from prose when the language is also free and reaches for something more than the sounds and patterns in our everyday communication. Unable in the fall to write down a single thought with their pencils, the children were finally producing these fresh observations:

Moods on a Foggy Day

When I look down to the cars they are moving so slow that I feel like moving slow too. And when I look at the sky it looks to me like it is going to come close to my window.

Girl

On a foggy day when I hear things, but can't see where they're coming from, I sometimes think that the fog has a mouth and can talk through it.

Girl

Some Reactions to a Day

The clouds are brushing their teeth and little spots of toothpaste are dripping down on the ground.

Girl

Today it looks like somebody is putting cotton all around the buildings.

Boy

On A Very Warm Spring-like Day in Winter

It feels like I can do what I want and spread out and do action.

Girl

I feel like taking an umbrella and going about 500 feet way up on the roof and then floating down and all the air will come in my face.

Girl

I feel like running so fast I can take off into the air just like an airplane.

Boy

Connections, insights

Let me ask again, "When is it poetry?" and close this section with a piece of writing that looks like prose and for the most part sounds like prose. Yet its basic idea expresses a poetic discovery. A surprising connection flashes, as the child likens the roaring sea to the bad-tempered lions. Here is that imaginative thrust mentioned above. For age eight this fresh insight is very close to poetry; more importantly, it reveals an "inventive, searching, daring" spirit.

The Roaring Sea and My Thoughts

The Roaring Sea goes on and on forever, with rolling waves. As it tumbles and rolls, fishes swim through it. It goes on past sandy islands, it goes on and on and never stops. I wonder where it does stop, nobody knows. As it goes on it looks like a lion in a terrible rage. But it must stop somewhere. And that place I do not know but I will guess, I guess it ends where a big forest comes and there is jungle and probably the bad-tempered lions meet with sea and make best friends.

That's what the Roaring Sea and my thoughts are.

Girl

References

ASHTON-WARNER, SYLVIA. *Teacher.* New York: Simon and Schuster, 1963.

ATWATER, RICHARD and FLORENCE. *Mr. Popper's Penguins.* Illus. by Robert Lawson. Boston: Little Brown, 1938.

HARRINGTON, M.R. *The Indians of New Jersey: Dickon Among the Lenapes.* Illus. by Clarence Ellsworth. New Brunswick, N.J.: Rutgers University Press, 1963.

LEVINE, RHODA. *The Quiet Story.* New York: Atheneum, 1963.

LINDGREN, ASTRID. *Pippi Longstocking.* Trans. from the Swedish by Florence Lamborn. Illus. by Louis S. Glanzman. New York: Viking, 1950.

MacDONALD, BETTY. *Mrs. Pigglewiggle.* Illus. by Hilary Knight. Rev. ed. Philadelphia: Lippincott, 1957.

NEAMAN, SOPHIA. *Raise the Bridge: Discovery in Creative Writing.* Unpublished Master's thesis. New York: Bank Street College of Education, 1967.

READ, HERBERT. "What is Poetry? An Afterthought" in *This Way, Delight: A Book of Poetry for the Young.* Selected by Herbert Read. Illustrated by Juliet Kepes. New York: Pantheon, 1956.

SEUSS, DR. *And To Think That I Saw It on Mulberry Street.* New York: Vanguard, 1937.

STRUNK, WILLIAM JR. *The Elements of Style.* With revisions, an Introduction, and a chapter on writing by E. B. White. 2nd Ed. New York: The Macmillan Company, 1972.

WHITE, E.B. *Charlotte's Web.* Pictures by Garth Williams. New York: Harper, 1952.

The nines and tens: self-discovery and self-understanding

Chapter five

Adolescence looms ahead tantalizingly. To ten-year-olds today—children going on eleven—and to some of the nines, it is only around the corner. Children of this age are not the children of a generation ago. Already many of them are struggling toward the independence and the new self-definition of the adolescent.

"Who am I, anyway?" the ten-year-old is asking himself. This is the big question confronting him. "What can I do? What can I become? Am I like the others? Are they like me?"

They see themselves on the threshold of adulthood, and they are turning an inquiring gaze toward us and our adult concerns. They want to understand more about death and love and war and sex and prejudice; they want to know how computers work; some of them have already experimented with drugs.

As their teachers we can best serve them if we can help them in their urgent effort to know who they are. If they can write almost every day, for instance, in a free form that I shall call poetry, then they have within easy grasp one of the most powerful tools man has ever invented to help him define himself, sharpen his awareness, and grow in his own directions.

Self-discovery through poetry

There are other forms of writing that are important for these children, and other forms of self-expression—particularly dramatics. But let us now put poetry first instead of last, and see what it can become in the hands of nines and tens and what it can do for them.

Poetry in the fifth grade: personal insights and expression

In a class of 20 fifth-graders, a racially and ethnically very mixed group, over half of them are reading on a second-grade level. About five of them are having difficulties learning English as a second language. It is February. A new student teacher has come to the classroom. She knows that the children have had good previous experience in writing, but she believes that they have not tried the kind of poetry she would like to see them tackle—poetry written out of their own feelings, poetry about themselves and their world.

The day comes when she suggests poetry writing. As she had anticipated, a groan arises from the class. She quickly explains that this is not going to be as difficult as they might think. All they are to do is write down things that go on in their heads. "Nothing goes through my head," a resistant child immediately replies. "A great first line for a poem!" the student teacher says, and at once turns and writes it on the board. The children catch on that what they say will be accepted, and some of them begin calling out other lines. And so the first class poem is composed and written on the board:

Nothing goes through my head
My head is eating and clothing and money
My head is a bikini
My head is a marshmallow
My head is a baseball
My head is the whole world
My head is talking and talking
My head is empty from everything the teacher says
My head is a clock

My head is a candy
My head is the Temptations
My head is the Supremes
My head is full of ideas

A "poem"? Yes, in the sense that it is full of playful, suggestive statements revolving around a central idea and sustaining a rhythm and, most importantly, truly reflecting the voices of the children. Certainly, though, it is only a beginning.

The student teacher, seeing the success of this method on the first day, subsequently begins each of her poetry sessions with a "class poem" which she writes on the board as the children call out the lines. Following the class poem, the children write individually. The topics suggested are always those that are close to the lives of the children. See what they do with candy:

Candy

I love candy
I will marry candy
I am the brother of candy
I love lollipops
I love sweetarts
I love strawberry stix, grape stix, apple stix,
    watermelon stix
Bubblegum
I work in a candy store
I wish I had all the candy in the world
I wish the whole world was candy
I wish I had a candy house!

Candy is their love, but they have hates too, and it is good for them to see that some of their hates are shared:

I hate chicken
Fish
Liverwurst
I hate spinach

Liver—I hate chicken liver!
You like chitterlings?
I hate vegetables
I hate potatoes
I can't stand broccoli
Onions make me cry.

As they hear each other's wishes, can they avoid recognizing that they are speaking honestly and often revealing very personal things to each other?

Wishes

I wish I had my own room
I wish I was sweet like sugar
I wish I had my own television
I wish I was a sparkling star over heaven
I wish I was a married man
I wish I had my grandmother back
I wish I had long hair
I wish I had a sister
I wish I had no school
I wish I was German and Hungarian and nobody
    understood me
I wish I had no sisters and no brothers
I wish I could see my real father
I wish I had a bird
I wish I was a magician
I wish I was a pickpocket.

As they dictate a class poem about brothers and sisters, they are opening up to each other even more and perhaps becoming more aware of their feelings:

Brothers and Sisters

I wish I had a brother
I wish I had twenty brothers

I wish I had a girl friend
I wish my brother could talk[1]
Brothers and sisters are good to have
But sometimes they get in your way
Sometimes I hate my brothers
But only sometimes
I hope I have a baby sister
My brother is a pest
He gets me in trouble
I want to kill him.

Their class poem about night not only enables them to share some of their uncomfortable feelings about night, but also leads them into the playful, metaphorical thinking that is so important in poetry-making.

Night

The night is dangerous
The night is very mysterious
The night is very frightening
The night is very exciting
The night is very misty
It covers all around
Like poison gas.

At night someone turns off the sun
Who?
A cloud.

The sun goes for a swim to cool off
It goes someplace to hide
It goes deep deep down
It plays hide and seek with the clouds
The moon is his wife.

[1]The brother referred to here is a deaf and dumb child.

Here are two of the individual night poems that followed the class poem. In the first one we see a boy openly expressing his feelings of fear:

The night is very scary
When my Mommy works late
I'm scared
and I hear noises in the hall outside
and mices running around the house
and when my Mom comes in
I be so happy
I run and get in the bed and go to sleep.

In the following we see how successfully metaphor has helped a girl grasp hold of feelings and thoughts she might have found too vague for precise, literal description:

The Noisy Despicable Night

The night is like ugly vampires
The night is like scary old birds
The night is bony with no bones
Inside a skeleton
The night is very old fashioned.

How did the student teacher help the children get started on this process of writing their own poems—a different matter from calling out lines for a class poem written on the board? Here are her own words:

In trying to build enough confidence in each child so that he believed in the worth of his own writing, I accepted tentative starts, retrieved crumpled papers from under desks and smoothed them out, and even pieced together torn-up pieces. I lavished praise on each effort. Later I was able to give constructive criticism to some children, in individual conferences only.

After each poetry-writing session, I typed up all the poems, correcting spelling and sometimes dividing lines. Seeing their work in this orderly and professional-looking version gave the children pride and confidence in what they had written. By posting the typed poems the next day, I was able to supply the immediate gratification that is important to many of these children. . . .

When I wrote poems on the board for discussion, I chose poems dealing with city themes, drawn from Richard Lewis's *Miracles* and Nancy Larrick's *On City Streets*.[2]

When they approached the subject of death, the children were apparently very challenged. Though not all of them wrote fully, they wrote thoughtfully and in a poetic line a step removed from prose:

Death is like a roaring thunder.
It's like something that hits you fast
and then you are gone.
I never been dead before
and I don't know what it's like,
But this is what I think it is.

Girl

Death is like a moment
or years of solitary
and silence.

Girl

What is death like?
It is like a spirit walking by you.

Girl

These children are groping to express big thoughts, and so is the little boy whose poem follows. He, however, brings the whole subject

[2]Quoted from a personal communication from Caroline Zinsser with her permission.

closer to himself and his life. His poem becomes a picture of himself, an attempt—no doubt unconsciously made—to arrive at some insights into his nature:

Death is like my heart is dying
Everything I see I could feel it in my heart
Gently and warm
Deep deep down
So warm and kind
Sometimes I feel as if my heart is broken
Sometimes I feel so sad that I think I'm alone
Sometimes I don't have any friends to play with or to talk to.

A picture of himself? Yes. In the classroom he was a lonely, clinging little boy, a little older than the others, a child without friends. His many poems—all of them dictated, for he could not be brought to writing in any other way—reflect his loneliness and sadness. But the very act of putting these feelings into words must have given him a certain satisfaction; this, of course, is one of the reasons for encouraging children to write about what most concerns them. Deeply disturbing feelings can sometimes be relieved through the healing processes of metaphorical expression. Of course, a child's teacher works in many ways for his well-being, too, and the child's poems give her added insight into what he needs. I quote here two more of this little boy's poems, outstanding for their use of metaphor:

Flowers

One day I went to the park
And I saw a lot of flowers.
Some were red
Some were blue
Some white, some yellow.
As I was walking
I turned around
And, when I turned around
The flowers were gone
Like if the sand

Swallowed them down.
They were gone forever.
They went to the middle of the world
And they never came back.

Life

Life is like a blackout,
So dark and far.
You feel so lonesome,
Like you were in a tall, tall building
That reached the sky,
Out of the world
So I could see other planets,
I could see the sun
And the sky.
So I only could see darkness.
Life is like a big, round, dark ball.
Life is like darkness.

In late spring the student teacher had to move to another school, but the children continued their poetry writing under the guidance of their teacher, who had worked closely with the student teacher from the beginning. Here the children dictate a class poem on what makes them mad and in their individual poems take the opportunity to express themselves on boys vs. girls and even on teachers (their teacher, of course).

Things That Make Me Mad

When my brother hits me
I bubble!
I feel like popping him in the face.
I feel to choke him
To strangle him
To stab him
Right in the heart!

Boy

Boys

Boys are dumb and very cockeyed
And wear cement shoes.
They are not respectful to girls.
I hate boys
Because they bite too many girls.
If a boy touches me
I'll knock him down
Straight to the ground.

Girl

Girls

I hate girls.
Girls wear funny colors
Like orange blouses
And pink skirts
And purple shoes.
Girls need plastic surgery.
Girls swear they're cute.
Girls aren't groovy.
Only boys have the hip tune.

Boy

Teacher

Our teacher teaches us every day
Like if she is going to teach us day and night!
But she is a nice teacher.

Girl

Teachers

Sometimes I hate my teachers
And sometimes I love them very much.
I can't stand the teachers that are bossy.

The teacher I have now isn't bossy
BUT
She is demanding.

Girl

Summer is like
The death of a teacher.
      —by Rhoda, the marvelous,
    the brilliant, the great, the stupid, the wonderful.

Girl

Rhoda doesn't tell us how she feels about this summer death of a teacher. We can guess, though, that many of the children—no doubt including Rhoda—would agree with the girl who writes below about the atmosphere in this classroom. It could not be otherwise, where there has been so much encouragement and acceptance.

Freedom

Freedom in this class is Love,
Everybody going around
Sharing their candy,
Giving books away.
And, if you don't know a math problem
We teach it to you right away,
And, we treat the teacher like a princess,
And we live like a great big family.

By the end of the year many of the children had developed really impressive powers as writers, which is not surprising in view of the consistent practice on personal themes and the exposure to the many voices of their classmates, as well as to poetry brought in by the teachers. After a trip to the zoo, see how expertly the children can put their observations into words, using metaphors and similes that come straight from their own level view; and how naturally their thoughts fall into lines rhythmically related to each other.

Monkeys

Monkeys are noisy little animals
Chattering away,
Never really saying anything.
I wish I knew what they are saying,
But only those who like monkeys know what they say.

Girl

The Elephant

He has a long trunk.
He eats peanuts and drinks water.
And when it's not hot out,
He puts dirt on his back,
His nose is like a vacuum.
He can vacuum up your floor.

Girl

Flamingos

Flamingos are very pretty.
I love their loud pink color.
They are very tall and slender.
They weigh approximately 75 pounds.
I think they're on a strict diet.
If they were human
They would be very feminine.
I love flamingos.

Girl

Finally, two more poems are offered here because of what they reveal about the children who wrote them and about the poetry-writing process, which enables children to touch and even to enlarge their feelings. The first is a mature statement made as a child looks around at her world. The second is an exuberant spring song and we might ask if the exuberance is only for spring or if it is partly for the joy of the poem itself.

People

I have a dream
That the world is going to be filled with paintings—
Paintings of people:
Tall people, thin people
Fat people and short people.
Kind people, good people.
And satisfactory people.
Fair people, excellent people,
Improving people,
Barely passing people,
And no passing people.

Girl

My Exciting Poem

Ha   Ha   Ha
Do you like spring?
Yes, I do
I just love spring
I could kiss spring from head to toe
If I were spring I would lighten up the whole world.
Some people said today is spring
And some said tomorrow is spring.
Don't talk about spring
Just love spring.

Girl

Poetry in the fourth grade: self-revelation

Can children younger than ten respond to an appeal to write simply and plainly about themselves and their feelings? There is no doubt that they can.

Across the hall from the fifth-graders whose work we have just seen, a class of fourth-graders worked in the same way, speaking directly about themselves and each other in their poems. These children were also a very mixed group racially and ethnically, and again

the poetry was written under the guidance of a student teacher working closely with the classroom teacher, in a room where there was
much stress on individual work, freedom of choice, and meaningful,
natural interchange.

It was easy for these children to write about something as close to
them as their hands and feet and mouths. Even these simple topics
gave them a chance to reveal a good deal about themselves:

My Mouth

I have a small mouth, but a lot
   comes out of it.
My father says if I don't shut that small mouth
   of mine
He will put his fist right in it.

Girl

My Mouth

I hate my mouth.
It gets me into trouble.
When I go out to play
My mouth says things I do not want it to say.

Boy

Hands

My hands get me in trouble
Because I get into fights.
I try to stop
But my hands get me in trouble.

Boy

My Feet

My feet make me wear shoes
   that I don't like

And then I get mad at my
    mother.
But I still wear them.

Girl

The following two boys appear to be pursuing insights into what
may be troubling aspects of their own behavior:

My Body

Sometimes my body hurts
    when I get nervous.
My heart starts to tickle me.
So I begin to laugh
Laughing and laughing all day.

My Body

My body keeps on shaking.
But I don't like the way it shakes.
If it keeps on shaking
I am going to punch myself in the stomach.

The children were asked to look at people around them, and they
wrote of love and hate in terms of specific experiences. In the following poem about love, a fourth-grade boy writes about a girl. There is
nothing unusual about this today, and the teachers in this class are to
be congratulated that a child will write so honestly on a paper that
will be handed in to them:

Love is . . .

Love is
    a pretty nice girl
    with a good dress,
        beautiful hair,
    pretty neat handwriting,

pretty nice legs and
a pretty nice face,
who says, "What you
lookin' at, man?"
very softly.

Boy

Hate is . . .

People that take things away from you,
People that fight for no reason—who
are stronger than you.
Someone who punches you in the nose and
you say, "Why you do that man?"
And then he hits your ear and then he says,
"I'm going to take those glasses off and
give you two black eyes."

Boy

From love and hate it is only a step to prejudice, which can be freely discussed in this free classroom where children who are black and brown and white live and work together. I select here five of the twelve poems that were written on this topic. In even this small sample, one can see how feelingly the children are speaking out and how they are thrusting around in an attempt to come to an understanding of what prejudice implies.

I am not prejudiced.
There are some people who do not like me.
    WHY?
So my mother is Black and my father is White.
I hate them.
They are prejudiced.

Boy

If I were black I'd feel what black people feel.
If I were black, I might be prejudiced against
    whites because whites would be prejudiced to me.
It feels like being shot when someone is prejudiced to you.
If someone hit me because they were prejudiced,
My heart would be stung, like being stung by a bee.

Boy

I am not prejudiced.
It is just that
When people start up
A fight
I do not
Like it!

Girl

Black is black
White is white.
So why does Black
Give you a fright?

I am black
You are white.
To me black is
A great delight.

Boy

Some people say prejudiced people are bad.
That is not true.
They are not really bad.
They just should not believe
        the way they do.

Boy (Same boy as directly above)

Of course, not all of the writing is on such serious themes. The
children go outdoors to the park and to the playground, and they find

lively words and rhythms and metaphors to express their light spirits. This is not surprising. Good writing always flows from a self that is being itself, and these children have had ample practice all along in being themselves with each other and with their teachers. The first poem below actually was not written with pencil on paper. It was called out from a branch on a tree in Central Park:

The Park

It feel good to climb,
I feel like I'm in Jamaica, man!
I like the park better than the city.
You have more lifetime up there.
You can do monkey tricks.

Boy

Spring and Summer

The sunshine and the playful wind
Make me feel as if I were shaking
          hands with spring.
The playground is as soft as
          chocolate pudding!
The children step carefully
          on the chocolate pudding.

The sun shining made the chocolate
          melt on the playground.
A boy slipped and said "Ouch   ooh   aah."
The sun made me red and hot.
It made me feel like a devil.

Boy

Finally, a girl writes about herself in a poem she calls "My Flag"— one of the most important poems in this collection because the child seems to be arriving at the understanding that in a poem one can make an exploration of oneself and a definition or redefinition of one's personality. Her poem begins with a simple matter of color choices; then she switches to something much more fundamental, as though suddenly realizing that she need not stay on a superficial level. Why does she call her poem "My Flag"? Has she glimpsed the symbolic functions of both a flag and a poem?

My Flag

I am a girl
Some girls like pink.
Some girls like red.
I am Catholic and
I do not go to church,
But I still believe in God.
I like strawberries.
    They are red.
I like apples.
    They are red.
I like watermelon 'cause inside of it,
    it's red.
Red is a pretty color,
And so is pink—for girls!

Several blocks away, other fourth-graders are working at the writing of poetry. As in the group we have just seen, these children have freedom to write in their own ways, but are helped by the teacher's suggestion of topics and reading of poetry on related themes. The children here, too, are far from homogeneous in both background and ability. According to their teacher, their writing skills range from second to ninth or tenth grade.

When the river was a topic, this picture of river and self was produced by a little girl:

River splashing on the shores
Telling of its water bright and emerald and beautiful,
Placing itself on the rocks,
Laughing to itself,
Gurgling to itself,
Being itself,
Flowing gently along its way.

One cannot be sure that the child is using the river as a symbol or making a statement about growing and being. She may not have known it herself, or not so explicitly that she could have said this about her poem. We can say it, however, knowing that children do find ways in their poetry to begin to realize themselves and to work at shaping and recognizing newly emerging thoughts.

The river topic seemed to be a fruitful one for a number of the children in this class, as it has always been for poets. How did the teacher approach it? We should explain in the first place that the teacher was a special teacher, a young man who came in to the class solely to work on writing with the children. The class was divided so that only eight or nine children were together for the weekly period of 20–45 minutes. Though the teacher's intention in the beginning had been to focus only on poetry, and though he never read aloud anything but poetry, it is interesting to note that the children themselves did not restrict their writing to poetry. After a period of uncertain beginnings and of asking for suggestions if they were left without topics, these boys and girls became avid writers, grabbing up their pencils as soon as they saw the teacher approaching and launching into stories and prose sketches as well as poems.

The river became a topic for discussion in a natural way, because the Hudson, familiar to all these New York City children, was very much in the news due to recent findings on the extent of its pollution. A number of the children wrote their first river poems on just this theme:

A Beautiful Pond

Once I saw a pond,
It was beautiful indeed.
It was made of beautiful diamonds and emeralds,
And this beautiful pond
Turned into a polluted river,
And that is called the Hudson River.

Boy

The above is a good attempt to make a poem that expresses feeling through images, though the boy reveals very little to the reader about himself. In the following poem, however, the child who wrote it makes his feelings known. We cannot escape the thought that he may have projected himself into this picture and expressed a wish on a very deep level. This was a boy who was going through a period of anger and hostility, always managing to come through as a negative force in the classroom:

So Polluted It Wouldn't Hurt It

I saw a polluted river so grimy, topped with scum,
And it wouldn't hurt it to throw in chewed
      chewing gum.
I'd hate to be a polluted river with a hat made
      out of scum.
And I'd hate people to throw chewed
      chewing gum.

In the next poem, the boy writer takes the opportunity to say something about a river and about himself and what he wants:

I'd Like A River

I'd like a river flowing through a jungle,
With no fierce animals,
Blue, with toads and lily pads,
And dogs and cats, friendly,
And everybody good.

While some of the children are writing these personally oriented poems, we find others who may be mainly taking pleasure in expressive words and images, though it would be a mistake to assert that in such poems there is no underlying symbolization whatever. In the following, the child's poetic instinct has led her to the discovery of onomatopoetic river words like "streaming," "shivering," "splashing". Note how the last two lines flow. No hard consonants appear at the ends of words to block the onrushing movement. Instead, the sounds of "y" and "ing" smoothly link the words and permit the "rivering river" to stream along just as the girl envisioned it.

In the night the river is a dark and
    beautiful streaming river.
In the day the river shivering with the
    most beautiful scene in the world.
In the sunset the river is overflowing with
    a beautiful red liquid.
In the morning there's a yellowy streaming
    lovely splashing rivering river.

How were these children taught to express themselves with so much meaning, relevance, and beauty? The only teaching was the reading aloud by the teacher of poems he liked and felt the children would like. There was no defining of what a poem is and no discussion of techniques—which does not mean that such discussions would always have been inappropriate. There were no corrections or suggestions beyond suggestions of topic. The reading aloud, however, must have offered the children a very significant training, because the teacher did not confine himself to the familiar poems that are apt to appear over and over in collections for children. He did not hesitate to read excerpts from thoroughly adult poetry when he found poems that he felt were within at least some levels of the children's grasp and had the power to extend their perceptions. For instance, in the opening lines from the beginning of "The Dry Salvages," T. S. Eliot's third poem in *Four Quartets,* the image of the river as a "strong brown god" is certainly one that many nine-year-olds can appreciate.[3]

Archibald MacLeish's river poem, "What Any Lover Learns," can be interpreted on more than one level. On its descriptive, surface level, it can break upon children's comprehension with an exciting impact:

What Any Lover Learns

Water is heavy silver over stone.
Water is heavy silver over stone's
Refusal. It does not fall. It fills. It flows
Every crevice, every fault of the stone,

[3]See T. S. Eliot, "The Dry Salvages," in *Four Quartets* (Harcourt Brace Jovanovich, Inc. 1943).

Every hollow. River does not run.
River presses its heavy silver self
Down into stone and stone refuses.

                    What runs,
Swirling and leaping into sun, is stone's
Refusal of the river, not the river.[4]

It should not be supposed that every time these fourth-grade children picked up their pencils to write, they produced poems as significant as their river poems. Indeed, they often wrote in prose; and there were days when some of them only fooled around with attempts at cleverness. (This was why the teacher at one point introduced them to limericks.) Not all the topics were as successful as the river topic, though there were good results with wind, seasons, weather, imaginary lands, and pets such as cats, dogs, and turtles.

Two final examples, from the wind and seasons poems, may remind us of the variety to be expected even within one class of children and of the fact that poetry writing serves children in innumerable ways, not the least of which is the push toward fresh conceptualizing, playful experimenting, and discovery:

When Autumn Comes

When autumn comes it is a fright.
I do not want to go.
After the go comes the word to
And after that comes school.

Boy

The Wind's Secret

The wind is a secret that opens thing's secret.
It opens the leaf's secret,
The tree's secret,

[4]"What Any Lover Learns" from *New and Collected Poems 1917–1976* by Archibald MacLeish. Copyright © 1976 by Archibald MacLeish. Reprinted by permission of Houghton Mifflin Company.

And even the scarecrow's secret.
The wind changes a hot summer day
To an enchanted magnificent world
Of play and excitement.

Girl (Author of "In the night the river . . .")

Coming to grips with the world

In a variety of schools and locales, other nines and tens are writing a variety of poems—for fun, for the joy of experimentation, and for self-understanding. To close this section, here are a few poems that bring us around full circle and remind us of the inquiring gaze these children are turning upon themselves and all the rest of us, poems of search for self-definition and for a bold grasp of our world—soon to become their world.

Two boys living three thousand miles from each other have found a theme that seems very suitable for preadolescent boys who are growing into their strength. These are poems glorifying the sense of body power:

The Heart

The heart
It pumps
Three hundred
Thousand
Gallons
Of blood
In one
Short day—
Enough
To lift
Five men
Twenty-five
Stories
Or drive
A truck
Away.

I like the feel of a tool,
A strong, sturdy power tool
A drill, a table saw, jigsaw, buzzsaw.
The vibrations give me a good feeling.

Two girls also living far from each other approach the problem of accepting death. The first child may not have experienced it personally, but she is thinking about it. She is not the first poet to take the falling leaves as a point of departure—Gerard Manley Hopkins' "Margaret are you grieving/ Over Goldengrove unleaving?" comes to mind at once.[5] However, her similes are singularly fresh and individual:

The Leaves

The leaves fall from the trees
Like red and brown comets falling from the sky.
They remind me of a locket
With a stem instead of a chain
And they fall off with a little push from the wind,
Like a big sister pushing down her kid brother.

The leaves crackle and crunch like crackers.
I feel sorry for the leaves as they burn and disappear.
But the smoke carries them up to heaven.
Everyone helps rake them up.
When there is a big pile, we all jump on it.

The leaves sound like they are laughing with us
But all the leaves have to die
Just like all people
Up in a cloud of smoke—go the leaves.

The other little girl, aged ten-and-a-half, wrote her poem at home following the death of a beloved mother's helper who had been with

[5]Gerard Manley Hopkins, "Spring and Fall: To A Young Child." In *The Golden Journey: Poems for Young People*, compiled by Louise Bogan and William Jay Smith (Reilly & Lee Company, 1965), p. 249.

the family for years. The poem is tangled and unclear, but this may be what to expect when a child opens herself to such a large and painful theme, and gropes for the symbols and metaphors that heal:

On the Death of Emma Lee

When one,
Long loved,
Is gone

Will my heart
Plant a seed
   In my mind?

May my mind lose
A pearl
   Of love?

Before my eyes
Will clouds
   Alight

And speech
   Sour sweet.

May I know
In my heart

She still lives,
Through drifts of sorrow.

Finally, let us remind ourselves of the poem about war quoted at the very beginning of this book. Written at home by a nine-year-old girl who often wrote at home, it has nothing to do with a school-assigned topic. However, it has everything to do with the fact that even children this young assess the world they are about to enter and do not shrink from attempting to say something about it though the task can be almost too much for their skills. Like the death poem above, this one is tangled; but anyone who reads it can sense its meaning and its power:

War

But why to kill a human body.
   To exchange thoughts,
and help each other.
   But just because the thoughts don't
latch, combine or go together
   Destroyed was blood, bone
brain that so carefully
put together make a human being.
But not just that have you destroyed
for God and love still
stand in sorrow.

Self-declaration through stories

Decision stories

Poetry for the nines and tens—yes. But also stories, when they can be genuine statements, not smoke screens.

How does a teacher help children discover the importance of what they can say in a story? On page 50 we had a glimpse of a fourth-grade teacher discussing bravery with her children, challenging them to think of the differences between moral and physical bravery. At the end of this discussion she gave the children an assignment to write a story about someone who had to make an important decision about right or wrong. She did not use the word "brave" but was indeed implying that bravery might be involved. Though she had no way of guessing exactly what the children might do with this assignment, undoubtedly she hoped that they might put themselves into the someone who was facing the decision.

As might be expected, several children wrote stories that were almost clichés about lying and stealing. I am not suggesting that no personal feelings found their way into these stories, or that they were without any meaning and value. Yet they didn't seem to reflect true incidents in the immediate lives of the children. However, in a number of the other stories, both girls and boys dared to write about difficult decisions they had faced in their own lives. Some of them made it abundantly clear through the warnings they printed in the margins and at the top of their pages that it took courage to reveal themselves in this way:

(TRUE)

Do not read to class!

One time in the beginning of school everybody hated me. They always were tesing me and fighting with me. So one day on a Wednesday I wanted to make a date with some one, I didn't want a date with Debbie. I always have dates with her, and it gets borring. So I called up Jane and she always tesed me. When I had the date with her she was very nice and from now on she's my friend. Now Ruth and Suzanne and Lucy and Marian are my friends now too.

Girl

Do not read to class
This means you teachers!

Once there was a girl named Leila. One day it was on a friday a girl named Jennifer called up Leila. Jennifer asked Leila if she could go swiming with her on sunday. Leila said "yes" on Sunday her best friend called her up and asked her if she could go out to dinner with her and then go to a play. She did not no whether to say no to her best frend or to go with her other frend she did not like so much. At last she desided to call up Jennifer and tell her she could not make it but she could do it next sunday.

Girl

| TRUE | | TRUE | | TRUE |

Do not read to class!

Once I was at a friends house and her brother was my brothers friend too, so my brother was there too. Well, anyhow, my friend had some sparklers (It's a kind of firecracker, it doesn't hurt at all). So all four of us went into the kitchen and lit some sparklers. Me and Johnny held them. (I was a little scared but I did it and it was fun). But then that night when I was supposed to go to sleep I couldn't so I wanted to tell my mother and father but my brother had said not to, so after a while I said to myself "I'm

The nines and tens: self-discovery and self-understanding

going to tell them tough on Johnny!" I gathered up a lot of coreage and went in! Well, it wasn't so bad. Johnny came in and it was sort of like a family talk!

Girl

The class was going to have a vote. Of what they thought they shouldn't have for lunch. Every one thought they shouldn't have mushrooms. Except Bob and he was afraid that he would be laughed at. So finally he said "I think we should have mushrooms for lunch." and then everyone laughed.

Boy

Family stories

Another setting: a private home where seven nine- and ten-year-old girls came together on Tuesday afternoons after school for a writing club. The mother of one of the girls, especially interested in creative writing herself, was the hostess, not actually the teacher. In her own words, she was "simply there" during the five months the girls worked on their 90-page book of stories about the Scale Family, a collection "joyfully conceived, lightly written, laboriously edited, and lovingly illustrated. . . ."[6]

The "Scale Family"? Who can account for this imaginative conception? The family—Major the father, Minor the mother, and the eight children, Big Do, Re, Mi, Fa, Sol, La, Ti, and Little Do—were a monkey family living in a jungle gym out in the woods. That is, this is the framework the girls established, but it was not one that bound them. In fact, it freed them to leap right into their own family situations. Three-fourths of the time the jungle gym was forgotten and the monkeys were sleeping in bedrooms, eating in a dining room, cooking in a kitchen. Like real-life boys and girls, they went Christmas shopping, got into quarrels and fights, celebrated birthdays and Halloween, played in the snow, had fun at the Fair (where they teased for sweets), experienced a first day at school, and often did what they should not have done and were punished by their parents.

[6]Quoted from a personal communication from Sandra Stone Peters with her permission.

The seven authors, though playing with high fantasy part of the time, were essentially creating a real family with its family life episodes and feelings, problems, and joys. In the process, as they wrote and shared their stories, they were undoubtedly learning more about themselves and one another.

Here are some of the stories by one of the ten-year-olds who was particularly insightful in her perceptions of motives and personalities. This excerpt from her first story, "About the Scale Family," introduces us to the scene. There are only seven children here, because the baby of the family, Little Do, has not yet arrived.

Once upon a time, there lived a monkey named Major and his wife, Minor. They had seven children named Big Do, Re, Mi, Fa, Sol, La, and Ti. They lived in a jungle gym surrounded by trees. There was a place near the jungle gym that had a piano in it.

Big Do was the eldest of all the monkeys and hard to get along with. Re was a quiet girl monkey and always trying to learn all she could.

One late Saturday when Re was working on her homework, she came to some problems she didn't know. She asked Minor, "Would you help me?"

Minor replied, "I'm sorry, dear. I can't help you now."

She went to Major but he was asleep. She went to Big Do. "Big Do, could you help me?"

Big Do answered slyly, "Yes, of course I can—but I won't."

"Now, stop it!" Re demanded.

"Stop what?" asked Big Do.

"You know," Re said, and she went out of the jungle gym.

She went for a walk through the dark woods. Then she met Mi. Mi was a jumpy girl a year younger than Re. She wanted everything to happen all at once. She was a proud monkey, too. Right now she was saying to Re, "Look at my beautiful grass hat! Don't you like it?"

"Yes," said Re, not thinking at all what Mi was talking about. She was thinking what it would be like to live in a quiet world where everybody agreed with each other. It would be nice, she thought, to have somebody give her a little time, at least.

She walked back to the jungle gym and went to the quiet

204

girl, Fa. Fa was a lot like Re, but had some of the boy's ways, too. She asked her how she would like to live in a quiet world. She said that she would like to.

Re went to her room and found Sol looking at her homework. Sol was a sort of snoopy boy, but was nice, too. Re asked, "Can you help me?"

Sol answered, "Well, I guess I could try." He was a very intelligent boy. He even knew almost more than Re did. . . .

The child author, in even this short excerpt, has demonstrated a keen sense of people and their individuality. In the next excerpt, note especially the interchanges—verbal and nonverbal—involving Big Do and his parents. With what skill the nuances have been perceived! In this chapter the family assembles to decide on a name for the new baby sister.

"Now, children," said Major, when all the monkeys were in Minor's room. "I want you all to be quiet when somebody else is talking. I think, because Big Do is the oldest, he ought to be first to say what he wants our baby to be named. Re will be next, then Mi, than Fa, and so on."

Big Do took a look at all his brothers and sisters and said, "Ha, ha, ha! I get to be first."

"Big Do!" said Minor, looking at her son with a fierce face.

"I think our baby should be named Little Do," said Big Do, with a look at his father, to see if that would be a good name."

His father gave a nod at Re, not paying any attention to what Big Do was doing. Re said quietly, "That would be a good name."

Her father gave Mi a nod. Mi said right out, "I think our baby should be named Bathazar Bab Scale."

"No!" shouted Minor.

"Wa-a-a-a," cried the baby, as if she didn't want that name either.

"I don't think your mother (or your sister) would like that name, Mi," said Major. "All right, Fa."

Fa said that she liked what Big Do suggested. Sol said that he liked the name Betsy, but his mother didn't. So he took Big Do's name. La said that she wanted the little baby to be named

Sing because she said that in her dreams, the little baby was always singing. But Minor didn't like that name.

Next came Ti's turn. He said, with a long sigh, "I want what Re has."

So they had a vote. Minor, Major, Big Do, Re, Fa, Sol, and Ti were the ones that took the name Little Do. The others wanted different names. The name turned out to be Little Do.

In the next stretch, which I quote in its entirety, the child author is rehearsing a mother's role. Here the wise mother, knowing her child's trouble with jumpiness and wanting to help her, restrains her irritation over the spills in the kitchen.

Mi Learns to Cook

One day, Mi came home heart broken. "Mother!" she cried. "I have to learn how to cook! I heard Miss Woozy-Loozy school teacher say it — wa — wa — ha - wa -ha -wa-la—sniff!" she cried.

"Oh, Mi! Cooking is fun. It really is," Minor said. "Don't cry."

"Really, Mother?" Mi asked. "Is it really fun—cooking?"

"Yes, of course," said her Mother, comfortingly. "Now, let me see. I wonder if I have a beginning cooking book," and she went to see if she did. "Oh, yes I do!" she said. "Now, Mi, come here," and Mi started her first cooking lesson.

But at first she didn't like it very much because she kept spilling everything. But her Mother didn't get mad at her. She knew that Mi was jumpy, and wanted her to get over it. So, Mi learned to cook.

Finally, in our last excerpt here, the author reveals an astute sense of a mother's ability to see through her children's behavior. It is fortunate that in this story writing, the child finds opportunities to use, deepen, and develop such insights.

The story begins with an early morning snowfall. Some of the children have been out playing in the snow and are now coming in to breakfast. But there is something wrong with La, who feels she has been left out.

Snow Again!

. . . La came in pouting because she was all alone with no one to play with.

"What's the matter, my dear girl?" asked Major of his daughter, La.

"No one will play with me," she answered. "I hate everyone but Mi." And with that, she stomped up to her room because she felt as if everyone were looking at her.

"That's funny," said Major. "La is always so—well, singy, if that's what you want to call it."

Minor went to speak to La. She felt her head and—she had a very hot fever!

"Why, La!" exclaimed Minor. "You have a very high fever! I do believe that you are sick." She went downstairs to tell the others.

While she was down there, La smiled. She liked to be sick (not to mention spitting up and that sort of thing), and have everyone be nice to her. "Just think! Me, being sick! I do believe that this is the fourth time in my whole life!" La thought. "Me, oh my! I am tired," she yawned.

When she was just about to go to sleep, a funny, slimy feeling came to her stomach. She went downstairs to tell her mother. "I feel faint, awfully faint, Mama. I don't feel well," she said to her when she got downstairs.

"Get to the bathroom, La, hurry!" said Minor.

La ran to the bathroom. She felt as if she were going to spit up, but could not. It would not come out.

"Mama," she cried. "I can't!"

"Can't do what?" asked Minor.

"Oh," cried La. "I can't—spit up. I can't!"

"Come here," Minor said comfortingly. "Come here, La."

La came, but didn't want to. Minor took her in her lap and held her close. "Darling," she said, "think of how you have hurt your brothers' and sisters' feelings by saying you don't like them. Think."

La thought, and suddenly she felt a little better.

"Lullaby, and good-night, with sweet roses so plenty," Minor sang. La had fallen asleep with a lovely feeling.

She dreamed that she was taking a tour to heaven. She rode

207

on a cloud. It was soft and fluffy. She had her new doll with her. Instead of being made of plastic, it was made of china. It had black hair instead of blonde. La loved black hair a whole lot. Suddenly, (in her dream) she felt herself bouncing up and down. "Oh, my stomach!" she cried. She opened her eyes. There was Big Do, bouncing her bed. "Oh, you—you, oh, oh," she cried. "My throat hurts." Big Do was scared half to death that La was going to tell Minor on him. He was just going out of the door when he saw Minor coming up the stairs. "Oh, oh," he thought. Suddenly, "What were you doing in La's room? Big Do, you know you weren't supposed to be in there," came Minor's voice.

"Oh, I was just going to see if La was awake," replied Big Do.

"Why?" demanded Minor.

"Because," Big Do answered slyly.

"Big Do!" said Minor angrily. "Now tell me what you did in there."

"I—I bounced her bed to see if she'd wake up. It was only an experiment. "Really, Mother, that's all."

" 'Really, Mother, that's all,' he says," quoted Minor. "Now, get to your room!"

"O.K." said Big Do, with a sad-like tone in his voice to make Minor feel sorry for him.

"Oh, pooh," said Minor, and went into La's room.

So we come to the end of the Scale Family Stories—for the seven children the end of an opportunity to explore themselves indirectly while at the same time knowing the joy of creation as authors. That it was indeed a joy for them to live for five months with this imagined family—"the very best friends that we ever found"—is attested to by farewell poems that were included with some of the stories, such as:

The Scale family are over,
We're so sad to see them go.
For us they were the
Very best fun that we will ever know.

Maybe they'll come again,
Another time, another place.

Maybe they'll come again,
In another language, by another race.
But for now the Scales are over,
We're so sad to see them go.

Children rarely have the opportunity in school to work together over a long period of time on a series of sketches that can be called a book. Couldn't such opportunities be found more often? A student teacher, an aide, or an interested parent might meet regularly with a small group, as the mother did in the case of the Scale Family project, not to teach or direct, but to be there for such help and encouragement as might be needed. Of course, there is no guaranteeing that another Scale Family would result. However, in an atmosphere where sustained effort and a spirit of mutuality are generated, such creative work becomes possible.

Note that the Scale Family stories were written by a group of girls. No boys were in the club. If there had been any boys, would they have been interested in these family stories? Perhaps not. It may be that at age nine and ten in our present social scene it is the girls, not the boys, who are preoccupied with family roles and the interactions of personalities.

Experimenting with styles

In another setting, a fifth-grade classroom in an independent school, some very similar family stories were written only by girls in a situation that allowed the children complete freedom to develop a story opening provided by the teacher. These opening sentences were neutral enough to permit expansion in any direction:

Mrs. Jordan put down her magazine and looked at the clock on the wall of the airport waiting room.

A voice from a loudspeaker said: "TWA flight 324 from San Francisco, Chicago, and Detroit has landed. Arriving passengers may be met at Gate 4 in three minutes."

Several people started to move toward Gate 4 and Mrs. Jordan walked along with them.

The nines and tens: self-discovery and self-understanding

The instructions given to the children were simply to finish the story about Mrs. Jordan in at least 150 words and give it a title.

One of the family-oriented stories delves into the difficult feelings of a young girl when she comes home from boarding school and is met at the airport by her new "mom"—Mrs. Jordan—who has just married the girl's father.

Another story presents family scenes centering around the visiting aunt who arrived at the airport. But a different element is added here. News broadcasts come in about strange flying objects and then about the arrival of little one-eyed creatures from another planet. The members of the family concentrate on trying to keep their little boy indoors and hiding their fright from him. Then comes a surprise ending:

> That day they played games with Timmy and thought up excuses when he wanted to go out. Then came the evening report. "It's O.K. You can stop your panicking. The creatures are Martians and are very friendly. They have learned our language and all they came for was to see what earth was like and to take an elephant back to Mars which we let them do. They are gone but they will visit often."
> The whole room was filled with sighs of relief.

A number of the stories by both girls and boys contained surprise endings. The teacher had been reading O. Henry aloud to the children, as well as other stories chosen to meet the children's needs for excitement and surprise and to carry them several steps beyond the TV dramas—*Batman* and *The Man from U.N.C.L.E.*—to which they were all addicted. Her readings had included, in addition to O. Henry's "The Ransom of Red Chief," some of Conan Doyle's Sherlock Holmes stories, Frank Stockton's "The Lady or the Tiger," Robert Louis Stevenson's "Dr. Jekyll and Mr. Hyde" (which had gripped the children more than any of the others), and some of G. K. Chesterton's detective stories. The skill with which they took over elements of these stories indicates that children of this age and stage are ready for some literary experimentation, that the search for their identity is not the only search that can occupy them as they write, and that involvement as it relates to school activities can include involvement in the exploration of varieties of literature and literary styles.

Here is a story whose indeterminate ending may reflect the ending of "The Lady or the Tiger":

> She was going to meet her friend, Dolores Jackson.
> When she got to Gate 4, she saw a queer thing. It was a green man!
> Just about a week before she had seen a movie about a green man. So she was scared, and screamed.
> The next minute she found herself in a hospital. Her friend (Dolores Jackson) was over her. She was trying to calm her down.
> Mrs. Jordan told her about the green man. But all Miss Jackson said was, "yes I know."
> Then Miss Jackson took her home.
> When they got home, Mr. Jordan asked what was wrong, for Mrs. Jordan was very pale. Miss Jackson said that she had a bad time.
> That night Mrs. Jordan told her husband what happened. But all he said was, "yes I know."
> Whether this story is true or not, is up to you.

THE
  N
  D

Girl

One of the boys, who is characterized by the teacher as "a natural writer," produced a first-rate detective story using secret codes and messages and an abandoned subway station for the hiding place of a satchel of loot. His laconic, suggestive ending may reveal the influence of the teacher's reading: "She [Mrs. Jordan] then went to the J.F.K. airport and took the flight to Tokyo. She traveled light. No luggage but a small brown leather satchel."

There are other stories bordering on science fiction or involving disguises or surprising meetings that are "twists of fate." The children were delighted with all these stories and chose three of them to act out as skits for the enjoyment of their parents at the parents' supper. According to their teacher, the rehearsals had been most unpromising. During the actual performance, however, the laughter and appreciation of the parents spurred the children into the spontaneous improvisation that is natural to them as ten-year-olds, and a wonderful time was had by all.

New awareness, new maturity

These fifth-graders, writing and acting out these often playful stories, were the children who listened with deep attention to their teacher's reading that same spring of a piece of literature of an entirely different order—Thornton Wilder's play "Our Town." They not only listened; they also began to read it themselves and to learn it. Then came the urgent request to act it—one scene of it, the return of Emily to her childhood home to relive her twelfth birthday.

Why should this adult play have had such an appeal to these fifth-graders? And was it an appropriate activity for them to memorize these lines and present a scene from this play to parents and other classes in the school? It is felt generally that children of this age should be composing their own plays, as a way of integrating and developing what they are learning, as well as fully experiencing the powers and pleasures—and the demands—of dramatic expression. The teacher of these children, however, reported that they had been an immature group. Here was a play they could understand, and as they read and learned it, they were putting some of their immaturities behind them. We already know what a push there is among nines and tens to try to identify with the adult world and its important concerns. Apparently this play, especially the scene of the return for the twelfth birthday, touched strong emotions in the children related to their growing consciousness of themselves. For this reason, it was very easy for these boys and girls to appreciate Wilder's poignant call to perceive and feel and look about at life as it is lived. And the fact that it was the children themselves who asked to do the play and to learn the lines, not at all at the teacher's behest, should indicate that they were pursuing something meaningful to them, no matter how others might look at it.

Certainly the adults watching the play were very moved. The

children had learned their lines easily and spoke them with little difficulty. Their whole demeanor was serious and involved; there was no snickering or silliness. The play was put on in the children's own classroom and was extremely simply done; there were no costumes, no scenery. The children who represented the dead in the graveyard sat in a little row of chairs, four rows deep, off at one side of the room. At the funeral, those who came to it walked in with umbrellas up to indicate the rainy day. When Emily returned to the world for her birthday, this all took place on the other side of the room, again without props except for one little basket the mother held in her hand and kept wiping to indicate her work in the kitchen. The children in the graveyard sat absolutely silently and solemnly.

So, we have come around to the point we made at the beginning of this chapter. The nines and tens—whatever else they are reaching for—are very basically concerned with the search for more self-knowledge and awareness as they move toward adulthood.

Awareness of others: social studies writings

This is the time to help children expand their new awareness. They are ready to understand the universality of some of their emotions and thoughts. It is only a small leap for them from their own fears and outrages and disappointments to those of an Indian, an ancient Greek or Egyptian. It is for this reason, of course, that dramatizations and role playing in connection with their social studies have such value for them. By putting themselves into the lives of others, they are able to sense the reality of people who lived long ago. They can do this in story writing, too, particularly if they write in the first person, attempting to be the Indian or the Greek, speaking his words, feeling as he might have felt.

The following two stories, growing out of a fourth-grade study of Egypt, reflect two different situations related to slavery. Obviously the teacher was trying to help the children do more than just damn slavery outright—as they no doubt tended to do—without some understanding of the varying circumstances that might have entered into the complicated picture of its existence. Of course, the stories also reflect other aspects of the children's study of Egyptian life.

Sapphira was up before the sun. Her father would be going to the slave market right after breakfast, and she wanted to watch him go. Soon she heard her father and mother talking. Her mother said to her father: "I'll need a girl for the kitchen and we do need a little girl for Sapphira. I am going to shave her head this afternoon and I think she is old enough to have a slave girl of her own."

Sapphira rushed into their room. "Shave my head," she interrupted.

"Sapphira," her mother shouted. "Don't you burst in here like that again. Of course, you're going to have your head shaved."

"Why?" asked Sapphira. "I don't wanna have my head shaved."

"Well, young lady, you are going to have your head shaved and I'll get you a wig just like mine. Now march down into the kitchen and tell Sabdolla to make breakfast. Your father and I will be down soon. Get dressed and help Sabdolla make breakfast. Now run along, little one."

After breakfast her mother and father got on a litter and rode off to the slave market. Sapphira ran down to Sabdolla who was sitting on the straw mat. "Sabdolla," she said, "what is it like to be a slave?"

"Well," said Sabdolla, "it's not a pleasant life. You're pushed around a lot and it isn't at all pleasant to be sold and sometimes separated from your family. But if you have a nice master life isn't so bad. Now run along and play. Your mother will be home soon."

The little girl trotted off down the road. She came back in a few hours and found her mother sitting on the porch waiting for her. She said that lunch was on the table so they both went in and sat down. Soon her father came in. "Did you buy the slaves?" Sapphira asked her father in a low voice.

"Yes," said her father, "and we bought a slave girl for you."

"Goody, goody," Sapphira's face beamed at the thought of having her own slave girl.

After lunch her mother said she was going to take her to the head shaver. They got on the little litter and rode off down the street. The head shaver was nice. He let Sapphira sit in a big chair next to her mother. Then he took a razor and in a second he had done half of her head. The other half he did in another second and gave her a wig. Her mother paid him three copper rings and then took Sapphira by the hand and led her to the mirror and put on her wig. Then they went back to her father and showed him how nice she looked. Then they all sat down and had dinner.

After dinner Sapphira went trotting upstairs to bed. She was very happy that she had a little girl that would work and do all her chores for her, and she was very happy with her new head now, even though she wasn't happy with it before.

Girl

Vuckie

Hi my name is Vuckie. I am a slave and I hate my master's guts and kidneys because all he does is sit and walk and buy slaves and all that. I am always hungry. And one day I hit upon a plan. It was: when I was sent to get some seeds with a bag I would go through the bakery to the granary. Before I got to the granary Kakyay would call me and start talking to me. Then, while we were talking he would hand me a small loaf of bread. I would put it in the bag and put the seeds on top of it. . . .

About two weeks later Vuckie's overseer sent him to get some seeds, he gave him a bag. Now, thought Vuckie. Here was his chance. He took the bag and ran across the fields and darted into the bakery and the rest went according to the plans. BUT, , , when he got back to the overseer and poured the seeds into the bowl the overseer asked what is that lump in the bag. . . . Vuckie had to say Kakyay gave it to me he said, in a very small voice. The next day Vuckie heard that Kakyay had been whipped. Vuckie vowed that he would make his owner sorry. A month later he told every slave he could trust to tell every slave he could trust that on this coming Friday meet at the old abandoned Shaduf and he would tell them his plans of escape. (Friday was a feast). Friday came and all the slaves met and ran away. They were never heard of again in Egypt.

The End

Boy

Not all of the social studies writing in the first person will necessarily take the form of prose. Here two nine-year-old boys—one in a class studying Mexico, the other the Greeks—use poetry to express the ideas and feelings that have come to them in the course of their learning. This can happen when the children become really immersed in a study that is much more than a quick overview and when they read widely, discuss and dramatize their new learnings, and live with magnificent photographs or paintings covering the walls of their classrooms.

My Eldorado

One day I went traveling way far to the West.
And there were perils on the way.
Like weird men eating serpents, and lions and tigers.
But it was worth it.
There were rows and rows of golden brick pyramids,
Houses arrayed with flowers.
It was called Tenochtitlan.
It was a beautiful city.
Then my men got greedy
And there were fields after fields of blood
And dead bodies scattered all over.
And then, the city.
It was destroyed.
The most beautiful city into piles of smashed bricks
And broken idols.
My Eldorado, ruined.
And then, the revolution.
Not a trace of my Eldorado.
My Eldorado, ruined.
The city, gone.

The Black Terror

Oh, giant terror sweeping
Through the land.
Just a black cloud of death
Killing woman, beast, and man.
All through the land

You see dying men.
And men aren't
The only ones,
Every living thing.

Why do the gods hate us?
What deed have we done that
Brought us this fate?
And whoever did it
We shall always hate!

Oh, gods, who did it,
Is it Jason, Theseus?
IS IT I?
Who is it?
Oh, mighty gods
On Mount Olympus?

In another Greek study, this one in a fifth grade, the children were touching upon primitive rituals. The child who wrote about "the whipping day" in the following story vicariously experiences a terrible incident.

The Whipping Day

It was the day the older boys were to be whipped on the altar. One of the mothers whose son was to be in it for the first time was very worried. She wondered how he would take it. Well only one child had died from it. Her son had a good chance. Other mothers were telling her not to worry. Their sons had been in it before. Only the mother whose child had been killed was worrying with her. All the other mothers whose child was to be in it for the first time had another child who had been in it before. She had only one child, so did the woman whose child had been killed. Her other children had been left on the top of the mountain to perish.

It was time to start the whipping. There was her son, he was pale. It was starting. What a terrible sight. Hardly any of the mothers were enjoying it. Her son was up now. It started again, she could hardly bear it. It was the whipping period, yet how could her son bear it? It hurt her very much every time the whip touched her son. How she hated the man who was whipping her son. Ah, it was over now. She was very happy. Wait a minute! Her son was dead. That's why he could bear it so long. He was dead!

THE END

Girl

Finally, here is a fifth-grader writing a long story from the point of view of an Indian in the early days when the colonists were first landing in America. In his story, growing out of a study of the settling of Jamestown, the child has moved far beyond the perspective of the third-graders whose stories on this theme we have already seen (pp. 151 and 152). Particularly impressive are his opening paragraphs, in which he reveals his close identification with the Indians:

Story

Out in the distance we saw them, huge canoes with trees on them and huge white sheets on the trees. They were White Men on the boats. I saw them first. I told my father, for he was the Chief of the tribe. Some day I would be the Chief of the tribe. I was the oldest son, for I was 16 years old. My name is Big Wolf. But, in the meantime, the strange white people came on shore. How strangely they were dressed! Their pants were wide and fluffy and they had large shirts. They had as much hair on their bodies as a bear. Not one of us had ever seen people like them before. When they came ashore, they started to speak to each other in some foreign language that none of us could understand. Then it happened. A deer came out in the open. One of the White Men saw it. He lifted a big stick up to his shoulder and pulled something on the stick. All of a sudden a deafening sound rang out, and a puff of white smoke came from the gun. The deer fell dead. We were all shocked from what they had done, for they had violated the number one code of nature: not to kill for pleasure. For after killing it they just left it lying on the ground to rot and went back to their ship. My father was enraged at them.

No more White Men came on shore that day. But, on the

next day, more White Men came. They had more thunder sticks and long hatchets. We all were puzzled. What were they going to do now? Then one of the White Men took one of the hatchets and started to chop down one of the trees. Again they had committed a sin. Then they started to chop off the branches. Then they started to take off the bark. That was like taking skin off a person. More than ever, we all knew that only one of our races could survive. The White Man comes here for the first time and starts to kill our game, steals our land and violates Nature's Law. Yes, it means WAR.

Growth and discovery through drama

A sense of fairness and justice

We have said that in dramatizations and role playing in connection with their social studies children can sense the reality of people who lived long ago. This is only one aspect of the value of a class experience in putting a play together, living the parts, and giving a final performance. It says nothing about the opportunities for learning—intellectual, emotional, and social—and the really joyful opportunities for self-expression and discovery.

Recently a fourth grade put on a dramatization of scenes from the *Iliad* as their culminating piece of work at the end of the year. For them it was the high point of the whole year, a unique experience in their group life.

Why the *Iliad*? Is this a suitable choice for fourth-graders? And how was this ancient poetic tale turned into a play?

As often happens with successful projects, this one grew naturally. The class had been studying ancient Mexico and had been thrilled to learn about the discoveries of archaeologists there. In fact, the basic work of archaeology—the unearthing of buried secrets—generally is of enormous interest to nine- and ten-year-olds, since these children are in a stage when mysteries, codes, and sleuthing have high appeal.

As this study of Mexico was drawing to a close, one boy in the class—a very good reader—happened upon a book that greatly excited him: *The Walls of Windy Troy* by Marjorie Braymer, a biography for young people about Heinrich Schliemann, the discoverer of the site of Troy. In fact, the boy stirred up everyone's interest, including the teacher's, in learning more about ancient Troy. The next step on the teacher's part was to choose a book to read aloud for the pleasure of the class. She brought in Jane Werner Watson's *The Iliad and the Odyssey*, a children's version, magnificently illustrated and retaining some of the poetic beauty of Homer's language. There was no idea in her mind at this point of leading the children toward the creation of a play. But the children were enthralled by this story of great heroes and their passions and aggressive actions. They began to bring their own copies of the book from home and from libraries to read along with the teacher as she read aloud. Soon there was no question of leading the children toward a play. All of them wanted it; all began to talk about the scenes that would lend themselves to dramatization.[7]

Consider the natural appeal of much of this material for nine- and ten-year-olds: the Greeks meet with their king, Agamemnon, to consider whether or not they should go to war to bring back Helen. This involves the basic question of fairness and justice, always of prime concern to children of this age. Another question of fairness arises when the great warrior Achilles quarrels with Agamemnon, who has appropriated one of the girls from Achilles' camp. Is Achilles justified in claiming that the king has no right to do this? Is he justified in stubbornly withdrawing from the battle? And now Achilles' best friend, Patroclus, who has put on Achilles' armor and gone out to fight the Trojan warrior Hector, is slain. The grief of Achilles can be deeply felt by children who know very well what it is to care about a "best friend" of the same sex. And they can identify with the passions of both of the great warriors, Hector and Achilles, as they come out to battle with each other. Then, after Hector and Achilles are slain, the wooden horse scheme! The trickery of it, the cleverness, the secrecy—what could be more appealing to fourth-graders?

The children easily agreed that the play's opening and closing scenes should revolve around Schliemann, showing him at the beginning as a boy reading the *Iliad* and vowing that some day he would discover the site of Troy; at the end, Schliemann the grown man, realizing his dream.

[7]For a fuller discussion of the meaning of this play to the children, see the teacher's own account: *Creating A Play With Children: "The Iliad,"* by Deborah Salzer (unpublished Master's thesis, Bank Street College of Education, 1969). Reprinted here by permission of the author.

Agreed, this is an intriguing story for fourth-graders. But how is it made into a play? Here the teacher must be given a good deal of credit for her part in helping the children produce a script. The children were encouraged simply to improvise the scenes while a tape recorder recorded what they said. If the improvisation was one that seemed fairly satisfying to everyone, then the teacher listened to the tape at home in the evening and typed out the scene. The next day the children could see their lines in print and could make whatever small changes they felt would improve the text or make the lines more natural to speak. Memorization of the parts came very easily, since the lines were the children's in the first place. Only one child had difficulty with the memorization. Because of this, her lines were cut down until they were manageable.

Improvising in this way, the children were often able to make the play sound like the *Iliad*. Immersed as they were in the great story, they took over some of the majesty of the language they had heard, particularly in scenes that were charged with emotion. And when they were speaking merely in their own contemporary childlike style, they were nevertheless completely involved in their parts, and the strength of their feeling gave their lines compelling simplicity, very much in accord with the spirit of the play. Now and then a too-colloquial line was altered by teacher and children together discussing its suitability—as when Mentor said to Hector, who was departing for battle, "Give it to him, man!" In the final script this became "You get him, Hector!"

See the blend of noble language and natural childlike speech in this scene of the "Grief of Achilles":

Scene Five: Grief of Achilles

Narrator: Scene Five takes place in Achilles' hut.

Ach: (*Alone on stage.*) I hope my friend Patroclus will come back alive. I'll feel awful if he is killed, even if he is helping the Greeks. I know I shouldn't have given him my armor. . . . (*as Antilochus runs on, breathless.*) Antilochus, what news of the battle?

Ant: Oh, Achilles! Patroclus is dead! He was killed by Hector, the great Trojan warrior.

Ach: (*Sitting.*) Oh, I knew I shouldn't have sent him. I knew it. . . . How long did the fight last?

Ant:	Not long. Patroclus fought bravely, but Hector was the stronger man.
Ach:	Did they take his armor?
Ant:	Yes, they stripped him of his armor and left him for the dogs. We could do nothing.
Ach:	My best friend deserved a proper burial. . . . Well, if they left Patroclus for the dogs, Hector himself will be food for the dogs! I'll kill him! I'll slaughter him! I'll take his armor and feed <u>him</u> to the dogs. I don't care about Agamemnon anymore. I'll fight for Patroclus! Bring my armor! Call the men to battle!
Ant:	The Greeks will welcome you!

And here is part of another scene, illustrating how easily the children were often able to improvise. The only changes that were made after this first improvisation were the removal of the opening words to the end of the previous scene and the redistribution of some of the longer lines so that other children would have parts to speak.

Planning the Wooden Horse

(In the battlefield, just after Paris has killed Achilles)

Men:	Hold it, hold it. Trojans! Trojans, hear me! Your great Paris has killed our best warrior. You think that you can beat us that way. I swear to kill Paris! Before you know it, all you Trojans will be food for dogs and vultures!
Ag:	You pigs, we'll defeat you easily.

(Greeks return to their camp.)

Ajax:	What's the matter, Odysseus?
Ody:	We won't be able to win this battle unless we can find some way to get inside those Trojan walls.
Ag:	Do you have any idea how?
Ody:	Not yet. I'm thinking. . . . We have to trick them somehow, but how?
Men:	Yes, I wonder . . .

Ody:	(*To himself.*) No, that wouldn't work. . . . How about a statue of something?
Men:	Hey, yeah.
A Greek:	A statue?
Ody:	A horse . . . and we could get inside of it.
Ag:	That's a beautiful idea.
Ajax:	Yeah, but what good would that do? How will the horse get over the wall? Remember, it's still wooden. It can't jump over it.
Ody:	We could trick them into opening the gates and letting the Horse inside.
Ajax:	That's right! That's right! Horses are their idols!
A Greek:	That's right!
Men:	But we can't fit about five thousand men in a big wooden horse.
Ag:	We don't have to. All we really need is about five . . . to open the gates!
A Greek:	Yeah!
Ag:	And then the rest can come in!
A Greek:	Right!
Ajax:	And once we're inside the walls, we're invincible!
A Greek:	But they'll open the walls?
Ody:	They'll have to, if they think it's a god.
Ag:	But there's one problem.
Several at once:	What's that?
Ag:	This Horse will take a long time to make.
Ajax:	Well, we've fought for three years, uh, ten years, and we can fight for another three. . . .

How were the parts chosen? The assigning of parts, of course, can bring in its wake one difficulty after another. Who should play the most coveted roles, and who should decide? In this case, the teacher made the decision that parts wanted by more than one child would be chosen by lot; and this seemed fair to everyone. Of course, it was not easy for the boys when a small, quiet girl drew the part of Achilles. However, the teacher was able to help the children see that each one of them could build his role into something strong and important; indeed, this is what happened as the children worked together on this play that was so vital to them and that made them a better functioning, better cooperating group than they had been all year. The role playing helped some of the children move into new positions in relation to their peers; the old social patterns of the class were loosened; one of the fearful children learned, through the role of Agamemnon the King, to speak out and confront the child who had bullied him all year; one whose relations with his classmates had been very childish learned in his role as Odysseus how to communicate more constructively; a boy who had been unmotivated and interested mainly in sports pitched in with zest when he drew the role of the heroic Hector and found himself elevated to new status in the classroom; and those children who had been poor readers gained new acceptance in their own eyes and the eyes of others when they discovered that they could read their lines on the typed sheets brought in by the teacher.

The play was produced very simply in a large classroom. The children had painted mural backdrops to serve as scenery, and their "wooden horse" likewise was a painting, mounted on a large frame on wheels. The "Greeks" could not only hide behind it, but also move it slowly into place. Dressed in unbleached muslin tunics, wearing helmets of tin foil, and brandishing their wooden swords and shields (made in the shop), the children were convincing players and conveyed excitement and emotion to their audience of parents and a few teachers and children. In their own eyes, they had become both adults and heroes.

A sense of history

The study of ancient Greece can also lead nine- and ten-year-olds into dramatizations that link the past with the present and provide a ground for enactment of themes that are of universal concern to the children.

In "The End of the Gods' Reign" by a class of fourth-graders, one notes first of all the children's sense of history and their grasp of a time line. This is beautifully evident not only in this particular play but in a poem one of the girls in the class wrote during the period when the children were studying Greece and developing their play:

Times

I often stop and sit and think
    That centuries are like a chain
Going link by link, over and over again.

Starting with prehistoric man
    When men could not do what we can
And then going up to Egypt Land,
    Where fewer things were done by hand.

After that comes the wonderful land of Greece
    Where they made up the story of the Golden Fleece.

Next comes the time of Etruria and Rome
    When the main thing in architecture was the dome.

Then there was a dark time

    It was the Middle Ages
Bringing with it Kings and Sages.

Next came the Renaissance with lots of art
    When Columbus went to the west world
And came back with a new heart.

Finally came the Modern Time with its train and plane,
Abolishing the ancient tools
Never to be used again.

Now here we are with rockets going into space,
    Every time bringing back knowledge
From an unknown place.

As the children in this class read and discussed the Greek myths, the question arose of what happened to make times change and old Greek gods fade away. In their play they grappled with one of the answers, a very large idea indeed—that mortals who have knowledge and skill do not need the old dependence on the gods. One can see also, in the lines about the death of the gods at the close of the play, that the children may have been dealing symbolically with their own concern with death. (Remember the scene from the play "Our Town" chosen by a group of fifth-graders—a day of life retrieved and re-lived.)

The children themselves conceived the theme of their play, wrote the lines—working on them in small groups—memorized them, and spoke their play with great power and emotion. It was given in a large room without a stage, costumes were simple and made by the children and teachers, and the setting was suggested only by painted murals.

Scenes I and II and an excerpt from the closing scene are presented here to convey the essence of the play.[8]

Scenes I and II

PROMETHEUS: Oh listen mighty gods of Mt. Olympus, I, Prometheus, creator of man, firebringer to mortals, will prophesy the future. Within the next 800 years Hebe, server of the immortals' ambrosia and Gannymede, cupbearer to the mighty Zeus shall attempt to deprive the gods of their power and their ambrosia.

(Curtain is drawn and next scene is gods at feast. Hebe and Gannymede are talking in the corner.)

ZEUS: Well, I see Prometheus' prophecy did not come true for today is the last day. It will never happen if it does not happen today. Gannymede is right here serving the ambrosia. Hmmmmmmmmmm, this is not ambrosia.

ATHENA: Perhaps this is part of Prometheus' prophecy. Yes, I am quite sure it is. Tantalus, that wary wretch, once stole the ambrosia. Gannymede has probably done the same thing to take it to mortals.

APOLLO: It is true, this is not ambrosia. We must question Gannymede.

PROMETHEUS: I see the future. Gannymede with Hebe is giving the ambrosia to some mortals. The mortals are making him their head god. They are believing in him more than in us. They are

[8]Presented here with permission of David Wickens, teacher.

building temples to him and letting other temples fall into ruins. They are not giving sacrifices to the other gods. The sacred fire has gone out.

ARTEMIS: Look, all gods, what are we doing here, just sitting here and feasting when we are being overthrown.

APHRODITE: Let us banish them. They are doing us no good so why let them stay here on Mt. Olympus.

HERMES: Yes, that is a good idea. I, myself, will bring them down to earth to make sure they will not escape.

ALL THE GODS SHOUT "YES."

ATHENA: Well, if we let him stay up here on Mt. Olympus, he will create more trouble. Mt. Olympus is too rich for him. If he goes down to earth it will be an ordinary place.

ZEUS: All the gods agree that Gannymede should be banished to earth forever. Gannymede, you are banished to earth forever. By this lightning bolt the judgment is sealed.

GANNYMEDE: May I say goodbye to somebody?

ZEUS: Yes, you may, but you must come back shortly for my son Hermes shall take you to earth.

GANNYMEDE: I will be back shortly, oh mighty Zeus. You will regret my banishment.

(Gannymede walks to Hebe at other end of stage as gods leave stage).

Oh Hebe, the gods are banishing me to earth. I plan to be a more powerful god than mighty Zeus. I will perform heroic deeds and I will teach the men manly skills.

(He lists the skills he will teach men.)

Hebe, will you teach the women how to:
(He lists the skills).

HEBE: I shall come with you. That is a good idea.

GANNYMEDE: But the gods will not let you. I shall change you to a staff.

In Scene III Gannymede and Hebe (who has assumed her own form) demonstrate by pantomime and dance how they show the skills of the gods to the people on earth. This is discovered by the gods and in Scene IV, at a great meeting in Zeus' palace, the decision is made that though their fate has already been decided they must fight Gannymede and Hebe. As Zeus says, "The mortals still respect us, still fear us, and still love us. We'll keep on fighting until we die. If we die Gannymede and Hebe will die with us. Let us make them flee until they die. Now to throw the weapons."

In Scenes V and VI, Gannymede and Hebe are attacked by thunderbolts, tridents, and arrows. "Help, Apollo's arrows," calls out Hebe. They decide they must take back all of the gifts they have given the mortals so Zeus will forgive them.

In Scene VII Gannymede and Hebe return to Olympus, beg forgiveness, and give back the gifts and ambrosia they had stolen. Apollo, however, perceives that they forget one gift they could not take back:

APOLLO: I, Apollo, will prophesy the future. The mortals will become more powerful. When Gannymede and Hebe took back the gifts from the mortals, they forgot one gift which they could not take back. The gift was intelligence of skills and art.

PROMETHEUS: I see the end of the Olympians. They will be forgotten, only to be remembered in tale and legend.

ATHENA: They do not need to depend on us anymore because of their knowledge and skill, given by Gannymede and Hebe.

ARTEMIS: But the mortals cannot exist long without our help. Who will take our place?

APHRODITE: The end of the trail of the gods is coming.

HERMES: Atropos is beginning to cut our strings.

APOLLO: I, Apollo can read the future. I can see that Gannymede and Hebe will stay alive while the other gods will die out.

APHRODITE: Through the ages, Gannymede and Hebe will change and become gods of other religions.

ATHENA: All of the other gods here will be known by other names to another tribe called the Romans.

ZEUS: The judgment has been passed. Gannymede and Hebe will judge right and wrong for eternity.

HEBE: Let us die with you instead of ruling on forever. I don't like the mortals. It is too much responsibility for even two minor gods.

GANNYMEDE: We cannot fight the fate of the future. Prometheus is dying!!!!!

PROMETHEUS: I am dying, oh Gannymede. Take my power of prophecy and my control of the mortals' fire.

HERMES: Atropos has almost snapped my string of life. Take my magic sandals and helmet and my wand and my staff. Now it will be your responsibility to lead dead souls to Hades.

APHRODITE: Oh Hebe, Lachis has finished spinning my thread of life and has handed it to old Atropos to cut it. Since I cannot live long I give you the responsibility of love, beauty and spells. Some of the things are the fountain of bitter waters, and the fountain of sweet waters and my spells and last, my wonderful magic belt of love that has brought me so many of my loves.

ARTEMIS: I, Artemis, will give you my powers, Hebe, for my life's string is almost cut all the way through. I give you my love of the chase, my hounds, my golden hinds, the harness to my golden chariot and my love and power over young children. My silver bow and arrows of sickness and death I give to you.

APOLLO: I, Apollo, will too give Gannymede the power of prophecy. Gannymede, you must take charge of the oracle. I will give you my silver bow with arrows of sickness and death and my flute of magic and spells.

ATHENA: Hebe, I, Athena, will give you my spear, helmet, and shield and knowledge of wisdom. I will also give you both the power to judge right and wrong.

ZEUS: I will give you my great thunderbolts and wisdom and power to rule over the universe. You must rule over the mortals. Make it rain when you think it is time to rain. Now I will go down and meet the other immortals and lead them to the Elysian fields.

As in the case of the *Iliad*, this play reflects some of the noble language of the Greek myths. The children have learned from their reading of Edith Hamilton, Padraic Colum, Sally Benson, and others. When Artemis, for instance, bequeaths her powers to Hebe, she speaks with nobility and beauty:

I, Artemis, will give you my powers, Hebe, for my life's string is almost cut all the way through. I give you my love of the chase, my hounds, my golden hinds, the harness to my golden chariot and my love and power over young children. My silver bow and arrows of sickness and death I give to you.

The children's contemporary style of speech is evident, too, as it should be in a play that comes from their own pens. When Hebe calls out:

Help, Apollo's arrows.

or when Artemis says:

Look, all gods, what are we doing here, just sitting here and feasting when we are being overthrown.

these are the words of children, not of gods. But the children spoke them as gods when they gave their play, because they were caught up in this legend of theirs; it was their own creation, their own conception. Over a period of weeks they had lived with the Greek gods and grown into their roles.

Other plays, other purposes

Another fourth grade created an original fairy tale, as it might be called, its setting the present and its themes built on everyday home and school situations shared in common by the children—not too unlike some of the Scale Family situations. However, magic enters and a fantastic land of opposites is created where everything taken for granted in our world is overturned. Such a play offers the children who create it numerous challenges and satisfactions—in the first place, the challenge of pinpointing those upside-down situations that will be universally understood and appreciated by a child audience. And as they work out these ideas, they have a chance to air the feelings they have about report cards, relations with parents, issues over eating, watching TV, and begging for money. This is putting language to work in the service of meaningful communication among classmates. Also, of course, the children are constructing a play, which means they must arrive at interesting, suspenseful ideas that will lend themselves to action.

The children learned how to do this by working out the ideas through improvisations, not by sitting in a circle or at desks and writing a play. That is, as ideas were suggested, they were tried out in action. These improvisations in turn helped in the selection and clarification of the ideas.

The final performance was entirely a matter of improvisation. The children had become very clear about the plot line, the characters, and their interchanges, and spoke spontaneously with no memorization of the dialogue—a superb exercise in learning to find the right word at the right moment. After the performance, several children felt that the play ought to be put into a written form to preserve it, and they produced the script from which I am quoting excerpts here.[9] Bracketed sections summarize omitted portions.

[9]Excerpted here with permission of Ruth Kaufman, teacher.

The Wearing of the Wings

[In Act I we see children who live in "Plainville" rushing out of school, comparing report cards. A strange shovel is lying on the stage. As various children happen to touch it, they are obviously affected by it, many of them beginning to walk in slow motion. Toward the end of this short act, our attention focuses on a brother and sister named "Ismeal"—as the children usually spell it—and Pinella, the main characters in the play. They are speaking of the low marks Pinella got in Arithmetic because she said 2 and 2 are 5. Ismeal got low marks in spelling because he spelled cow with K.]

> Ismeal: I sounded it out phonetically. What more does she want? (He sees shovel and picks it up. They wish they didn't have to go home.)

(Pinella tells him to put it down, it's rusty and he's got enough junk in his room now. His mother is complaining all the time she can't keep it clean.)

> Ismeal: Look it's a good shovel. It works. (He examines it and discovers writing. They read the writing— brushing off dirt as they read. They read it a second time more smoothly.)

> SHOVEL SHOVEL IN MY HAND
> PLEASE TAKE US TO MAJIKLAND
> CHILDREN CHILDREN HOLD ON TIGHT
> I'LL QUICKLY TAKE YOU OUT OF SIGHT.

(White lights go out and colored lights go on and off. Crash sounds.)

> (Shovel pulls children off stage as curtain closes. They continue journey in front of curtain across stage.)

END OF ACT I

[In Act II, Scene I, Ismeal and Pinella find themselves in the town of Majikton, where everyone is wearing wings. The inhabitants flock around the children, question them, and explain their wearing of the wings: "Many many years ago when the first people came here they said, 'Let's be different from other

*people.' '' Wings are offered to Ismeal and Pinella, who gladly
accept them.*]

Ismeal: I feel like one of these people now.
Pinella: I don't feel like a stranger with these wings on.
  I'm thirsty.
Ismeal: I am too.
Pinella: There is a lady carrying water. Let's ask her for
  some.
Ismeal: We are thirsty. We've travelled a long distance.
  May we please have some water?
Pinella: I'd like some water, too. PLEASE.
Old Woman: PLEASE? Is that a way to speak? Be respectful
  young man! Where's your manners? Say GIMME
  when you ask for something.
Ismeal: O.K. Gimme some water, please.
Old Woman: Remember your manners. Say Gimme, don't say
  please.
Pinella: Gimme some water, too. We're thirsty.
Old Woman: Water you want? I just paid $2.00 a quart for this
  water. Drink milk if you are so thirsty. (Mut-
  tering—water indeed. . . .)

ACT II, Scene II

[*Scene: Pinella and Ismeal are wandering around town looking
at windows. Pinella looks through a window at people sitting in
dining room. She calls Ismeal to come see it too. Two prop men
hold up window for them to peer through. In front of window
family comes in, places tablecloth on stage ready for mealtime.*]

Mother: Come to the table children.
Carmine: I'll go wash my hands, mother.
Mother: Never mind dear, I love nice dirty hands at my
  table.
Carmine: May I have some spinach please?
Father: What did you say, Carmine?
Carmine: May I have some spinach?
Father: What is the correct way to say that?
Carmine: Gimme some spinach.
Mother: Did you finish your strawberry ice cream?

The nines and tens: self-discovery and self-understanding

Carmine: Do I have to?
Mother: Of course, now go on . . . eat . . .
Carmine: Aw, do I have to? I don't like it.
Mother: You have to eat it. It gives iron, and it is good for your teeth.

* * * *

Ismeal: (*at window*) Excuse me, can you help us. . . .
Mother: Certainly. (*Very warm, friendly person.*) Won't you stop by for a minute and have dessert with us?
P and I: All right. (*They walk around and sit down. Window disappears.*)
Mother: Carmine, pass the spinach to . . . What did you say your name was?
Ismeal: I'm Ismeal and this is my sister Pinella.
Father: Carmine pass the spinach to Ismeal and Pinella.
Pinella: I thought you said dessert.
Mother: I did, and spinach is dessert tonight. Aren't you lucky?
Ismeal: (*stage whisper*) This place sure is different from the U.S.A.

* * * *

Father: O.K. kids get ready for T.V.
Johnny: Aw gee. We wanna go to bed.
Father: No, now put on channel 7 for the Flintstones.
Johnny: Oh, no. If we watch anything we want to watch 3 star news.
Father: Your mother said to watch something else for a change.
Mother: I'm fed up with all those news programs and educational programs you insist on watching. They're simply horrible.
Johnny: But we enjoy watching them. They're fun.
Father: It is not fun for us. Change that channel now. Hurry up before I make you stay up another half an hour later to watch the Three Stooges Playhouse.
Cathy: Do we have to have our usual snack of potato chips?
Mother: Of course, what else?

The nines and tens: self-discovery and self-understanding

| Johnny: | Can we have liver tonight? |
| Mother: | O.K. But do not make a habit of it. |

* * * *

Pinella:	Do you go to school?
Cathy:	Yes, we do, why?
Carmine:	Would you like to see it?
Ismeal:	Yes, sure.
Mother:	(children rise and she puts arms around them) Tomorrow the children will take you to their school.

(Mother takes off apron and changes into teacher as she crosses stage)

Prop man walks across stage slowly with sign saying: NEXT DAY

Children take place for school room scene.

ACT II   Scene III

(Children are seated on floor in rows simulating classroom.)

Teacher:	Attention. Good morning, class. Now we will practice our arithmetic combinations. How much is 2 and 2?
Child:	2 and 2 are 5.
Teacher:	Correct. How much is 3 and 3?
Child:	3 and 3 are 7.
Teacher:	Good. How much is 4 and 4?
Child:	4 and 4 are 9.
Teacher:	Splendid, you have been studying. Now . . .
Ismeal:	But 2 and 2 are 4 and 3 and 3 are 6 and 4 and 4 are 8. . . .

(Boy rolls over on the floor in laughter. Class laughs.)

Teacher:	Enough children, nonsense. Whoever taught you arithmetic? Let's try to explore problems now. What's yours, Cathy?
Cathy:	I bought 2 pairs of blue wings and 3 pairs of red wings. How many pairs of wings do I have?
Child:	6.

Teacher: Good work.

Ismeal: We didn't learn arithmetic that way in Plainview.

Teacher: Next problem.

Child: One day the children made 4 hats for a party. The next day they made some more. Then John counted the hats and said we have made 9 hats. How many more did they make the second day?

Child: 4.

Teacher: Correct.

Ismeal: That's not the way we learned it in America. Imagine, Pinella. You wouldn't have failed on your report card if you learned here. Remember your mistakes in arithmetic?

Pinella: But these are silly mistakes.

Teacher: Stop that talking, next problem. Andy had 5 toys and Brian gave him 3 more. How many did he play with? Is that addition or subtraction?

Child: Subtraction.

Teacher: Right.

Ismeal: Wrong.

Teacher: It is correct. You try to give us a problem, since you seem to be so smart.

(Pinella and Ismeal discuss it and decide to do an easy one the class can readily see and understand.)

Pinella: I have 5 fingers on one hand. I have 5 more fingers on the other hand. How many fingers do I have? Add them.

Ismeal: You get an answer of 10 naturally.

Child: No, the correct answer is 11.

Ismeal: How do you ever figure that out? Count them.

Child: Sure, I'll count them. 10, 9, 8, 7, 6, on one hand, and I add the other hand of 5 fingers. So I have 11 fingers.

Child: We all know that easy one.

(Whole class agrees with child)

Ismeal: But you're wrong . . . *(protesting and mumbling . . .)*

Teacher: See, you're wrong. Enough of this arguing. We are wasting valuable time. Let's review our spelling now.

The nines and tens: self-discovery and self-understanding

[*Teacher asks for the spelling of "cake" and other words begin-*
ning with "c" such as "care," "cars," "cow," "cut." The chil-
dren all spell them with a "k."]

Pinella: But cake is spelled c-a-k-e and care is spelled c-a-r-e
            and cars is spelled c-a-r-s . . .

Teacher: What are you saying? Of course it is not. SOUND IT
            OUT PHONETICALLY. You can HEAR the K sound.
            Can't you?

Pinella: Yes, we can but . . . (*dejected*)

Ismeal: (*bends over and whispers to her*) Well, they won
            another argument. Wish I could persuade OUR
            teacher of that spelling. Then I wouldn't have failed
            on my report card.

Teacher: Quiet now. I bet you children haven't been taught to
            read either. Oh, it's later than I thought. Class dis-
            missed. (*Teacher walks out*)

                        *   *   *   *

[*A bell sounds in the distance. It is the Good Humor Man. One of*
the girls, Lynn, rushes to her mother who is approaching with
packages in her arms, and begs for money for a cone. The mother
corrects her when she fails to say "Gimme" instead of "Please,"
and refuses the money, because she wants the child to help her
carry the packages home. Tears follow, and when the child
complains "You don't love me any more," the mother gives in
and produces the money. The Good Humor Man, boisterous and
jolly, arrives on a highly decorated tricycle. Children step up to
him and ask for spinach pop, or a cone, or a spinach sickle.
Before he rides off he asks Ismeal and Pinella if they want a
chocolate covered spinach pop.]

I and P: (*politely, but strained*) No thank you. (He goes off on
            bike.)

Pinella: What a horrible thought.

Ismeal: These people wear wings, but it doesn't seem to
            make them angels.

Pinella: I'll be happy to get back home again.

Ismeal: I will be too.

Pinella: This certainly is a strange land.

Ismeal: I've had enough of it.

Pinella: I have too. Let's go home now.

Ismeal: If we can find the shovel.

(They hunt all over the stage, calling shovel, shovel . . . etc.)

Pinella: Do you think the magic shovel will get us back home
again? *(Build up some suspense in the audience.)*
Ismeal: Well, we can always try it:
Shovel, shovel in my hand
Please take us to Majikland
Children, children hold on tight
I'll quickly take you out of sight.
Ismeal: Nothing is happening. It isn't working.
Pinella: Perhaps the words are wrong. Let's try saying: Take
us OUT of Majikland.
Shovel, shovel in my hand
Please take us OUT of Majikland
Children children hold on tight
I'll quickly take you out of sight.

[*The front red lights and the rear amber lights flash on and off.
The cymbals clash and then quaver as the curtains close.*]

THE END

The children in this teacher's classes, though not specially selected
or gifted were good writers year after year. They not only improvised
and wrote plays successfully; their poems, stories, and essays were
impressive. It is almost always true that in a classroom where children
can dramatize, the writing skills improve markedly. For these children who wore the wings, writing came easily.

From Majikton to outer space:
half-magic worlds and science fiction

Children who are not too old for the make-believe of wings and magic
shovels enjoy other forms of imaginative writing about strange,
half-magic worlds and people. Some of these stories of the nines and
tens are striking in their inventiveness. It is hard to know, of course,
how much the children may be borrowing from television and the
comics or other reading. If they are borrowing, however, they have

The nines and tens: self-discovery and self-understanding

selected and absorbed some arresting ideas, and it is important for us to recognize the appeal to them of this mind-stretching fantasy.

The fifth-grade boy who wrote "The Little House" below invented something so imaginative that one is perfectly willing to overlook the collapse of the story at the end.

The Little House

One day when I was walking through the woods I saw a little house and I went in. In there I saw drapery that looked like silk. Then I saw an umbrella that looked like the sky at night with little specks of light in it. As I wandered through the halls I saw a broom that looked like a tree with branches growing from it. I also saw a pencil like a snake with a cup on its tail and a pointy nose.

Then I had my biggest surprise. I saw a man whose skin and bones were as soft as butter and his arms were as big as the Nile River.

The man said to me, "What are you doing here?" in a loud voice that sounded like a locomotive.

When I heard his loud voice I started to run. As soon as I got out of the house and the woods I called the police. The police took the man to jail and I lived happily ever after.

The nine-year-old boy who wrote the next story presents us with a transition from reality to fantasy almost worthy of C. S. Lewis. (See especially *The Lion, the Witch, and the Wardrobe.*) This piece of writing was stimulated by the teacher's suggestion that the children invent and write about imaginary lands. This is the teacher whose children produced the river poems we saw earlier.

Andy Island

One day I made a boat out of metal. Then one day I decided to take my boat out on the river. When I was in the middle of the river, I was in a whirlpool. I was going so fast that I ended under water. On an island! I got off of my boat, and I mapped the island.

After I made the map, I set up a hut. Three days later I went out fishing in my boat, and I ended up in the whirlpool! Ten seconds later I was in my house!

The next story—from a classmate of "Andy"—comes from our contemporary world of wonder-working pills and drugs:

Invisible

There was a man who invented a pill he thought would make him invisible. He took the pill and his skin turned clear. And from that year, month, week, day, hour, minute, second forth he walked around with all his insides showing.

Boy

Another boy in this class chooses the moon for his setting and encounters a monster there, but the point of his story takes us to a plane somewhat removed from that of the monster stories of our younger children. Something else is at work here: a sophisticated imagination enjoying its own cleverness in creating a new, slick version of man vs. monster.

To the Moon

I went to the moon and saw a monster. He looked at me and I looked at him; then he tried to soop me up. I jumped out of his way and ran to a shack and met a skeleton. He said "Boo" and scared me out of my wits. So I ran without any wits. Then I stopped and went back. I wasn't afraid because I didn't have any wits.

Moon men figure also in this story by a fifth-grade girl. But this child, like the boy above, is interested not so much in a horror story as in novel concepts. She is moving toward a more developed form of science fiction than we have seen in most of our children as she begins to think realistically about the possible characteristics of creatures from another planet. In this respect she is like the girl (p. 210) who conceived of Martians visiting the earth for the sole purpose of seeing what the earth was like and taking an elephant back with them:

One day when the moon men came down on the earth they were scaring everybody out of their wits. Their space craft was smaller than one window. It was so small the space men had to be smaller than their space ship. They were frightening because they were talking through their body instead of their mouths which they used only for eating. The moon men wanted to become earth men.

Of course, there are some ten-year-olds, and older children and adults, who read space fiction mainly because it provides fascinating glimpses into a half-possible future, where robots and computers take charge and spaceships travel to distant unknown planets where evil creatures may lurk—modern counterparts of the old fairytale giants and trolls and witches.

The following is such a story, written by a ten-year-old boy. He has obviously learned a lot from reading or TV and in this story is probably enjoying maneuvering his children and robot into a victory over invading monsters. (His teacher will have to discuss with him the mistake he has made in conceiving of a spaceship landing on a star rather than on a planet near the star.)

The Universal Two

Once there was a spaceship called the Universal 2. It was like a flying saucer. Its mission was to land on Alpha Centauri, our nearest star. It was launched from Cape Kennedy on the date of March 12, 1972. There were a family of 5 people, a navigator, and a robot, who was used as a computer, in the spaceship. The commander, Jon, was the husband. His wife's name was Merin, and the children were Milt and Bill, and Mr. West, as the navigator.

At the speed of 25,000, the spaceship took a week to pass the solar system. When they almost reached Alpha Centauri, they met a cosmic storm. It was filled with electrical charges but the ship went through the cosmic storm safely. There were four cells that were broken after the cosmic storm, and they had to use their emergency cells. They were lucky. They reached Alpha Centauri and at last, landed on it.

After their landing, they fixed the cells. It took them one month to fix it. At last the cells were fixed. "Tomorrow we will lift off," said Jon. "Allright," West answered. In the afternoon, the children were playing outside. When they came back, they saw their parents and their navigator had been put into the freezing unit in the spaceship. And the robot had been put into the lower deck. His batteries had been taken out. The monsters were invading the ship!

The children sneaked into the spaceship from the back door, and into the lower deck. They found the robot's batteries and put them into the robot. Then Bill told the robot to be quiet.

And soon, they lift off Alpha Centauri. But the monsters turned the ship in the opposite way. So the children and the robot made plans to turn back the ship. And the robot gave each person a shock, and the children tried hard to throw the monsters overboard, or tie them up in order to get their parents and the navigator out of the freezing unit. After a hard time, they got rid of them all.

And at last they were on their way back to earth. And at last they landed on earth from a year of being lost in outer space.

Finally, here are stories by several children who are beginning to make small statements about society and thus are on their way to becoming writers who can make the most of science fiction. As Sheila Egoff has said, writing of the characteristics of science fiction today, although it can be the literature of pure escapism, "it may also be the vehicle for biting criticism of contemporary society," a literature that makes "large statements about our transitional society."[10]

There are no large statements in these children's stories, but there are small statements revealing children who are mature enough to begin thinking critically about their society and contrasting it with others that might exist on other planetary worlds or on their own planet in a far future.

The first story was written at home—it was not a school assignment—by a ten-year-old boy who was probably thoroughly enjoying the adventure and the chance to vicariously feel such super body strength. He may also have been enjoying his intellectual grasp of the mechanisms that could lie behind the production of "weak man" as well as "superman."

[10]Sheila Egoff, "Science Fiction," in *Only Connect*, ed. by Sheila Egoff, G. T. Stubbs, and L. F. Ashley (Oxford University Press, 1969), pp. 384 and 391.

The boy's mother found this story lying on the dining room table one morning and explained that the dining room in relation to birthdays was important in their home. Birthday presents were always placed in the dining room, so the birthday child could see them first thing upon coming downstairs in the morning.

It was Nov. 10, 1968, my 11th Birthday. I went donestairs and found a time machine in the dining room. I tried it out and went to the year 2000, but the controls broke. I remembered it was my Birthday and that I had 10 dollars with me. So I went to the newstand to buy a comic. And unlike the presents comics these were all about topics like weak man. I then understood why. We have comics about superman because we don't have one. They had comics about weak man because they were superstrong from a special pill.

I took a pill and found that I could fly. So I flew right through the time Barrier and crashed into the garage because I hadn't perfected my flight manuevers. I flew to my school every day and the first day, I opened a book and tore it apart because I didn't know my own strength.

In the next two stories there are prophetic references to populations of skeletons and to a "big Empty filled with ruins" discovered in the far future. It is hard to believe that the two boys who wrote these stories were not intending some commentary on our society, though possibly the adult reads in more than the boys meant to put there. The first child is a ten-year-old, the second one aged nine.

It all started on December 11, 1964 when the teacher asked each child what he'd like to be when he grows up.

There were twenty-seven children in my class. First came Tom, he said he'd like to be a fireman because they help people.

After a while my turn came. I said I would like to be an Astronaut to explore the outskirts of the universe and to know all the space equipment.

Soon school was let out. After watching some science fiction shows I went to bed and had a dream. I was to be the Astronaut to land on Venus. After the take-off I got very sleepy so

I went into the freezer room and slept forty days. When I came out of the freezer room I found I was off course. I saw a planet in the distance. It looked similar to earth. I called it Paradise II. When I landed I found there was only skeletons. Immediately I took off. For forty years I searched for earth. Finally I found it. I landed only to find earth had a population of skeletons also, only they were alive.

Then I woke up out of my dream and went to school.

The Time Machine

Chapter I "The Time Machine"

In the year 1951, in a little farm in Connecticut, there was a little family. There were two boys. Their names were Bill and Ed. Ed was walking, and he saw a sphere. He got in it.

Chapter II "In the Sphere"

He was sitting in the seat. He pressed a button on his shirt and away he went. On a little panel it said: 1962-1963-1970-1991-2090-10,000.

He stopped and got out and looked and saw a robot with abcdefghijklmnopqrstuvwxyz on it, and he saw galpuveas and such and such.

Chapter III "The Machine"

He was astonished. He saw a machine, and it had a light and conveyor belt. There were little balls on it. He got in his time machine to the five trillionth century and stopped and got out and looked around. He saw a big Empty filled with ruins. So he got in and went back home and lived happily ever after.

Finally, from a fifth-grade girl we have an uncomplimentary picture of the behavior of Earth people toward a Martian. It is hard to know if the child herself saw all the implications of the episode involving Mr. Horner and the Martian. She is more concerned with the need to create a happy life for her character who is "different" and ill-treated. Yet the groundwork seems laid here for the kind of space fiction story that can take a good cold look at our planet Earth.

The Cross-Eyed Martian

There was once a cross-eyed Martian who lived on Mars. He was a nice Martian, but the other people were not kind. He would help other people. One day the cross-eyed Martian took a trip. He got in his space-ship and started from Mars. He did not like Mars, so he kept going and going, until he saw a planet where he could stop at. Suddenly he saw a planet: it was the Earth. He stopped on that planet. He landed in the weeds where nobody lived. So he got out of his space-ship and started looking around. And soon he got to a little town called Jamestown, a man named James Horner owned that town. There were a few people living there, but the cross-eyed Martian looked so unusual that people started coming down from their houses and they looked surprised too. Mr. Horner was walking toward the Martian, as soon as he got there, they both stared at each other and soon Mr. Horner asked him a question, "Who are you?" The cross-eyed Martian said, "I am a Martian from Mars, I am cross-eyed." And Mr. Horner said again, "What are you doing on Earth?" He said, "Up on Mars the people treat me very mean, so I came down on Earth." "But you cannot stay here," said Mr. Horner. "Why?" said the Martian. "Because you are not like us." So the cross-eyed Martian turned sadly away and started back to the space-ship.

Meanwhile back up on Mars a woman broke her leg and they were looking all over for the cross-eyed Martian, because he was a doctor. Soon the cross-eyed Martian started to his space-ship and he started it up. He went back up to his planet, and as soon as he got there he went up to his house and closed the door. A man was crying. He said to the Martian, "My mother broke her leg. Can you help her? She is dying," he said. "I will help your mother if you ask everybody to be kind to me." So the man said, "The whole planet will be kind to you, but just help my mother before she dies." So he got the medicine kit and he went up to the lady and helped her. She was saved, so all on planet Mars were happy, and they had a party for the cross-eyed Martian. They loved him. He never left the planet again. He lived happily ever after.

Moving beyond the horror story

Even ten-year-olds, I have said, can begin to grasp the more serious implications of science fiction. However, the time may come when a teacher sees the science fiction interest so dominant in her class that nothing else seems to get through.

One teacher of a fifth-grade class of capable boys and girls in Spanish Harlem—children who were turning eleven—worked at just this problem. She had been encouraging and providing time for the children to write stories of their own choosing. The children wrote in little 6″ × 6″ booklets constructed of drawing paper and helped each other illustrate the booklets. They wrote whatever they wanted to write, and the stories were enjoyed by all, including the teacher. No corrections were made.

What this meant to one boy in the class is expressed in a little note he added at the end of one of his booklets:

About the Author

To tell the truth, I really do like school work and things that have to do with hard working.

When I came here to New York and went to P.S. 108 for the first time, I was put in a class I loved very much. It was Miss Levitt's class.

I was the smartest one in that class and soon had to be changed to Miss Dermer's class. There I learned more and more and was better in all different kinds of sports. My favorite sport is basket-ball.

Here in Miss Dermer's class I had more time to write stories and books like this one. Never in my life did I ever want to write so much until I got in this class of more work and more activities.

Many of the stories were full of imagination, and even some of those that may have been TV-inspired were well conceived and offered more than TV horror. But Miss Dermer began to feel that too many of the stories stemmed directly from TV science fiction and carried no challenge to the children to use their own ideas or go beyond horror and destruction. So she began to help the children find real-life subjects for their stories and other writings. She was asking not for blandness, but for reality. She got it in some moving stories, true pictures from the New York City scene. For example:

The Day Jim Got Shot

Once there was a boy named Jimmy. He was 21 years old and he wanted a job. He asked his parents if he could work in a liquor store. His parents said "Yes, you may." The next day he started working. He worked from 8:00 A.M. to 11:00 P.M. Day after day he worked carrying boxes of V.O. and 7 Crowns and stuff like that to the basement.

One day he was in the liquor store with his friend. They were working. All of a sudden two men came with guns. One man asked for a bottle of V.O. When Jimmy turned to get the bottle, "Bang." They shot him. They had the other man with a knife on his throat.

They took the money out of the cash register. Then they ran.

A man came in and saw Jimmy on the floor. He quickly called the police. The police got an ambulance. They took Jimmy to the hospital. When his mother heard what happened, she cried, and cried.

She went to the hospital every day to see him.

Then the next day he died.

Boy

There were other stories more reality-based than the outer-space thrillers, yet touched with the play of imagination, such as a story of the dilemma of a very tall boy who took reducing pills only to find himself growing too short.

Real-life stories also resulted from a class discussion on old people, stimulated by an article all of the children had read in the weekly newspaper distributed in their class. It is hard to say to what extent the children were able to concern themselves with the plight of the elderly. But it must be remembered that in Spanish Harlem the presence of grandparents in the homes is not unusual.

Thoughts on Growing Old

Growing old is a difficult situation. Growing old is like losing your life. If I were old, I would feel lonely because there is nothing to do or see but sit and rock in my rocking chair.

Old people get sick not just because they get a disease but because they are missing their young life. At night and during the day, they can only see darkness. Things that are getting them sick is watching the young people doing things that they can't do anymore. Being in a nursing home makes old people seem sicker than they are, too.

Old people are usually poor because they can't work anymore. People are rude to them and throw them out of their homes because they don't have enough money to pay for the rent. People should try to treat old folks better because soon they'll be old folks, too.

Girl

If I were eighty-five, I wouldn't have any strength and I might not be able to walk anymore. I would be nervous and sometimes I would feel awful. I wouldn't be able to play with my grandson. I wouldn't be able to run because I probably would need a cane. I would feel lonesome especially when I would have to live by myself because no one wants me around anymore. I wouldn't have the power to work hard or to lift up heavy things.

Worst of all, I wouldn't be able to play like when I was a little boy.

Boy

Miss Dermer also introduced the children to haiku poetry, often very appealing to fifth- and sixth-graders. The formal structure—five syllables in the first line, seven in the second, and five in the third—presents a challenge. Furthermore, the children are not too young to grasp that the essence of the poems must be created through skillful handling of implication, suggestion, and mood, rather than through forthright, explicit statement.

Among the many that were written, these three stand out as particularly arresting. (The first two are by the same girl.)

Beautiful flowers
Gathering in the warm sun
In nice wild colors.

Air you can not see
Wrapped up around the world
Breathing life to us.

Life for a flower
Is living in great beauty
And dying young.

Boy

Finally came the "Who Am I?" experiment, one that carried with it a great deal of excitement for most of the children. Miss Dermer, inspired by a TV program, began by asking the children one by one to say who they were. This was a little difficult in the beginning, so a switch was made to each child writing in private about himself. The reader will see that the children have picked up some threads from each other, but there is still much here that is individual. It is no wonder that eventually a place was made on the "Who Am I?" TV program for the children of this class.

These "Who Am I?" statements were not written as poetry and were not called poetry by the teacher or children. However, they have much in common with the fifth- and fourth-grade poems presented at the opening of this chapter. All of these children—some of them already feeling surprisingly adult—want to look inward and discover the emerging new person. There are many ways to help the process along.

I'm a boy of my own feelings and my own looks,
I'm a human being just like everyone else.
I get mad very easy.
I can't say that I'm smart but I'm smart enough.

I like to do things other people might do.
Sometimes I feel a little lazy but why?
That's what I keep asking myself.
I do the type of things that's fit for me to do.
I'm a big brother to my little sister.
I'm a student of class 5-317 and a member of P.S. 108.
I probably can do things that I think I can't do.

Boy

I'm a boy who has no friends except two boys and a girl who I like
   very much.
I'm a boy who everyone thinks can't draw.
I'm a boy with a bad temper. But I can hold it.
I'm a strong boy but people think I'm weak.
I'm a boy who tries to make friends with boys and girls but often
   they turn me down.
I'm a boy who is very intelligent.
I'm a boy who is in love.
I'm a talented boy.
I'm a boy who can sing like Johnny Mathis, Elvis Presley, and the
   Temptations.
I am a genius.
I'm a boy who can't be stopped when I get really mad about
   somebody.
I am short. I am an American.
I am like a comedian.
I am a boy who gets easily turned off by his work when at home.
I am a boy who wants to be skipped to the sixth grade.
I am a boy who can't wait to be a man.
I am a boy who likes kid stuff.
I am a boy who is full of tricks to get things.
I am a boy who has a room of junk.
I am a nuisance to the teacher.
Do I like myself?
Sometimes I don't like myself but I really like myself.

Where am I going?
Who knows?
   Not even me.

Boy

The nines and tens: self-discovery and self-understanding

Who am I?
A girl
L _ _ _ _
A human being
Person
A very big girl
A person who is growing up.
A human being that is going to be somebody.

Do I like myself?
Yes.
I think inside I am a good person.
People like me so I like myself.
I am the youngest one in the family.
But everyone still likes me.
I like myself because I do lots of things.
I try very hard.

Girl

Who I Am

A boy
F _ _ _ _
Human being
Person
I'm smart.
A body of cells
I feel good.
I like sports.
I want to be an F.B.I. man.
I'm strong
I'm healthy.
My skin is tan.
People like me.
I love science.
I'm in the fifth grade.
I like people.
I like my friends.
I love my mother.
I love my family.

I have a best friend.
I like books.
I like my teacher.
I want to go to college.
I like school.
I love peace.
I love this!!
I'm lazy.
I'm a clown.
I'm a brother.
I get in trouble. I pray.
I want this school to be good.
I care.
Sometimes I don't.
I'm sometimes happy.
I love happiness.
I can't stop!!
I like myself.
I love films.
I love everyone.
I love playing.
I love this.

Boy

Exploring characters,
situations, experiences

Another way to deal with the science-fiction interest is to try to help
the children broaden their understanding of what science fiction can
be at its best. Let them read—or let the teacher read to them—some of
the good writers whose stories are centered in earthbound dilemmas
and belong to the literature of commentary and character. True, there
are not many really outstanding science or space fiction stories for
children as young as nine or ten. The majority of space writers who
are addressing themselves to children are aiming at young teenagers.
But no ten-year-old should miss Jean E. Karl's *Beloved Benjamin is*

Waiting, in which communication from outer space reaches an unsuspecting child; or *The Forgotten Door* by Alexander Key, a story that has much to say about some of our values and ways as seen through the eyes of a small boy visiting this planet. Somewhat similar, though more difficult, is Patricia Wrightson's *Down to Earth*, in which earth inhabitants have a hard time believing that a visiting space boy really is a space boy. Interesting differences are brought out between the perceptions of earthmen and spacemen. Even more exciting is *The White Mountains* by John Christopher, the first of a trilogy about "Tripods" from outer space attempting to conquer the earth. The struggle of a group of earth inhabitants against these terrible Tripods, who destroy in their captives all will to dare and be free, makes a thrilling story. Good readers of ten and eleven should be able to handle this book and would probably stick with it because of its excitement even though parts of it might not be clearly grasped. Likewise, good readers no older than ten are known to tackle with enthusiasm Madeleine L'Engle's *A Wrinkle in Time*, winner of the 1962 Newbery Award for the year's most outstanding piece of American fiction for young people. This is a story not only about a journey to a sinister planet to effect a rescue, but about the relationships of the young people who undertake this perilous mission, and the powers that enable them to overcome evil.

Well within the reading abilities of many nines and tens are the less demanding Mushroom Planet stories by Eleanor Cameron. They are not commentaries on our society, but they offer believable children and the excitement of secret space trips undertaken for constructive purposes. Also constructive, and in a class by themselves, are the Danny Dunn science fiction books by Jay Williams and Raymond Abrashkin. In *Danny Dunn and the Voice from Outer Space*, events lead up to a breathtaking climax in which a communication from outer space is received and decoded. Definitely a book for children with background and keen interest in science, it is not easy reading, but could be handled—if not devoured—by just the right ten- and eleven-year-olds.

The fare is richer for children of twelve, thirteen, and fourteen. They can go on to other more difficult books by Alexander Key, John Christopher, Robert Silverberg, Donald Suddaby, and William Pène du Bois, as well as H.G. Wells and Jules Verne. And why not also Swift? *Gulliver's Travels* is a book for children young and old, as well as for adults. Even nine- and ten-year-olds can follow the beautiful exactness of Swift's prose; and the adventures of Gulliver among the Lilliputians—especially as illustrated in the Duell, Sloan, and Pearce volume—offer them food for thought and the enlarging experience of exploration in a miniature world.

Reviewing books

Many teachers prefer not to require book reviews, arranging instead for discussions in which children can share their enthusiasms and discoveries. Is there really any other purpose, they ask, in requiring a child to review a book he has read? Some teachers ask children only to describe one moment they think others would like to hear about. Some suggest that the children write a few sentences about the way a book has made them feel or about a situation or dilemma in a story that was similar to one they have experienced. The hope here is to help children know themselves better, to make deeper connections with themselves through their reading. Still other teachers give children opportunities to dramatize portions of books or to draw and paint whatever they may want to after their reading. Older children, sixth-graders, can profit from and enjoy studying one of the characters in a book they've liked, learning how to tell others what sort of person he is by documenting what they say, using appropriate quotations to back up their statements.

Another form of book review, often chosen by children who are good readers and writers, is simply the retelling of the story. This, of course, is what Tolstoy found true of his children in the Yasnaya Polyana School: ". . . the same pupil who weeps over the composition on a bench will excitedly describe the feeling of love or anger, the meeting of Joseph with his brothers, or a fight with his companion. The subjects of the compositions were naturally chosen from among descriptions of incidents, relations to persons, and the repetitions of stories told."[11] Repeating a story they have loved may give children a chance to live with it longer, integrate it, make it their own. And the act of writing itself may become more pleasurable when the content

[11]Lev Nikolaevich Tolstoy, "The School at Yásnaya Polyána," in *Tolstoy on Education*, translated from the Russian by Leo Wiener and with an Introduction by Reginald D. Archambault (The University of Chicago Press, 1967), p. 289. Reprinted courtesy of The University of Chicago Press.

can be so easily summoned up. Furthermore, children who rewrite stories are sometimes attempting to reproduce the author's style. This in itself may present an attractive challenge. And certainly it is an exercise that can help them strengthen their own skills, as well as develop appreciation for the power of language to shape itself, take on color, and speak in a variety of voices.

The boy who below retells *The War of the Worlds* has managed—for a ten-year-old—an amazing replica of the dry, clipped, controlled style H. G. Wells has adopted for telling this chilling story. The boy is telescoping in what he writes and even distorts some of the details. Nevertheless, what he has remembered is astonishing, particularly since he is remembering so accurately the manner of Wells. Here is the beginning of his review:

The War of the Worlds
by H. G. Wells

It all started out when me and Professor Ogilvie were walking along one night in England, and saw something fall out of the sky. People thought it was a meteor, but we thought it wasn't. We were going to investigate.

When we got there, we saw a pit with a huge cylinder sticking out of it. People started to gather around, and Professor Ogilvie went down to inspect it. We knew it wasn't a meteor after we had taken one look at it. We wondered what was in it. It took quite a while until people would believe that this strange object had come from Mars.

You must understand that this was the year 1890. People did not know much about space then. Even the scientists like Professor Ogilvie did not have much information. He was the first to go down into the pit, and he was the first to die. Strange-looking creatures came up from the pit and, as the people started to run, the creatures would aim one of their tentacles, and a heat ray would fire. This is what killed Professor Ogilvie.

The following is an excerpt from a nine-year-old girl's long review of *Huckleberry Finn*. The child was a great reader and loved to write, and her command of English, both written and spoken, was excellent.

In this retelling she was probably making her first attempt to use a grammar unlike her own:

This story takes place a little before the Civil War.

THE ADVENTURES of
HUCKLEBERRY FINN

You don't know about me if you haven't read a book by the name of THE ADVENTURES OF TOM SAWYER. But that ain't no matter. The Widow Douglas took me in to try to civilize me. But that wasn't half the worst of it. Old Miss Watson, her sister, was my main teacher. One day the judge, (judge thatcher) called me in and gave me six thousand dollars, which was my share of the money that me and Tom had found. I didn't know what to do with it so I asked the judge to keep it for me.

Since the widow Douglas took me for her son, pa disappeared but I don't mind that at all. One day, after supper, I walked up to my room, and open'd the door, and there, sitting on a chair, was pap. For a long time we just stared at each other. Finally pap said, they told me in town you was agoin' to school, said you was better than your pa!!

He picked up a pikture, what's this, he asked. It's something you get when you do your lesson well, I said. He threw it across the room and warned me not to let him catch me around that school. But I kept goin any way. One night, pa came in the window, drunk. C'mon, he said, we're agoin'. Goin' where? I asked. You'll see. Pa took me about three miles up the river and then we went across to the Illinois shore.

No less impressive is the ease with which boys who are sports lovers are able to adopt the vocabulary and style of the sports reporting they expose themselves to during their out-of-school hours. The excerpt below comes from a child who, according to the teacher, often had difficulty writing. It would be an excellent story for the teacher to use in discussing with the class the concept of writing with a particular audience in mind. The children will easily recognize that the vocabulary and style that reach one audience will not reach another, and they may like to try to identify various styles of writing, including not only the styles but the audiences and purposes behind the writing. As a matter of fact, the teacher of this boy's class did lead the children into some study and writing of newspaper headlines, an exercise they greatly enjoyed.

Zoom-Ooops-Splutter

It was a football game—the Dallas Cowboys vs. the Baltimore Colts. The first big play was in the first quarter, first and 10 to go. It was a pass, a 90 yarder. Did you read it right? A 90 yard pass from Baltimore's Johnny Unitas to Baltimore's Tom Matte, and he ran for a touchdown.

The Colts were in the lead all through the first and second quarter. Second big play—first and 10 to go. The Cowboys quarterback yelled. It was a triple reverse and then a pitch out from the quarterback, Craig Morton, to the running back, Dwain Thomas. He ran for a touchdown and the score was tied 7–7.

Half time went on. And then the game started again. It was the 3rd quarter and the Coyboys' kick off. It was a beauty by Clark. It was a 40 yarder. WOW! . . .

Studying the good writers

Fifth-graders are not always too young for a broader and more direct attack on style than we have indicated so far. Often it is best to let them write entirely in their own ways, either experimenting or learning simply from exposure, as the fifth-graders we've already seen (on p. 210) learned about surprise endings from exposure to O. Henry. A teacher can easily find out if her children respond well to discussions about an author's style and to suggestions about using some of his techniques in writing assignments.

One fifth-grade teacher interested some of her class in thinking about Kenneth Grahame's writing. Just how did he create such a vivid and warm effect in his description of Badger's room in The Wind in the Willows? What is the importance of mentioning light and color, odors, textures? The class discussed other rooms they had read about and remembered. And the teacher introduced them to a description none of them were acquainted with. It appears in an adult book, yet it held great appeal for them—the description of the kitchen in Alfred

Kazin's *A Walker In the City*. How did they feel about this room? How did Kazin manage to stir this emotion?

After these exposures to Grahame, Kazin, and others, the children were asked to write about a room of their own choice. In the three examples that follow, the influence of the discussions pinpointing the importance of attention to sensory details is quite evident. (Where the idea of "Dr. Dog" came from, however, one cannot guess.)

The big red brick fireplace sent out a growing glow of warmth and light, the black pot hanging on its nail. The old mahogany huch, with the best blue dishes and boles on it. In the center a dark mahogany table that seems a mile long, with the white embroidered tablecloth. The two big light brown woven chairs on either side, with a red home spun pillow on each catching the fire light. The two long benches by the table. The walls glisting from the strength of the glow. And the brown earth floor well packed down.

Girl

It was a cold summer night the wind was blowing the rock chair.

The fire was burning the sparks hitting the screen.

The door opening and closing.

The sofas were covered with sand.

At the beach with the waves crashing against the shore.

The other chair was sandy too   the table with a fruit bowl on it was gleaming in the fire.

Boy

As the sun rises in the morning, Dr. Dog rises. He looks around his room. His chair was sagging as if a whale had been in it. The door, a bright red, creaked as Dr. Dog opened it to see if his new furniture had arrived. No, it hadn't. The curtains were drawn. His bed was unmade. The sun rays lighted up his room as he opened the curtains. For a dog he had a tremendous amount rooms. (one) As he cooked his breakfast he could smell the bacon cooking. He ate it with a content feeling.

Boy

A fourth-grade teacher shared with her class at Christmas time her enthusiasm for Dylan Thomas' *A Child's Christmas in Wales.* She first talked with the children a little about Thomas' imagery and use of words, and when she read parts of the poem aloud, the children listened with enjoyment. Here was a writer, it seemed, who had something fresh to offer to both children and adults.

The following day, after more discussion of the especially interesting words in the poem, the teacher asked the children to try their own piece of writing about Christmas: "A Child's Christmas in New York." Here most of the children went their own ways, unable to become young Dylans. Though they could feel the appeal of Thomas' style, the nostalgic appeal of his content was not really for them. Perhaps they were still too close to the joys of Christmas, too much within the living experience, to be able to write with anything resembling the free flow of Thomas' emotion. For many of the children the writing assignment became a matter of literal recall and listing of the events of Christmas—though not without sparks of childlike joy, excitement, and poetry. A few of the children—those who seemed especially appreciative of Thomas' imagery—did try to play with words and discover new combinations and metaphors:

> On Christmas eve it was very nice. not a sound nor a mouse
> in the house. but there was something worng with this house
> there wasn't and didn't feel like anything would come
> down from the sky like maybe little white faces or something
> like that. It was cold out like one little drop of a cold tear or
> maybe a very, very freezing little finger   a baby's finger. . . .

> . . . They sat at the window sill and watched each icicle
> fall down. It was like seeing santas come down the chimney, like
> gingerbread in the mist of snow.

Strained? Unchildlike? Too much effort showing through? Possibly. But strain is unavoidable when a child—or anyone else, for that matter—is reaching out to experiment. Better to reach and try, and grasp for a new way, than to settle for what is safely and narrowly known.

The most important part of this exposure to Dylan Thomas may have been the exposure itself, rather than the writing attempts that followed—exposure to a new voice, to the knowledge that an artist can make language spring up into new sounds and forms; exposure also to a teacher's enthusiasms, bringing the children in contact with the teacher's personal life, her reading, and her feelings about it. When a teacher can invite children in to share with her the ground she is clearing for herself as she reads and learns, it is likely that all of them will learn in new ways.

Reading aloud from autobiographies

Teachers can also share their own reading with children when they discover—often in autobiographical writing—passages that might remind the children of what they know or have experienced, but have let slide into unawareness; or passages that may introduce children to what they have not known, yet might be able to discover if they sharpened their powers of observing and knowing.

It was the reading aloud of Wilder's *Our Town* that may have aroused in the children who heard it a more alert consciousness or comprehension of feelings already there. (See p. 212.)

Of course, not all fifth-graders are ready for *Our Town*. Nor would all of them be ready for—or interested in—the suggestions I am about to make. These represent my enthusiasms. Let them stand as possibilities, not only for ten-year-olds, but for older children as well. Teachers, knowing their own children, will make their own search and bring to their children the choices that are appropriate.

Colette, writing of her childhood in *Earthly Paradise,* describes with a wholly enveloping sensory vividness the gardens, the sky, and the land she knew in rural France. In the following passage, the reader becomes this child, out walking in the almost dark morning before dawn. Children who have never had this experience can have it here, or they may recall that they have indeed had such moments, not under Colette's skies, but even in the city, up on the fire escapes and down in the streets on clear, early mornings—moments of glorious being, worth searching for, worth knowing again and again:

> Those were summers when the heat quivered up from the hot yellow gravel and pierced the plaited rushes of my wide-brimmed hats, summers almost without nights. For even then I

The nines and tens: self-discovery and self-understanding

so loved the dawn that my mother granted it to me as a reward. She used to agree to wake me at half past three and off I would go, an empty basket on each arm, toward the kitchen gardens that sheltered in the narrow bend of the river, in search of strawberries, black currants, and hairy gooseberries.

At half past three, everything slumbered still in a primal blue, blurred and dewy, and as I went down the sandy road the mist, grounded by its own weight, bathed first my legs, then my well-built little body, reaching at last to my mouth and ears, and finally to that most sensitive part of all, my nostrils. I went alone, for there were no dangers in that freethinking countryside. It was on that road and at that hour that I first became aware of my own self, experienced an inexpressible state of grace, and felt one with the first breath of air that stirred, the first bird, and the sun so newly born that it still looked not quite round.[12]

Or try passages from Laurie Lee's autobiography, *The Edge of Day*, so full of vivid sensory recollections. Or introduce Gavin Maxwell's story of early years, *The House of Elrig*, detailing a boyhood spent with great happiness exploring the Scottish moor. This is a book that might particularly interest (in parts) those children who have read the author's *The Otter's Tale*, a children's edition of his well known *Ring of Bright Water*.

Even if a teacher should find that the natural world of the moor and the boy's love of it, as recalled in *The House of Elrig*, is too remote for her children, she could share with her class the prank of Gavin, Robina (daughter of the headmistress), and a boy named Vivian, the three of them clambering over the high roof of their boarding school late at night. Let the children ponder—not necessarily discuss— whether they themselves ever dared, as Vivian did, to open themselves up in some way to the lure of the sky and the night.

Robina's favourite playmate was a boy named Vivian, a vivacious and beautiful ash-blond with such a fine soprano voice that he sang in distant cathedral choirs. With him, and

[12]Colette, *Earthly Paradise* (New York: Farrar, Straus & Giroux, Inc. and London: Martin Secker & Warburg Limited, 1966), p. 7. Copyright © 1966 by Farrar, Straus, & Giroux, Inc. Reprinted by permission of the publishers.

sometimes with me, by invitation, she broke such school rules as she dared, exploring the vast rubbish dump behind the chapel (a tangled mass of rusty iron in which treasure was constantly and confidently expected), raiding the larder, smoking her mother's cigarettes, or climbing about the roofs and the fire-escapes at night. It was on one of these last escapades, with moon and stars bright beyond the darkness of the tall chimneys, that Robina dared Vivian to sing. He sang, first "Heilige Nacht," quite softly but with intense emotion, then "Adeste Fideles," beginning almost muted, but slowly allowing the full volume of his voice to take over the first refrain so that it soared wild and high and infinitely pure into the brilliant sky, and my throat contracted as if I wanted to cry.[13]

Children can become better observers of what lies around them through exposure to the perceptive eye of the artist-writer. Joyce Cary, for instance, in his autobiographical novel, *A House of Children*, writes of reflections in a way that might stimulate children to become more aware of moving reflections—on ceilings and windows, on parked cars, and on wet streets—a part of the visible world yet often simply not noticed because they are superimposed on the known concrete reality. Children who are beginning to study some of the techniques of the good writer need to know that they must learn to see if they are to make the most of their abilities. Let them see the wonder of Joyce Cary's house by the shore, Dunamara, filled with reflected ocean waves:

. . . When the tide was up and the sun or moon shining, especially at a spring tide, the long white front of the house was in movement with reflected waves. The walls rippled with hollow curves of pigeon grey and palest yellow, a ghostly sea, which, on the tall twelve-pane windows, became so solid in colour and form, gold and blue, that one seemed to be looking through the glass at actual water. The house seemed to be full of sea; until, of course, one turned round and saw the real sea so

[13]Gavin Maxwell, *The House of Elrig* (London: Penguin Books Ltd, 1965), p. 103. Reprinted courtesy of the publishers.

miraculously real in its metal weight and powerful motion, its burning brightness, that it startled. One gazed at it with astonishment as if one had never before seen such an extraordinary and glorious object.

I must have turned myself hundreds of times to catch the sea in its realness. . . .[14]

Finally, let children rediscover what many of them already know but may have overlooked, thinking it of no importance. Read to them in Vladimir Nabokov's *Speak, Memory* his recall of the colors he associated with the sounds of letters when he was a young boy. This will lead the children not only into recall of their own color and letter associations, but possibly also into awareness of other sensory associations well-known to them but unpredicted, unguessed by any of us.

On top of all this I present a fine case of colored hearing. Perhaps "hearing" is not quite accurate, since the color sensation seems to be produced by the very act of my orally forming a given letter while I imagine its outline. The long *a* of the English alphabet (and it is this alphabet I have in mind farther on unless otherwise stated) has for me the tint of weathered wood, but a French *a* evokes polished ebony. This black group also includes hard *g* (vulcanized rubber) and *r* (a sooty rag being ripped). Oatmeal *n*, noodle-limp *l*, and the ivory-backed hand mirror of *o* take care of the whites. I am puzzled by my French *on* which I see as the brimming tension-surface of alcohol in a small glass. Passing on to the blue group, there is steely *x*, thundercloud *z*, and huckleberry *k*. Since a subtle interaction exists between sound and shape, I see *q* as browner than *k*, while *s* is not the light blue of *c*, but a curious mixture of azure and mother-of-pearl. . . .[15]

[14]Joyce Cary, *A House of Children* (New York: Harper & Row, Publishers, Inc. and London: Curtis Brown Ltd., 1956), p. 53. Reprinted by permission of Harper & Row and Curtis Brown Ltd., London acting on behalf of the Estate of Joyce Cary.

[15]Vladimir Nabokov, *Speak, Memory* (New York: G. P. Putnam's Sons, 1966), pp. 34–35. Copyright, 1947, 1948, 1949, 1950, 1951, by Vladimir Nabokov © 1960, 1966 by Vladimir Nabokov. All rights reserved. Published by permission of the author.

Drawing on their own observations, one group of children explored some of their sensory associations in the following ways:

Poems We Made Together

Rain drops are like
   glass falling down
   little people falling from the sky
   a song
   snow
   a lot of tears without salt
   a hose
   a shower
   drips in a sink when you forget to turn it off

Grapes are like
   purple and green diamonds
   cherries
   big green marbles
   a little nut
   little purple rocks, a piece of clay
   a king
   gush
   little birds eggs
   soft acorns

A sponge is like
   seaweed
   a marsh
   a thick sweater
   something soft
   a foam bed
   a grassy thing
   a cloud
   wet sand when the tide has gone out
   a sponge fish
   the moon's surface

The nines and tens: self-discovery and self-understanding

A shooting star is like
   when Apollo 13 went up
   a flash light on a ceiling
   an egg dropping
   a bullet
   a falling rock which has been thrown up
   a home run hit
   a rocket
   a piece of tin foil falling in the night.

A Class of Tens and Elevens

References

BENSON, SALLY. *Stories of the Gods and Heroes.* Illustrated by Steele Savage. New York: Dial Press, 1940.

BRAYMER, MARJORIE. *The Walls of Windy Troy: A Biography of Heinrich Schliemann.* New York: Harcourt Brace Jovanovich, 1960.

CAMERON, ELEANOR. *The Wonderful Flight to the Mushroom Planet.* Illustrated by Robert Henneberger. Boston: Little, Brown and Co., 1954.

———. *Stowaway to the Mushroom Planet.* Illustrated by Robert Henneberger. Boston: Little, Brown and Co., 1956.

———. *Mr. Bass's Planetoid.* Illustrated by Louis Darling. Boston: Little, Brown and Co., 1958.

———. *A Mystery for Mr. Bass.* Illustrated by Leonard Shortall. Boston: Little, Brown and Co., 1960.

———. *Time and Mr. Bass.* Illustrated by Fred Meise. Boston: Little, Brown and Co., 1967.

CARY, JOYCE. *A House of Children.* New York: Harper & Row, 1956.

CHESTERTON, G. K. *Father Brown Mystery Stories,* edited by Raymond T. Bond. New York: Dodd, Mead & Co., 1962.

CHRISTOPHER, JOHN. *The White Mountains.* New York: Macmillan, 1967.

COLETTE. *Earthly Paradise.* New York: Farrar, Straus, & Giroux, Inc. and London: Martin Secker & Warburg Limited, 1966.

COLUM, PADRAIC. *The Golden Fleece and the Heroes Who Lived Before Achilles.* Illustrated by Willy Pogány. New York: Macmillan, 1962.

COOLIDGE, OLIVIA. *Greek Myths.* Illustrated by Edouard Sandoz. Boston: Houghton Mifflin, 1949.

DOYLE, ARTHUR CONAN. *The Boys' Sherlock Holmes.* Revised edition. Howard Haycraft, editor. New York: Harper & Row, 1961.

EGOFF, SHEILA, G. T. STUBBS, and L. F. ASHLEY, editors. *Only Connect.* Toronto: Oxford University Press, 1969.

ELIOT, T. S. "The Dry Salvages," in *Four Quartets.* New York: Harcourt Brace Jovanovich, 1943.

GRAHAME, KENNETH. *The Wind in the Willows.* Illustrated by Ernest H. Shepard. New York: Charles Scribner's Sons, 1908, 1933.

HAMILTON, EDITH. *Mythology.* Illustrated by Steele Savage. Boston: Little, Brown & Co., 1942.

HOPKINS, GERARD MANLEY. "Spring and Fall: To A Young Child." In *The Golden Journey: Poems for Young People,* compiled by Louise Bogan and William Jay Smith. Chicago: Reilly & Lee Co., 1965.

KARL, JEAN E. *Beloved Benjamin is Waiting.* New York: E. P. Dutton & Co., 1978.

KAZIN, ALFRED. *A Walker in the City.* New York: Harcourt Brace Jovanovich, 1968.

KEY, ALEXANDER. *The Forgotten Door.* New York: Westminster, 1965.

LARRICK, NANCY, editor. *On City Streets: An Anthology of Poetry.* Illustrated with photographs by David Sagarin. New York: M. Evans and Co., Inc., 1968.

LEE, LAURIE. *The Edge of Day: Boyhood in the West of England.* New York: Morrow, 1960.

L'ENGLE, MADELEINE. *A Wrinkle in Time.* New York: Farrar, Straus, & Giroux, 1962.

LEWIS, C. S. *The Lion, the Witch, and the Wardrobe.* Illustrated by Pauline Baynes. New York: Macmillan, 1950.

LEWIS, RICHARD, collector. *Miracles: Poems by Children of the English-speaking World.* New York: Simon & Schuster, 1966.

MACLEISH, ARCHIBALD. *The Collected Poems of Archibald MacLeish.* Boston: Houghton Mifflin, 1962.

MAXWELL, GAVIN. *The House of Elrig.* London: Penguin Books Ltd., 1965.

———. *The Otter's Tale.* New York: E. P. Dutton & Co., 1962.

———. *Ring of Bright Water.* New York: E. P. Dutton & Co., 1961.

NABOKOV, VLADIMIR. *Speak, Memory.* New York: G. P. Putnam's Sons, 1966.

O.HENRY. *The Ransom of Red Chief.* New York: Hawthorn Books, 1970.

SALZER, DEBORAH. *Creating A Play With Children: "The Iliad."* Unpublished Master's thesis. New York: Bank Street College of Education, 1969.

STEVENSON, ROBERT LOUIS. *Doctor Jekyll and Mr. Hyde.* Revised edition. New York: Washington Square Press, 1972.

STOCKTON, FRANK. *The Lady or the Tiger and Other Stories.* New York: Airmont Books, 1968.

SWIFT, JONATHAN. *Gulliver's Travels.* Edited by Elaine Moss. Illustrated by Hans Baltzer. New York: Duell, Sloan & Pearce, 1964.

THOMAS, DYLAN. *A Child's Christmas in Wales.* New York: New Directions, 1959.

TOLSTOI, LEV NIKOLAOVICH. "The School at Yásnaya Polyána." *Tolstoy On Education.* Translated from the Russian by Leo Wiener. With an Introduction by Reginald D. Archambault. Chicago: University of Chicago Press, 1967.

TWAIN, MARK (SAMUEL CLEMENS). *The Adventures of Huckleberry Finn.* New York: Crowell, Collier & Macmillan, 1962.

WATSON, JANE WERNER. *The Iliad and the Odyssey.* Pictures by Alice and Martin Provensen. New York: Golden Press, 1964.

WELLS, H. G. *The War of the Worlds and The Time Machine.* New York: Doubleday, 1970.

WILDER, THORNTON. *Our Town: A Play in Three Acts.* New York: Harper & Row, 1938.

WILLIAMS, JAY and RAYMOND ABRASHKIN. *Danny Dunn and the Voice from Outer Space.* New York: McGraw Hill, 1967.

WRIGHTSON, PATRICIA. *Down to Earth.* New York: Harcourt Brace Jovanovich, 1965.

Eleven, going on twelve: new awareness and abilities

Chapter six

Our children have become sixth-graders—the elevens, as they are called in some schools. In other schools, where there are open class-rooms, they may be grouped with children a little older and a little younger. What interests us here is not so much the exact age or grade as the fact that now we are dealing with children who show new abilities and self-insights, as well as new awareness of what is going on in the outer world of political and social reality—awareness that can bring questioning and discomfort with it. These are children who also know the discomforts of young adolescents whose daily social interactions can be of all-consuming concern.

When they sit down to write, it is important for these children to know that the purpose of writing is to try to say something that is meaningful to them, no matter what the degree of their writing skill. And we do not imply that any one genre or cluster of topics is more meaningful than another. Playful, imaginative, and even satirical experiments with language; more serious stories, essays, editorials, myths, plays, and poems; personal writings in prose about thoughts and feelings related to the self and the events of daily life—all of these are meaningful.

Here are examples of the writings of our contemporary children of eleven or a little older. They are of course no more than suggestive of efforts others might want to make.

Reality

We know that a great many children today have been strongly affected by the anxieties of the adults around them over the recent war in Vietnam and the ever-present threat of the atomic bomb. The following pieces are not at all atypical of the concepts and feelings that many of these children have tried to handle. The first piece is by a low-achieving boy. Obviously he has violent and revengeful feelings he must express before he can move on to constructive thoughts and wishes. But he does move, and it is fortunate that he and his teacher have not let the poverty of his skills prevent him from attempting to say what he has to.

IF I was the richest Boy in the world I would buy my own house Buy my own property Buy some Body guards to protect me. I get some Judo experts to teach me judo   I would give money to the poor people pay my tax pay rent. send 1 million dollars to the poor people. make Busness buy my own stores to make more money. send money to the children that have no mother or Father hire 25 Butlers and 25 mades get all children who have no mother or Father   Let the mades and Butler take good care of them   get there own privet doctors get them all kinds of toys. And then get my revenge on those people that live down town who are almost rich   Those mean people who are greety and don't give money to the poor people.   and try to make peace with white people and the negroes. and make peace with the cuba and china Vietnam aso. And let us discuss why we are fight for nothing killing each other for nothing I'll tell them Lets Be Like Brothers Lets all be together Find the things in life dicover the universe see IF theres Life in other planets and what we learn We'll teach them what they Learn Let them us and other Let us all Be united together. Lets be Like Brothers and sisters Stop Fighting Like dogs and cats Live it up. Like humans should.   the end

Boy

272
Eleven, going on twelve: new awareness and abilities

Hurrah for the A-Bomb

The beat grows quicker
Lights begin to flicker
BOOM
And all is still.
The ravage-wrecked houses
In a storm of death
With half-dead things
Struggling weakly
Spasmodically
Through the radioactive rubble.
Here and there
A house is standing
With thirst racked throat
Demanding, demanding.
This is the A-Bomb
Oval of destruction
Helping the population

Reduction.

Girl

Thoughts of death and age and time passing

Some fifth-graders have written about elderly people with feelings of identification and sympathy. We also saw fifth-graders using *Our Town* to express their own awareness of the passing of time and the need to love and hold the present moment. (See p. 212.)

The first poem below, "By the Lake," is a sixth-grader's version of this call to keep hold of the vividness of the present, "to remember it, and live with it" so that it will not be lost. The poem speaks in an easy, childlike voice, sometimes in rhyme, sometimes not, in compelling simplicity.

The other four poems say a good deal about the maturity of the children who wrote them—or if not maturity, then a reaching toward it, a wish to know, to comprehend what lies beyond their own eleven-year-old reality.

By the Lake

By the lake it's cozy indeed
The wind seems to whisper
All through the trees.
How cool and pleasant it is here
not too close and not too near.
But free, with nothing to fear.
The moss has conquered all
the earth that is surrounding
the lake, making a bed for animals
around. But forget that now, and
think of the past, remember the
evening, remember it last?
Remember the stars shining through
the trees, remember the bugs, do
you remember? Remember it, and live
with it, for if you do, that thought
will always stay with you.

Girl

The old turtle pushed its way up the hot rock,
Slipping part way down
And then starting upward again with a strong will,
Panting thirst conquering its throat.
Its short arms and legs pushing,
Straining the reluctant muscles
Until it finally reached its goal,
A victory against old age.
And then one swift movement of a single finger
Knocked the limp turtle down.

Girl

A Death Song

Could this be it!
A soft humming
as I sunk to the ground,
the birds chattering, the leaves

Eleven, going on twelve: new awareness and abilities

falling, they all seemed
to fade away through
darkness and then I knew
that I must go slowly
slowly, I must go.
Goodby, goodby, goodby life.

Boy

The Ending of the Ways

The sweetness of the stream is less,
The brightness of the sun is dimmed,
The darkness is a pool of black,
And I am standing on its rim.
The stream—a trickle on the moss,
The sun—a pale ray so thin,
The once firm soil now is cracked,
And I am sinking in.

Girl

In A Park

Pigeons run around, aimlessly looking for food.
But the elderly man or woman, in lonely a mood . . .
They too might be hungry for food.
Not only those who are hungry for food sit in
park benches, but those who hunger for beauty
They can find in the park.

Boy

The real world of the inner life

The room was silent, all except the scratching of pens on
paper. Andy looked timidly around the room. All heads were
bent except his. He bit his fingernails fervently and stared again
at the test paper. His long, thin, bony knees shook underneath
the desk. Andy leaned his head on his hand and bit the ends of

the pen. His long neck craned and peered at the paper. Suddenly the bell rang. Andy jumped and heaved a sigh of relief.

Out in the hall some boys were talking about the test. Andy strode over to them with an expression he hoped looked perfectly at ease. He started telling them how he didn't care at all about "a dumb old test," trying to keep his voice smooth while his wide blue eyes looked down upon the group anxiously. Andy's long fingers grasped often the edges of the books he was carrying as he moved along to the next class.

Girl

The Shiny Apple

Janey's stepmother set a big, shiny apple on a small silver tray and satisfied, she let out a sigh. Her name was Laura and immediately she had before her all the roles of a mother. For her husband had three children and she found herself faced with responsibilities galore. She had won the affection of Mark, 15 years, and Dolores, 12, but she could not even obtain a smile from Janey. Cold and unresponsive are the words that well described Janey's attitude toward her new mother.

Now looking out the window at Janey's frolicking with her friends, Laura shivered. For she knew that when Janey came inside the smile would leave her face and she would just sit and think with a big book on her lap. Laura wanted so much to be close to Janey, to hug and kiss her. Somehow she felt closer to Janey than she did to Mark and Dolores. She saw herself as a child and she realized how much alike she and Janey were.

She looked back at the apple and smiled again. When Janey opened her lunch bag at the picnic she would pull out the big, shiny apple that Laura had washed and polished so carefully. Janey would see the apple and smiling she would throw out the core. At the door she would call, "Mommy, I LOVE YOU." Yes, she'd call her "mommy." Then Janey walked in sullen and sad, ate her dinner and went to bed.

Laura watched Janey walk off to school clutching the little brown bag with the big, shiny apple in it. Watching the clock the day ticked away and Laura could see Janey sitting on Bonnie Hill eating her apple as she pulled out the grass smiling and . . .

The picnic was over. Janey's class was returning to school.
On the top of the grass a shiny red apple lay uneaten, untouched.

Girl

Hey! Did you see that boy
that walked down the street
he is the boy I love
but he doesn't love me.
Whenever he sees me
he turns around his face.
He knows how I feel
and wants to go away.
I just can't live without you,
I just told him today
he looked a little sad
and said, "I think it's late."
I stood there crying.
but knowing that is true
that you can't love a boy
if he doesn't love you.

Girl

What steps does a teacher take when such papers as the three above
are brought to her? What will lead these boys and girls into still
deeper and broader knowledge of themselves and possible new directions for their writing?

She might ask herself: Have they studied the myths in depth—
Greek, Norse, Babylonian? Children who have insights such as revealed in these papers are certainly ready for the knowledge and
passions the myths embody. They can recognize, as Susanne Langer
has said, that myth is "a story of the birth, passion, and defeat by death
which is man's common fate."[1]

[1]Susanne K. Langer, *Philosophy in a New Key* (Mentor Books, New American
Library, 1958), p. 157

The real world of myth

All of us who have read Herbert Kohl's 36 Children remember how his sixth-graders were drawn to the Greek myths. They wrote their own myths and their own versions of the Persephone story, revealing their personal involvement and their individual interpretations of Persephone's relationships with Pluto her husband and Demeter her mother—interpretations that depended entirely on what the children were projecting from their own feelings and experiences.

Recently in a class made up of nines, tens, and elevens the children's work centered for a large part of a year on a study of the life of the ancient Greeks. The reading of the myths had brought special enjoyment, particularly as presented in Ingri and Edgar Parin d'Aulaires' Book of Greek Myths, Olivia Coolidge's Greek Myths, and The Iliad and the Odyssey: Adapted from the Greek Classics of Homer by Jane Werner Watson. Here were stories of adventure, strength, daring, challenge and adversity, deception and comedy—many of them revolving around domestic problems not at all unfamiliar to these particular children. The myths were read and then dramatized in simple, informal presentations requiring few props and few rehearsals. A small group might practice for three or four days and then perform for the rest of the class right there in the classroom. The teacher noted that the heroic parts were frequently taken by just those children who needed to feel more strength and belief in themselves. With the right intuition—bearing out one of the major premises of the value of creative dramatics—children sought out the parts that would help them grow.

From reading and dramatizing, the children moved on to writing their own myths, centering on "creation" themes. The teacher helped them see that the invention of a myth need not be a formidable task. She reminded them of the great variety in the myths they had read and pointed out that a five-line myth might be just as valid as one of three pages.

In the example that follows—the work of one of the oldest children in this group—it is easy to detect the possible projection of personal feelings. A sibling rivalry theme is dominant.

Creation Myth

In the beginning, mother sky was all alone, very bored of just sitting alone. After years of boredom, she had two children,

Cause (girl) and Ham (boy). They spent many years playing and growing flowers and vegetables, and picking vegetables and fruit from the trees that grew there.

When they grew up, they had their own houses and their own gardens and their own work. But Ham became very troubled by Cause. Whatever Ham did, Cause did better. Ham had a garden, but so did Cause only Cause's garden was twice as big and grew twice as quick. Ham had a dog and so did Cause, but Cause's dog did tricks. Ham was very discouraged and one day got a sudden urge to kill Cause. One day he took Cause out to his fields to show her how well his corn was growing. When they got out there, Cause complimented Ham on his corn and knelt down to draw him a picture of her corn in the dirt. When Ham saw this, he realized her corn was twice as tall. Out of a sudden urge, Ham picked up a log and killed his sister, Cause. Mother Sky would never forgive Ham, and banished him from her land. She cried for nine days and nine nights without stopping for a minute. She buried Cause in the flood, and washed all the evil of Ham away.

Girl

Stories of the creation of man and the earth were of course encountered in the children's reading, and toward the end of the Greek study the teacher introduced other myths about beginnings. The Greek creation versions were compared with the Babylonian and Hebrew, as told in the Gilgamish story and in the first part of Genesis. To help the children make the transition from Genesis to the scientific thinking of today, Roger Pilkington's In the Beginning: The Story of Creation was read aloud and discussed. Pilkington translates the Genesis version into terms twentieth-century children can understand and appreciate.

That some of the boys and girls in this class were intrigued by these stories of beginnings is evident in the myths they themselves wrote. Here was their chance to invent, while at the same time keeping one foot on the familiar ground of Earth. The author of the first story below, for instance, is fantasying about the gods, yet trying to realistically keep in mind the task facing those gods who wanted "to make things to go on the Earth." What did they need to create, to make it "like the way it is now"? Our child has done some good thinking as she decides to have the gods provide for animals, things that grow from the ground, man, and "someone to teach man everything they needed to know."

Koosaleez, the goddess of the plants, married Skibela, the god of the waters, and they had four immortal children: Kistaj, Racales, Melbourne, and Bransha. They were the less important gods.

Then Koosaleez and Skibela had another child, and this was the Earth. And the four gods made things to go on the Earth. Kistaj made animals; Racales made things that grow from the ground; Melbourne made man, and Bransha made someone to teach man everything they needed to know.

And that makes it like the way it is now.

Girl

Once upon a time, there were stars and only stars. And they dropped an egg. Out of the egg came a tree, and the tree grew eggs, and the eggs turned into more trees. The trees dropped grass which grew bugs, and water and flowers. And the stars dropped animals, and animals made humans, and humans live.

Boy

In the beginning, everything was black. And from blackness was born Unes, the god of blackness. After a while, Unes got very, very cold. So he made a giant ball of fire. Sparks flew from the ball of fire. Some of them stayed firey, and later were called stars. Some of them cooled and became planets.

Unes, after a while, got bored, and made people to amuse him. He'd watch what they'd do, and listen to what they said. If you ever go way out in outer space, you'll find a giant star which was the great ball of fire that started everything.

Boy

In the beginning, when all the hot lava was flying around in outer space, there were little orange seeds getting caught in the lava which was slowly being turned into Earth.

Eleven, going on twelve: new awareness and abilities

When Earth cooled, and the air was warm, little plants grew from the orange seeds. They were weird shaped with a big round end. One of the planets was different, and suddenly it popped! . . . From it came a big puff of smoke that went up into the sky. It was the god Arfa. Arfa was all powerful. Arfa was male-female. As time passed, the other plants opened and little creatures crawled out. Arfa did not like the looks of these little creatures, so Arfa decided to change them into prettier creatures. And also, he called them "Human Beings."

Arfa built shelter for them and gave them food. Now some of the weird creatures Arfa did not change. They were left alone, but each one of the creatures were different. Arfa decided to call the left over creatures "animals." Some of the plants the creatures came out of got bigger, and some smaller, some Arfa called trees, some bushes, some flowers, some grass, but they all were plants.

They all learned to live with each other, and after each generation, they looked different and nicer.

Girl

The children's myths were bound together in rexographed booklets—one for each child—entitled "Creation Stories," and it is interesting that the class decided to include at the end of the booklet a few of the creation accounts they had written as an outcome of their tadpole and embryo studies with the science teacher. That they could group the tadpoles with the gods and the stars is a tribute to them and their grasp of the dimensions, great and small, of creation. It is a tribute to the teachers, too, for encouraging this grasp and for conceiving of curriculum as a large whole made up of interrelated parts.

Here are some of the children's science stories:

I am a bird in an egg. I wonder if I will ever get out of here. Probably I will. It's sort of nice here.

What will happen once I'm out? It's strange. Maybe I can find out. I'll try and break the shell with my beak.

I'm coming out. Oh, wow! Hello world.

Girl

A frog's egg, then a tadpole, then a frog

Everything's dark in here. It's cold, wet, and tight in here. I've been in here a long time and I'm sick CREAK! of this egg. My egg has hatched! I'm free. Weeeee! It's fun swimming in the water. I can't wait to grow up and become a frog! _____ Gee, I've grown up to be a frog. I wonder what it's like on dry land. I think I'll take a peek out of the water. __ Wow! I think I'll go a little further. Now I can go in the water and on dry land.

Boy

A frog will not feel as much at home on land as in the water because it had spent more time in water than on land.
As an egg
A frog's egg is soft and laid on a rock. A frog can't see out of an egg.
As a tadpole
When first born, everything is bright to a tadpole. Everything is warm and wet, and it can swim very well.
As a frog
When a frog gets out of the water, everything is drier than in water. A frog can feel wind and other things that he might not feel in the water.

Boy

From creation myths to world cultures

It is only a small step from a focus on the gods to a focus on man and his beliefs about his own creation and his obligations to gods and other men—in short, a focus on the ways man builds a culture around himself, providing for the rituals and laws and customs he needs.

Children whose studies take them in this direction are beginning to delve into social anthropology, whether or not they hear this term in their classrooms. To put together the pieces that make up a culture and to begin to see the whole taking shape is an exciting exercise for elevens, one that many of them are intellectually ready for.

282

The authors of the "Creation Stories" moved on later to think about laws in relation to towns. First they conceived of a possible town—strictly an invented one—then its laws, keeping in mind the teacher's suggestion: "If we first invent a place, how can we discover more about it through the laws its people had?"

Other classes of elevens have found the study of utopias stimulating and have tried to conceive of a utopia of their own, taking into account all the aspects of living for which provision must be made.

In one school the elevens invented whole cultures—some of them very primitive—in connection with their study of mythology. Their attempt was to see how the customs, institutions, and religious attitudes might be interrelated. For instance, in "Made Up Religion" below, the child takes a mythological religion as a point of departure, describing some of its rituals and moving out to include not only beliefs about the creation of man, but also about reasons for "good" and "bad" events in the lives of the people.

Made Up Religion

In the religion I will write about the people worship and worry about their future years of life. They call themselves Worrews. The Worrews worship the god Future.

How man began has been a problem in many religions, but the Worrews quite firmly believe that man grew out of a leaf. They are not supposed to be seen playing with or damaging leaves because it would be like ruining the life of another man. On a special night the Worrews would gather all the leaves they thought necessary and put them in a circle. Then when the god Future passed by that spot they would all turn into men. No one would ever see him change the leaves and no one tried because they knew it would break the spell. Even if they did try to see they would only see a huge cloud to be removed in the presence of no one.

The people die when Future is angry with them for committing a sin or when they reach the age 100 because Future knows it would be unpleasant to get past that age. The people are dressed in leaves and a mattress made of leaves is put in the coffin when they die. I will tell you a bit about the bracelets they

Eleven, going on twelve: new awareness and abilities

have now because the coffin is decorated with the scenes that are on the charms of one of the two bracelets. If the person is good it will have good scenes and vice versa.

Some beliefs they have are that they shall all have two charm bracelets. One with scenes that they would like to happen in their life and one bracelet with things they would not like to happen to them during future life. If something from their good bracelet happens they have a year of good luck and if something pictured in the charm of their bad bracelet happens they have bad luck all year. Another belief of theirs is that they think each first day of the New Year they need to make a sacrifice to Future to thank him and to make him go on doing services for them. The sacrifice they pay is to (one leaf per 5 persons) throw a leaf into a bubbling, leaping bowl of red flame. It is like sacrificing a person because by and by the leaf would turn into a person anyway. Even though most people would consider this a sad time they don't because it is the beginning of a new year and they have hope of a good year so they make toasts in favor of one and have the great rejoicing of the year.

Girl

The next step for these young anthropologists might be to move completely away from myth to the cultures of either the world today or the immediate past and to give up invention and focus on such facts as working anthropologists have painstakingly winnowed out. For some of the most able children, the reading of *Ishi, Last of His Tribe,* by Theodora Kroeber, might provide an exciting introduction to anthropology. This is the story, written particularly for young people, of Ishi, the last Yahi Indian of California. The author's account for adult readers, *Ishi in Two Worlds,* which brings Ishi out of his primitive world and into the modern one he lived in for five years, can also be read—at least in parts—by good eleven- and twelve-year-old readers.

Children can discover anthropology also through the reading of Margaret Mead's *People and Places,* which not only describes several differing cultures in detail but introduces the reader to the common concepts and problems all people have had to deal with while building their ways of life.

Creativity through poetry

Poetry's musical shapes

The creation of myths and imaginary cultures has great appeal, as we have seen. An altogether different kind of creation, however, also interests elevens and twelves, particularly those children who have a good ear for language. They can understand more now than they used to about the relationship between form and feeling in a poem. It becomes clearer that a poem's form can accent its meaning and that a poem can be thought of as a musical structure whose phrases, words, and rhythms create pace and texture and emotion, all springing full-bodied from the force of feeling in the poem—dictated, in fact, by the vital presence of the feeling.

Here are two poems by a so-called low-achieving boy.[2] Without training in this direction from the teacher, but possibly under the influence of our contemporary rock balladry, he produced two ballads of his own, full of musical repetition. He lined them on the page in his own way:

Halloween

Halloween, Halloween
   Trick or treat
Halloween, Halloween
   Lost my treat
     Lost my money
      Lost my treatbag
       Lost my honey
        But I haven't lost my greeting.

Sally and Ted

Sally has a doll that goes
Mom-mom, mom-mom, mom-mom.
Ted has a dog that goes

[2]From *Somebody Turned on a Tap in These Kids*, edited by Nancy Larrick (Delacorte Press, 1971). Copyright © 1971 by Nancy Larrick Crosby. Reprinted by permission of the publisher.

Bow-wow, Bow-wow, Bow-wow.
My father has a wife that goes
I love you, I love you,
I love you. And my sister
has a boy friend that goes
Do you love me, Do you love me,
Do you love me? And my
Sister's boy friend has
a little sister that cries
and cries and cries.

The End

When a child shows such a talent, what can the teacher do to help in its development? The boy may already be familiar with the ballads of Rod McKuen, but it is unlikely that he knows the musical voice of Carl Sandburg. The whole class might enjoy listening to poems read by Sandburg himself on the record *Carl Sandburg's Poems for Children* (Caedmon TC 1124). Here a new dimension is added to the written word. The poem becomes music, though not actually sung.

The author of "The Hawk" below might also appreciate the expressive voice of Sandburg. Note how the boy has found a way to emphasize dramatically not only the sudden down-flying of the hawk but the contrast in the aftermath, expressed in the slow words "too late, too late." This is a good example of the way a poem can flow into a form that accents its feeling:

The Hawk

A mighty hawk flies over the land
    searching for its prey,
While the squirrel in the tree below looks
    for a place to hide,
But it is too late, too late.
The hawk gets set,
   and then,
        down
           down
               down
                   down it comes
until it's too late, too late.

He carries off the carcass to his young ones.
But he will return to the horror of other squirrels.
And for them
        it will be too late, too late.

The next five poems are full of sound and rhythm effects that create both the music and the substance of the poems. In "The Wind" there are suggestive wind words—whirring, whistling, sweeping, swaying sweetly—and there are sweeping rhythms varied in the middle of the poem by the two rhymed lines, "Oh, the trees/ swaying in the gentle breeze," suggesting a calmer movement. At the end the pause and the short phrase effectively silence the poem.

The Wind

The wind went whirring, whistling through the trees
in sweeping motions caressing the limbs.
Oh, the trees
swaying in the gentle breeze,
the limbs swaying sweetly in the wind
her branches mingling with the wind
until there was no more whistling, caressing.

The wind was no more.

Boy

"Trees," another wind poem, has playful repetitions, images, and rhythms. The fact that the child has not lined the poem in the conventional way makes for no difficulties whatever for the reader, who is easily caught up in the echoing phrases. In fact, the tumble of words in the first paragraph—all one long sentence without punctuation—in itself helps build the image of the glittering leaves and darting "playful puppy."

Trees

They sway in the wind as if they
are about to snap but then all of a
sudden it springs up like outstretched

arms reaching for the sun which glitters
and shines upon its many leaves like
a playful puppy darting in and out
sometimes hidden from view.
   "Yet it is only a tree, only a
tree, only a tree, only a tree," whispers
the wind while it rustles the leaves.
"So, it can't be a puppy, can't be a puppy,"
echoes the wind. "Someday it may
be chopped down into firewood for some
lucky child, lucky child, lucky child,"
whispers the wind.

Girl[3]

The following ocean poem must have delighted its author. She hit
upon the felicitous combination, "Ocean blue, Ocean thunder," and
with the rhyming word "under" she makes a suggestive picture of the
thundering sea. Then she skillfully switches to slow, one-syllable
words, showing how quiet it is in the undersea world. She has also
found other descriptive sea words—"curls" and "swirls"—to evoke
her "different kind of world."

Ocean blue, Ocean thunder
But one day when I went under
This ol' ocean turned all clear
Nothing under here to fear.
   Quiet, cool, clear and green
   So much down there to be seen.
Such a different kind of world
Completely filled with curls and swirls.
That's my ocean, blue and thunder.
Different though when I go under.

"Night Poem" creates an atmosphere of mystery and magic. A
strange presence hovers over the poem, rising from the quiet, slow

[3]From *Somebody Turned on a Tap in These Kids,* edited by Nancy Larrick (Delacorte Press, 1971). Copyright © 1971 for Nancy Larrick Crosby. Reprinted by permission of the publisher.

rhythm of the short lines and the evocative words and phrases: "misty-shady," "twinkling/with stars' light-fill," and "time's sand."

Night Poem

I saw a lady
as I walked down
the misty-shady
walks in time's gown

her face was yellow
her feet and arms white
her tresses mellow
although bright

her dress was darkness
and still
it was twinkling
with stars' light-fill

she moved with grace
o'er the trees
her veil of mist
pirrouetted
in the breeze

a dark-faced man
dressed in black
over time's sand
carried her back

he was the Night
she the Moon
the Sun rose in the morning
like a Golden Balloon.

Girl

"Old Woman," with annotations by the child herself, experiments with slow rhythms, pauses, and voice effects that will give the images dramatic reality and crystalize the feeling the girl is putting into the poem.

Old Woman

(Read slowly with pauses	She sits, . . .
in a meditative voice)	She sits, . . .
	She sits and rocks and knits, . . .
(faster)	She thinks, . . .
	Of what she'll wear, . . .
	And - what - when -worn - did
(Light headedly dying out)	fall, . . .
(Build up)	To molten, mildewed masses, in
	her trunks of finery, . . .
	And yet, . . .
(small pause)	She, well-wrapt in soft, gray old-
	ness, . . .
	Hears the swish of silk, of satin,
	still upon the floor, . . .
	Time is gone, . . .
	But she is left,
	A relic of herself,
	She sits, . . .
	And the snow falls.

Girl

How have these particular children learned to write such poetry? Is there a way to teach it? We can point out that the author of "Old Woman" was a member of the small group of children who read their poetry aloud to each other, sometimes offering comments on the appropriateness of the reading voices in relation to the qualities of the poem. (See p. 47.) She had also heard Edith Sitwell's *Façade* record and had had a chance to note what a gifted poet-reader can do with the voice. By and large, for all of these children, though they were not in the same class, exposure was the teacher. The children listened to a great deal of poetry, old and new, free and structured, read aloud by their teacher, by themselves, and by poets on records—e. e. cummings, Yeats, Robert Frost, and others. If they discussed poetry, it was not in terms of lessons on how to achieve sound and rhythm effects; rather, the children were encouraged to point out and speak about what they had noticed and what had especially made an impression on them. Sometimes, indeed, these discussions did center on words that seemed particularly effective. Most important, the children were given frequent opportunities to write. In this way they could make their own discoveries through many trial attempts; and no doubt for them as for all practicing poets, the right "effects" simply descended on them at times, born of their feeling, their engagement, and their growing skill with words.

A teacher can build up her own background in the aspects of poetry discussed here by studying David Holbrook's The Exploring Word and Flora J. Arnstein's Poetry and the Child, two books that may be found particularly helpful. Also suggestive is Kenneth Koch's work with children on sound effects, described in his Wishes, Lies, and Dreams. There is, of course, no one guide to use and no one way to learn to become a "poetry teacher." Some of the best teachers have taught themselves. They use ideas that spring from their own knowledge and love of poetry, and they make discoveries along with the children.

An experiment with haiku

When a teacher finds herself with a class of elevens who are resistant to poetry—or who think they are—this is the time for her to use her ingenuity.

In one such class a young student teacher undertook an experiment with haiku poetry that turned out to be highly successful. That is, children who were not writing found out that they could write and that they had something to say.

The student teacher knew that writing haiku poetry usually appeals to tens, elevens, and twelves. Its seventeen-syllable, three-line form (not always followed literally by translators) gives it a non-frightening brevity; the requirement of five syllables in the first line, seven in the second, and five in the third, presents an attractive challenge; and the underlying haiku concepts—that the poem rests on overtones suggesting more than is said, that it usually records a high moment in a clearly sketched picture, and that it often contains a contrast setting off trains of thought and feeling and suggesting "the point where the momentary intersects the constant and eternal"[4] —are well within the children's grasp.

[4]Donald Keene, Japanese Literature (Grove Press, 1955), p. 39.

Here, for instance, are examples of haiku attempts by sixth-graders from two schools, the first two from a New Jersey school and the other from a school across the continent in Oregon. The boy who composed the first poem used a thoroughly contemporary subject—why shouldn't he?—but successfully suggested the high moment and the overtones:

Standing on the mound
Starting to wind up   and then
He throws the ball in.

Boy

The nest is quiet!
The mother bird is quiet
The egg is breaking.

Girl

Spring is like a snail
crawling with his heavy shell
toward the burning sun.

Girl

The student teacher, before reading haiku poetry to her sixth-grade class, conceived of ways to illuminate the nature of the poetry by exploring with the children some of its relationships to other art forms. She knew that she could take several days—not necessarily consecutive days—for this haiku project and she came to it prepared with materials and ideas.

On the first day she began by reading a few of the poems by the old haiku masters—Joso, Basho, Issa, and others—avoiding the word "poetry."[5] For example:

[5]Peter Beilenson and Harry Behn, translators, *Haiku Harvest*. Decorations by Jeff Hill. Japanese Haiku Series IV (Mount Vernon, New York: Peter Pauper Press, 1962), unpaged. Copyright © 1962 by Peter Pauper Press. Reprinted by permission of the publisher.

Eleven, going on twelve: new awareness and abilities

AMONG THESE LOVELY
   CHERRY BLOOMS,
   A WOODPECKER
HUNTS FOR A DEAD TREE

Joso

AN OLD SILENT POND . . .
   INTO THE POND
   A FROG JUMPS,
SPLASH! SILENCE AGAIN

Basho

SHAKING HIS LOOSE SKIN,
   A TIRED OLD HORSE
   SCARES AWAY
A WHITE BUTTERFLY

Issa

The children's first reactions were that the poems were "strange." So
Mrs. Wegman, the student teacher, talked a little about what the poets
were trying to do, pointing out that the attempt was to suggest perceptions, insights, and feelings that could be captured in other arts as
well, notably in music and painting. After reading one or two more
poems, she showed the children a picture of the koto, a traditional
Japanese stringed instrument, and played a record of koto and flute
music (World-Pacific 1424). To our western ears this music is indeed
suggestive and elusive in melody and rhythm, though the flute tones
have perfect clarity. It seems to be sketching its musical meanings in
phrases that we ourselves must interpret—just as we must read between the lines of the haiku poem. Throughout, the mood is lyrical
and meditative. The parallels with haiku poetry are unmistakable.

After playing the record, Mrs. Wegman showed the children a book
of sumi-e ink-brush paintings (*Sumi-e in Three Weeks* by Sadami
Yamada). Here again there are clear parallels with haiku poetry. With
a few strokes of the black ink, the picture is brushed on to the white
paper, which serves as a blank background suggesting spacial depth.
There are no decorative embellishments. An image arises from the

deft and delicate strokes, as haiku images arise from the open structure of a few succinct words.

On the second day, pursuing her plan to illustrate the relationship of haiku poetry to other arts, Mrs. Wegman projected on an overhead projector a photograph from the book *Children of Many Lands* by Hanns Reich. The photo shows a smiling Chinese woman—obviously well-dressed and well-fed—sitting on a chair in a market place beside her three heaped-up baskets of rice. Almost in front of her, on the ground, is a wretched, bony little boy, holding out an empty bowl toward the photographer. The implicit contrast and its overtones need no comment.

On this day, also, Mrs. Wegman brought in a box containing all the necessary materials for sumi-e painting—ink stone, ink stick, and brushes—and invited the children to paint. They did this without hesitation, since they were children who had had years of experience in the art workshop in their school.

When the sumi-e materials were not in use, they were laid out in careful arrangement at one end of a long shelf under a window, the Yamada book beside them. The children's paintings—many of them very successful indeed—were posted on a bulletin board near the shelf.

At the other end of the shelf, an attractive display began to take shape. In the first place, the shelf itself was made beautiful. Its rough, paint-worn surface was covered with pieces of black and white paper laid down in an interesting size-and-shape arrangement. Then, carefully placed on the paper, so that each object had its own space around it, were the following:

- A long dry pod
- Pieces of dried moss
- A feathery weed
- Small sticks of intricately eaten-away wood
- Interesting stones
- A small twig from an evergreen tree
- A small bone
- A large slab of tree bark

- Shells
- A pine cone
- A dark brown branch of eucalyptus
- Prickly burrs

Two books of haiku poetry were included with the display, and above the shelf was posted an explanatory, hand-printed label:

> Some of these materials are described by Japanese poets like Basho, Buson, and Issa in traditional haiku verse (cf. the book of sumi-e paintings).

Nothing had been said so far about the children writing their own haiku, but at least one girl had gone ahead on her own after seeing the projection of the photograph:

She has bags of rice
Spare some for a starving child
He has none at all.

A haiku poem? Perhaps not, in the true Japanese sense, though it has the correct form and springs from emotion expressed with restraint. The important point is that the child wanted to write it.

Now Mrs. Wegman suggested to the whole class that they try some haiku, stressing that for this first attempt they forget about an absolutely accurate syllable count, instead trying to express something with feeling. "I bet you couldn't write about blood and killing," a boy objects. "That isn't so. You can write about anything."

With this encouragement, the writing began—as it might not have

Eleven, going on twelve: new awareness and abilities

if the children had been asked to produce only the purest haiku. The purpose here was to help resistant children begin to find satisfaction in writing, whatever the results might be.

So, blood and killing were indeed included in the poems, as well as other aspects of life not usually touched upon by the Japanese poets. These two poems came from the pen of one boy. (Note that he manages to contain each one within seventeen syllables):

> The cool dark alley lightens
> The street gangs run, the alley
> runs in blood.

> The knife is bloody and cold
> The blood runs hot
> The bloody flower is hot.

A boy who was known to the teacher as a very fearful child wrote:

> In fear he walked, in fear he ran
> In fear he hid . . .
> In fear he died.

A girl, who explained that she was thinking of death at the time, wrote a poem full of suggestion and overtones:

> They are old men,
> Raising but a feeble hand,
> And looking toward the sky.

Strong interest in the civil rights movement was reflected in this poem by a girl:

> A Black man and a white man
> friendly conversing.
> May it always be this way.

A boy who grasped the idea of the contrasts often implicit in haiku produced, among others, these three (the first one was written following a morning walk, when the boy had climbed the wall referred to):

> The clean, rich boy climbs
> the wall of the ugly dirty
> alley.

> Look into the New York skys,
> first the grand sunset, a little lower,
> the grand flag, a little lower, the
> dirty slums.

> The chickens with high voices,
> are in the cellar, while the cow, with
> voice low, is in the pasture.

Another boy, who could take only a tongue-in-cheek approach, managed nevertheless to catch the idea of the surprise climax or revelation often expressed in the third line of the haiku poem:

> I tightened my hold and stabbed
> it in, then, turned the crank.
> When it was sharp I yanked it out:
> I had sharpened a pencil.

Meanwhile a number of girls were writing poems that caught a good deal of the haiku spirit:

> The crest of the wave
> Laps along the shore all day
> And covers the bugs.

> I read to a child
> She listens and falls asleep
> The clock keeps ticking

A feather from
the great white bird
floated gently to the
sea.

Yesterday I saw a stone dragon
all covered with snow.

Many more poems were written than are quoted here, some children producing from five to twenty haiku. They were not all shared with the class, though Mrs. Wegman picked out some by each child to read aloud. Sensing the children's reticence, she did not reveal names, but indicated whether the poem was by a girl or a boy. The children listened intently and quietly.

So, in a few days—and more skillful planning by the teacher—interest was stirred and the children wrote. Later in the year the class moved on to a study of Chaucer. Here again rich background materials were provided, and the creative drama and art expression that resulted were very impressive. These were children who rose up quickly out of their childlike resistances when the teacher placed them on her own level and shared her knowledge of history, authors, poets, and artists.

Inventive, searching

In a final look at the potentialities of the elevens and twelves as writers, let us turn to some of their purely imaginative creations.

Over the years these children have learned to write concisely and clearly, with sensory vividness and few clichés. They are all children who by and large have achieved this mastery in one of the best ways known—through writing, talking, and reading.

The Book

I ran upstairs to look at the book my great uncle (he was supposed to have been a very strange man) had given me. When I took it off the shelf it seemed to be much bigger than it had been. Never were there such beautiful pictures, a marvel to the eye. Closer and closer I bent over the pictures so as to examine their details. To my great surprise the images began to move and enlarge, then suddenly they sprang out of the paper. Absolutely delighted I began to join in their frolicsome jig. We went spinning around and around. My head was whirling, the room was sheer bedlam!! Suddenly, in a flash!! everything stopped. There was silence, I opened my eyes (which had been shut during the dancing) to see the room in absolute order, not a figure to be seen. Slowly I walked out of the room forgetting the book for the while, thinking only of the dancing.

Several days later I brought my brother to see the pictures. He looked at them and saw nothing out of the ordinary. But I knew and saw the book. The marvelous book my strange uncle had given me was not so ordinary.

Girl

This child is not only inventing magic; she is enjoying exclusive prerogatives. Only she can know and see the marvels in her book. This, of course, is one of the functions of fantasy for its inventor.

In her writing she suggests very well the spinning and whirling of the dance and then its sudden end. That she has used two clichés—"frolicsome jig" and "sheer bedlam"—is not surprising. She is old enough now to be picking up common expressions, as all adult writers tend to do involuntarily. This is something for her to work on in the days ahead.

One is reminded, in her story, of the picture book dreamed of by Elise in Hans Christian Andersen's fairy tale *The Wild Swans*. Elise saw the figures not only coming alive and walking out of the book, but skipping back into place as she turned the pages. One wonders if our child author may have been influenced by this story. If not, and if she does not know Andersen, now is the time for her to discover him and his delicate world of magical objects.

The Magic Globe

"Mom, what can I do?" Kathy whined. "I'm tired of being in the house."

"I'm sorry, but you'll have to stay inside. After all, you've just had the chicken pox. Why don't you go up to the attic and putter around?" her mother suggested.

Kathy swished her long brown pony tail and walked slowly up the stairs to the attic. She opened the door. Everything was covered with dust. There was a heavy musty smell in the air. She looked around uncertainly, wondering where to start. In one corner were some old chests, along one wall was a table with some decaying boxes on it, but what attracted Kathy's attention was an ancient globe of the world standing in the middle of the floor. It seemed mysterious and inviting. Kathy felt as though she was drawn towards it. She walked over to it, examined it, then spun it around. Dust rose up from it, and Kathy coughed. As she went downstairs, questions came to her mind: Who did the globe belong to? And why was it in the attic?

But these questions were forgotten when she heard the radio. "A large portion of Australia was suddenly completely blacked out!" the announcer was saying. "A witness reported that everything suddenly went black, like a fast eclipse, then became light again! Cause unknown. Further reports tomorrow!"

Kathy felt very weak and sat down. Australia was the country she had touched when she spun the globe!

"Mom, uh, well, where did that globe up in the attic come from, Mom?" she faltered.

"What globe? We don't have a globe!" her mother exclaimed.

Kathy ran to her room, her mind in a whirl. Could the globe be . . . magic?

That night, Kathy lay awake, distressed. If she had caused the blackout . . . how could she be sure? Should she try it out? But finally Kathy fell asleep from sheer exhaustion.

Next morning Kathy raced up to the attic as soon as breakfast was over. She had made up her mind. Looking over the globe, she unwisely (as it is densely populated) chose France. Carefully she put her hand down there, then picked it up. She ran downstairs, slamming the door behind her.

Sure enough, an hour later, she turned on the radio to hear the now familiar report of a blackout <u>and</u> in France! Now Kathy was sure. The globe had to be magic!

300

"Kathy, isn't that the craziest thing? Blackouts without any cause!" her mother scoffed as she listened to the radio.

"Mom, I've got to tell you something. Well, I think that the globe—well, and me too, uh, sort of caused those blackouts!" Kathy stammered.

"Kathy, what are you saying? You'd better come lie down. I don't think you're over the chicken pox yet!" Kathy's mother ordered.

There was no protesting. Kathy followed her mother and let her put her in bed. Kathy soon fell asleep. When she woke up she decided to take another look at the globe. She snuck upstairs because she didn't want to be seen, opened the door cautiously, and peered inside. The globe was gone! She rubbed her eyes and looked again, but the globe didn't appear.

"I guess it was just a dream," she thought sadly.

But moving closer, she saw on the floor, which was covered with dust, a circle that was clean. It was exactly where the globe had been!

"Hmm . . . I wonder . . ." Kathy said softly to herself as she walked slowly downstairs.

Girl

Here again we have a creator of magic who enjoys exclusive possession of her power—though "enjoys" is hardly the right word. Power to this extent is both mysterious and frightening, and it must be cushioned by the existence of an illness and the presence of a mother.

The child has written a masterful little mystery story in extremely competent prose. She has made us see the dust in the attic and smell its musty smell. We feel along with Kathy the weakness that makes her want to sit down after the Australia blackout; we hear her stammering as she speaks. That our author is really still a child is revealed only in the phrase, "She snuck upstairs. . . ." Yet after all, this expression is such an apt one that time may eventually remove it from its present nonstandard status.

(Untitled)

I got in my little space ship and started off. I splashed in the water and I went down and down, and there was a big hole, and I went down it. It was all dark and it was like a tunnel. I drove hours through the tunnel, seeing fish, big and little.

Then it was all bright. When I came to the end of the tunnel, there were millions of rocks, and no one was around. I heard voices and all these fish came out and they stood there and looked at me. Then suddenly, they all started shrieking, very loudly. I started my ship up and drove off real fast. I could hear them still and I thought my ears were going to break. I got to the end of the tunnel. I still heard them. I drove home and just sat on the chair feeling dizzy.

Girl

Here the child is able to give us in just a few lines a whole adventure, neatly begun, neatly ended. It is a frightening adventure, and its ambience of dark, and light, and noise is well sustained throughout. Perhaps it is brief because the child herself found her own invention disturbing. To encourage her to extend her story might be a mistake.

A teacher might find a way, however, to help her become more precise in her choice of words. The umbrella word "all" is an easy trap for the writer. We have here not only "all dark" but "all bright" and "all these fish." And why is our girl in a spaceship for an underwater trip? She and other children in the class might enjoy and profit from some exercises in clear and accurate description.[6] Her imprecise phrases, of course, should not obscure the achievement: an original story full of invention, a story for our time when underwater exploration is uncovering strange truths. Has the author seen the TV underwater programs of Jacques Cousteau? Has she read Cousteau's *The Silent World* and *The Living Sea*? These might be appropriate books for her at this time.

The Map

It all started a few years ago when an unknown person lay in his death bed. In a few moments he would be in heaven, or in hell. I never found that out. Everybody had left the room. No not

---

[6]See, for instance, Edward B. Jenkinson and Donald A. Seybold, *Writing As a Process of Discovery: Some Structured Theme Assignments for Grades Five Through Twelve* (Bloomington: Indiana University Press, 1970).

quite everybody. His eighteen year old nephew was still there. In the last minute his uncle asked him to come to his bedside.

The uncle gave him a map. His last words were, "I was the only one who knew, now you are." His nephew looked at the map. He couldn't figure it out but he kept it as a memento of his uncle. Years went by. He was in Yale University. Then one day, (in fact it was Oct. 10, 1965), a map was brought to Yale. He looked at it, then at his uncle's map. They were the same. He puzzled over it. Yale's map was a pre-Columbian map of the New World as they had pictured it. Then he noticed on the back of his uncle's something he hadn't noticed before. It was a picture of a trail in the Adirondack Mountains and of an arrow pointing to a hole in a mountain. Inquiring at an Adirondack Mountain Club headquarters, he found the trail and the hole. He decided to try to go down into it. He got the equipment he would need. Seven hours later he was still descending. He stopped to rest. Then he got to thinking, could this be an undiscovered land of which the maps were really made of? Another hour passed by. He saw light beneath him; it was coming closer! closer! His hand slipped! He grabbed frantically to keep his hold. His head hit a rock. Everything went black. He was dead, just like his uncle. The difference was his uncle had someone to give the map to. He didn't.

Boy

What is the author trying to convey in this story? Perhaps he is mainly playing with that always fascinating theme of "What if?" involving the chance happening that changes the whole course of events and brings possibility to an end, right at the edge of discovery. Of course, he is playing, too, with a strange geographical idea that is an intriguing one even though its details are not very convincingly presented. What convinces us is the complete closure at the end of the story, the black and sudden gap; the nothingness. The boy has handled this extremely well in his short sentences. He has found, as a mature writer would, a style that is very well-suited to the suspense of his subject. True, his redundant "of" ("of which the maps were really made of") betrays his inexperience, and a more seasoned writer might not have let the author's "I" in. Nevertheless, he has created a story that has some of the flavor of the great storyteller Frank Stockton, who is fond of shutting doors on his readers. To have arrived at this stage of mastery in writing must in itself be a source of considerable satisfaction to the author.

A Trojan and the Sword Fixer

> Clang! Clang!
> "Aw darn, my sword broke. I better go to Matt, the metal man. He can fix a sword very fast. Hi, Matt."
> "Oh, hi Hector. How are things going at the battle field?"
> "Not so well."
> "What are you doing here, Hector?"
> "My sword broke. Will you fix it for me?"
> "Sure thing I'll have her fixed in a jiffy."
> Clang! Clang! Clang!
> "There you go, Hector, as good as new. That will be . . ."
> "Yes, yes I know. Ten dracmas and if you're a soldier, 5 dracmas. Well, here you go, Matt. I'll see you after the war is over, if not sooner."
> "Well, good by Hector."

Boy

"So, the old Trojans were human beings. Take them out of the grand old poems and they might have sounded like this." With a little more maturity and historical grasp, the author would probably put slightly different words into the mouths of Hector and his metal man. For now, however, he is to be congratulated on his fresh insight and his ability to give the reader a wrench away from old habits of seeing. He is not alone, of course, in this kind of invention. He belongs to the decade that has produced the musical, *Jesus Christ Superstar*.

Spelling? Yes, the boy still has something to learn about drachmas.

(Untitled)

I awoke one morning and looked out of the window. There was a clear blue sky and the sun actually poured through my brass rimmed full length mirror. I had found the mirror the night before up in the attic. As I thought of how the brass shone, my mirror began to glow and I looked up and saw myself. I think it was beckoning for me to come.

Well, curiosity overpowers most anything. I came to the figure or reflection—I was never quite sure what it was. It started to say something in a high pitched singing—

"Step inside step inside the mirror." Over and over again it repeated "Step inside the mirror." I thought it foolish but, willing to try anything, I stuck my hand through the mirror. And I drew it back stunned. My hand had gone through the mirror. Very cautiously, I stepped into the mirror.

Suddenly the sun that poured through the mirror carried me upward. Before I had time to see inside the mirror, I was plunging through space. Right behind me was the brass rimmed mirror.

Then as quickly as it had started, the sun beam stopped. I fell through space. I saw the brass rimmed mirror! I grabbed the brass with my hands and felt the rest of my body sinking into a crystal clear pool without holding my breath—sinking, sinking, sinking, sinking.

The next thing I knew is my beautiful mirror was shattered in thousands of pieces, and I was sprawled out on the floor.

Girl

Reading this remarkable fantasy, one completely suspends disbelief and accepts the rising of the mirror up and out of the room—just as one accepts the falling of Sendak's Mickey down from his bed into the Night Kitchen. Of course, part of the appeal of this adventure lies in the use of a mirror as an object of miraculous power. Perhaps no one of us, exposed as we have been to Lewis Carroll and his Alice, can remain entirely insensitive to the potency of mirror magic—though even without Lewis Carroll, who would doubt that a certain amount of magic can be summoned up from a mirror by anyone who has a mind to do so? The poet Sylvia Plath writes of a mirror and a woman (the mirror speaks):

Each morning it is her face that replaces the darkness.
In me she has drowned a young girl and in me an old woman
Rises toward her day after day, like a terrible fish.[7]

Plath's mirror drowns a young girl. Note that our young writer sinks into her strange, brass-rimmed mirror as into a crystal clear pool.

All that is left to say here is that the child knows very well how to grasp hold of magic and handle it convincingly. Are her effects so striking partly because she stays with the concrete details all the way? The reader is with her every moment, listening to the mirror, drawn to its glow, stepping in, then plunging, sinking, and finally sprawling as the mirror shatters. The child writer is scarcely still a child, yet she has retained that childlike sharpness of the senses that can light up a writer's thoughts and words and keep him exploring his own individuality.

Now let her go on to the invention of longer stories. What she has written here is little more than an introduction, a trial attempt; and she seems to be standing on the brink of a shattering experience without drawing close enough to perceive its symbols. Let her read Tolkien—especially *The Hobbit*—and Lloyd Alexander, author of the Prydain chronicles, and not only delight in the wizardry of their creations but live for a while with myth-size moods, emotions, and struggles. Let her go back to Lewis Carroll, step into that mirror— ". . . certainly the glass *was* beginning to melt away, just like a bright, silvery mist."—and explore with Alice the enormities, vexations, and mysteries on the other side of the glass.[8]

References

ALEXANDER, LLOYD. The Prydain Chronicles. New York: Holt, Rinehart & Winston, Inc. (*The Book of Three*, 1964; *The Black Cauldron*, 1965; *The Castle of Llyr*, 1966; *Taran Wanderer*, 1967; *The High King*, 1968).

[7]Sylvia Plath,"Mirror," in *Crossing the Water* (New York: Harper & Row Publishers, Inc., 1971), p. 56. Copyright © 1963 by Ted Hughes. Originally published in *The New Yorker* and reprinted by permission of Harper & Row, Publishers, Inc. and Olwyn Hughes.

[8]Lewis Carroll, *The Annotated Alice: Alice's Adventures in Wonderland and Through the Looking Glass*. Illus. by John Tenniel. With an Introduction and notes by Martin Gardner (Clarkson N. Potter, Inc., 1960), p. 184.

ANDERSEN, HANS CHRISTIAN. *The Wild Swans.* Illus. by Marcia Brown. New York: Scribners, 1963.

ARNSTEIN, FLORA J. *Poetry and the Child.* New York: Dover Publications, Inc., 1970.

AULAIRE, INGRI D' and EDGAR PARIN D'AULAIRE. *Ingri and Edgar Parin d'Aulaire's Book of Greek Myths.* New York: Doubleday, 1962.

BEILENSON, PETER and HARRY BEHN, Tr. *Haiku Harvest.* Decorations by Jeff Hill. Japanese Haiku Series IV. Mt. Vernon, New York: The Peter Pauper Press, 1962.

CARROLL, LEWIS. *The Annotated Alice: Alice's Adventures in Wonderland and Through the Looking Glass.* Illus. by John Tenniel. With an Introduction and Notes by Martin Gardner. New York: Clarkson N. Potter, Inc., 1960.

COOLIDGE, OLIVIA. *Greek Myths.* Boston: Houghton Mifflin, 1949.

COUSTEAU, JACQUES-YVES and JAMES DUGAN. *The Living Sea.* New York: Harper & Row, 1963.

COUSTEAU, JACQUES-YVES and FREDERICK DUMAS. *The Silent World.* New York: Harper & Row, 1953.

ETO, KIMIO and BUD SHANK. *Koto and Flute.* Hollywood, California: World-Pacific Records, WP-1424.

HOLBROOK, DAVID. *The Exploring Word.* Cambridge: Cambridge Univ. Press, 1967.

JENKINSON, EDWARD B., and DONALD A. SEYBOLD. *Writing As a Process of Discovery: Some Structured Theme Assignments for Grades Five Through Twelve.* Bloomington, Indiana: Indiana Univ. Press, 1970.

KEENE, DONALD. *Japanese Literature.* New York: Grove Press, 1955.

KOCH, KENNETH. *Wishes, Lies, and Dreams.* New York: Chelsea House, 1970.

KOHL, HERBERT. *36 Children.* Illus. by Robert George Jackson III. New York: The New American Library, Inc., 1967.

KROEBER, THEODORA. *Ishi in Two Worlds: A Biography of the Last Wild Indian in North America.* Berkeley & Los Angeles: Univ. of California Press, 1962.

―――. *Ishi, Last of His Tribe.* Drawings by Ruth Robbins. Berkeley, California: Parnassus Press, 1964.

LANGER, SUSANNE K. *Philosophy in a New Key.* New York: Mentor Books, New American Library, 1958.

LEE, LAURIE. *The Edge of Day: Boyhood in the West of England.* New York: Morrow, 1960.

MEAD, MARGARET. *People and Places.* New York: World Publishers, 1972.

PILKINGTON, ROGER. *In the Beginning: The Story of Creation.* Drawings by Piet Klasse. Nashville, Tenn.: Abingdon Press, 1966.

PLATH, SYLVIA. "Mirror," in *Crossing the Water.* New York: Harper & Row, 1971.

REICH, HANNS. *Children of Many Lands.* New York: Hill and Wang, 1958.

SENDAK, MAURICE. *In the Night Kitchen.* New York: Harper & Row, 1970.

SITWELL, DAME EDITH. *Façade.* Music by William Walton. Columbia, ML 5241.

TOLKIEN, J. R. R. *The Hobbit.* Boston: Houghton Mifflin, 1938.

WATSON, JANE WERNER. *The Iliad and the Odyssey:* Adapted from the Greek Classics of Homer by Jane Werner Watson. Pictures by Alice and Martin Provensen. New York: Simon & Schuster, 1956.

YAMADA, SADAMI. *Sumi-e in Three Weeks.* Rutland, Vermont: Japan Publications Trading Co., 1964.

A final word

What we have been saying indirectly at the end is what we said explicitly in the opening pages of this book. Whoever tries to write creatively enters an enormous room—an exciting, luminous room—whose ceilings and walls are vaguely defined, whose doors are everywhere standing open. For any child who explores it, the guidelines are clear: essential at all stages are live senses and feelings, involvement, knowledge and skills, inventiveness and daring. The writings that result may not all appear to be remarkable as products, but this is not crucial. What is of first importance is the quality of the child, the person himself, as he moves out and among others. If the doorways are now broadening for him and he is gaining perspective on himself; if he has found new resources in words, new surprise and power and delight; if he is becoming skillful in clarifying and giving shape to his thoughts and feelings; and especially if he has begun to discover his own individuality as he works at his stories and poems and plays, then he has in his hands a potent force: belief in his own truth. He is becoming that free and powerful person—interesting to himself and to others—who can open the book that has been closed and find "still more pages possible."

Looking ahead

Thirteen

Thirteen . . .
is like
getting off a merry-go-round
and going on the roller-coaster.
You want to become an adult,
to leave the merry-go-round,
yet . . .
because you're afraid
of the roller-coaster
with its
ups and downs.
That's thirteen.

Girl